THE LIVING END

ROGER STARR

THE LIVING END:
The City and Its Critics

New York

Coward-McCann, Inc.

For Fifi

NOTE

My employers, the members and directors of Citizens' Housing and Planning Council of New York, Inc., have been struggling for nearly thirty years to achieve better housing and more effective city planning. In my gratitude to the Council for permitting me this extracurricular activity, I must make clear that the ideas contained here are mine; it must not be assumed that they reflect official views of the Council itself, or of any of its members.

Chapters VII and IX have appeared, in somewhat different form, in *Horizon,* and I am grateful to that publication for permission to re-use the material herein. Part of Chapter XI, also in somewhat different form, was published in the *Pratt Planning Papers,* a quarterly devoted to questions of city planning, which also has graciously allowed me to restate the ideas to which it first gave currency.

I am especially thankful to Marian Sameth, associate director of Citizens' Housing, who assisted in more ways than I care to remember. Mildred Black, a member of C.H.P.C.'s staff, was as helpful as she was patient in preparing the manuscript for the printer. I must thank also Monica Raymond, Elsie Woods, and Ruth Dickler for their aid. But the responsibility for the content is mine alone.

—ROGER STARR

CONTENTS

Introduction | ONE CITY

WHAT, another book about The City?

Suddenly it seems that anyone who has traveled by subway from Bowling Green to Times Square, or taken a taxi from the Edgewater Beach Hotel to the Loop, must hasten to the typewriter and set down his experiences, preferably between hard covers.

Living in a city is no longer regarded as a temporary necessity, perverting man's essentially rural nature; it is now generally accepted that our ancestors slid from the trees to stay, and that we had better reconcile ourselves to the pavements, or find a way to reconcile the pavements to us.

This view is based on no new evidence. Men are now bothering to examine old facts. European men have for so many centuries been deserting their rustic homes that in retrospect they seem to have been born with a drive for urbanity far more important than their alleged attachment to the soil. Every schoolboy knows that history has been on the side of cities. In the eighteenth century cottage workers deserted their villages to cluster around the steam engine; electrification speeded the concentration. Now that it is stylish to study urbanization, men are noting that the internal combustion engine has made further growth of the cities inevitable. The gasoline motor makes the city's transportation truly flexible; the large diesel engine will, in the end, make it nearly unnecessary for anyone to live on the farm.

Already, in the industrialized sections of the United States, a cow is merely part of a machine to bottle milk; chickens and turkeys are carefully raised without being permitted to touch Mother Earth: she contaminates them. Farther West, the successful farmer has become an absentee owner: he lives apart from his lands, which are planted, cultivated, watered, and harvested by contracting teams with giant, mobile factories. The hired hand has become an industrial work force; its very numbers will diminish as its mechanical productivity rises. The work force moves across the landscape; it is no more rural than an army. And the stalwart husbandman, displaced, will move to The City.

Even when one is told that the pace of the transformation is slow, portentous warnings of doom are difficult to avoid.

Politically, in the United States, The City has received new attention. After these many Jeffersonian years, the Supreme Court has established the principle that an urban vote is to be the equal of a rural vote. And Congress has established a federal department whose sole concern is The City.

And the flood of books, articles, speeches, and television programs devoted to The City continues to swell. The books, in particular, have been so many that they have coalesced into a special City of the Imagination, a baffling complex of the impressions made by real cities on the minds of different observers. All who have read the books find themselves living, at least in part, in that City of the Imagination. With a little digging we may be able to uncover some assumptions shared by the writers who are describing The City in so many ways that do not match, and who call on The City to mend itself, with so many contradictory injunctions. A study of these assumptions might even lead us to the development of a few strategies of our own for dealing with the most pressing problems of The City: its racial tensions; its architectural disappointments; its transportation burdens; its patchy, stubborn poverty; its politics.

Faced with what seems to be the limitless growth of The City and its institutions, observers tend to fly in the opposite direction, placing hope for salvation on The People. But the miracles expected of The People seem to ask quite a lot of the men and women who actually live in cities. Can one devise strategies for The City that can be executed by the people who live in it?

No examination of The City can be helpful if it depends on thinking of men and women as abstract repositories of good or evil; no strategy for city problems can help unless it projects men and women as we are, not as we might like ourselves to be. The people of The City are various and contradictory, neither saints nor always devils; not always right, or patient; they are happy, puzzled, long-suffering, peremptory, anxious, agreed on almost nothing, but in some way not ever quite defined, holding among them the fates of their neighbors, their city, and perhaps the world. No book that insists on seeing them as they are can be entirely redundant.

Part I | **EASY ASSUMPTIONS**

I. A HUNDRED CITIES—A HUNDRED CRITICS

IT all seems so easy; the issues, so clear.

In a hundred cities throughout the nation a thousand citizens approach their officials in the council rooms, board rooms, hearing rooms of their marble, limestone, brick, and clapboard City Halls. It is hard enough for citizens to free themselves from the grip of daily life but, once in the hearing room, to move forward to speak involves new arrangements, made only because the matter is so urgent, the Right Thing so clear. Babies are left behind in someone else's arms; older children, holding balloons with slogans dabbed on them, are urged to stand quiet for only a minute; hats, cases, newspapers, umbrellas, rubbers, are dropped on the benches. The citizens walk to the rostrum, microphone, speaker's stand, while behind them others cheer, applaud, stamp their feet in unison, and sometimes hoot and laugh ("We will have no demonstrations of any kind. . . .")

From coast to coast, the words so often begin the same way: "My friends told me I was wasting my time coming down here, you've all got your minds made up already, but I came anyway, because I said to myself, if only they knew what the people want (or don't want: *pick one*) those officials of ours, your honorable bodies, would (or wouldn't: *pick one*) . . ."

What do the people want? What would or wouldn't the officials do?

Obviously the officials *would* build the new bridge that's so badly needed to get people from the new suburbs into town. Automobiles are backed up three miles every afternoon at five o'clock; the jam is even worse mornings; some people are leaving the city for good, simply because it's too hard to get things done, and every day the shopping centers in the suburbs are doing more business, while the department stores in the city are doing less. Last week, one of the three best-known department stores in the city closed down, and put 300 people out of work, many of them too old to find new jobs. What will happen next week, or the week after, to another 300 jobs if the new bridge isn't built?

Or, quite as obviously, if they knew what the people want, the officials *would not* build the new bridge. It would destroy 300 homes, nice homes with gardens that people have worked on for years. There are plastic pools on the front lawns in summer, where cast-iron elks once grazed beside concrete bird baths. The approaches to that new bridge will knock out the neighborhood just like a bomb. It used to be one of the very best sections of the city, and it's still mighty good; we know how to destroy such neighborhoods, but does anyone know how to make them?

Obviously, if they knew what the people want, the officials *would* build the new housing project. When it's built, 500 families will be able to move into it, and out of decrepit firetraps where twelve people burned to death last winter (we saw the face of one of the children at the window on the third floor, and she wouldn't jump, and no one, no one who heard her scream will ever forget it). We know those houses, where water won't reach the fourth floor, and mice race you for the groceries every night, where a thousand coats of paint have blurred the outlines of the wooden cabinets as sickness blurs the face of an old man. We know those buildings where you can't scrub the smell of beans, garlic, and lard out of the floor boards; where the darkness in the hallways has become part of the wall; where one hardly dares open a silent door, for fear of finding something terrible forgotten on the far side.

Or, quite as obviously, the officials *would not* approve the new housing project. It will put out of business twenty-four small shopkeepers, too old to start again elsewhere, some of whom have lived in this section for twenty years, some of whom started here when the trolleys used to pass on their way to the picnic grounds. Some of them don't even speak English, and they always gave credit to the people who needed it, not like the A&P and the other chains where they don't even know your name, and don't want to. Build the project and what happens to them, and to the old people living in the old houses, looking out at the street and seeing now and then a familiar face? If something happens in the night, there's always someone to hear, and Mr. Schultz, the druggist, you can talk to him. Don't they know this isn't a slum, not a real slum?

Obviously, if they understood what the people want, these officials *would* rebuild the four blocks of the downtown business district, or at least where the downtown business district used to be. Everyone who has lived in this city knows that the Central Plaza Hotel was one of the city's best hotels, opened the year we became a state, and the former territorial governor came to the opening night banquet, toasted Mrs. Stevenson, the owner's wife, in vintage champagne, and everyone ate oysters brought all the way from the Gulf. But it hasn't had an overnight guest with a suitcase in four years now; all day long those men sit in what used to be the lobby, squinting out above the paint line on the windows at the hot summer street, waiting all day for nothing but that single moment when the room clerk and manager, his sleeves rolled between wrist and elbow, reaches up, pulls the little brass chain, lights the green-glass-shaded bulb floating in the motionless air like a small model of Saturn in the barren sky. Next door, a bankrupt laundromat fills what was once the livery stable; the only living business establishments on the four blocks are two cheap restaurants, their menus written in white paint on the windows; three bars, where they sell you whiskey at ten cents a shot; two liquor stores whose trade is confined to pints of California muscatel. Properly used, this land could produce new jobs, new income for the city, bring new industries, help us to regain our place as the leading and most progressive city of our part of the country.

Or, just as surely, these same officials *would not* rebuild the four blocks of the downtown business district. This is the Skid Row of our city, and we should not touch it until we know what to do with the men who hang out there. Removing the cheap saloons and the restaurants and the broken-down hotels will only scatter these men all over the city, turn them into the good neighborhoods, cast them loose to drift where they will. Besides, the Central Plaza Hotel is the finest structure in the city; the cupola on top with its four arched windows is the unique signature of its architect. The mannerist Ionic columns supporting the angular pediments over the windows are a subtle nineteenth century adaptation of the Farnese Palazzo. To tear it down in the hope of stimulating the uncertain glory of a business revival is sheer vandalism. Besides, you really don't know if you can get any business to come in here anyway.

And so it goes.

That's what the people want.

On the other side of the rostrum, microphone, speaker's stand, the officials look out, or down at the speakers. Sometimes they themselves say something, ask a question, or pound with a gavel, demanding silence. For the most part they sit quietly, listening to whoever is speaking, or watching the others in the room, sometimes turning to whisper to a colleague or a messenger from the outside. What are they, the officials, thinking?

Who speaks for the people? If democratic government means that the will of the people must be paramount, who decides what is the people's will? Is it that decision demanded by the greatest number of speakers? The decision hurting the fewest people or hurting them least? Helping the most people even a little? Is there a compromise? What is cowardice?

As the voices continue, the officials shift wearily in their chairs, and from time to time, raise their eyes above the citizens ranged before them, above the clock on the rear wall, even above the ceiling molding (needs paint), and then, by closing their eyes with a splendid effort of will, they sometimes manage to see, not the people, but their city, and the sweep of its nearly overwhelming needs.

Like a lumpy bed on a sleepless night, no inch of which is capable of providing the slightest, momentary comfort, so the imagined city frets the fancy of the officials, back and forth from traffic jams to tax deficits; from insufficient police salaries to the unknown terrors of school integration; from dwindling commerce to industrial relocation; from slum inspections to the shortage of nurses in the public hospitals.

Never before in the history of the United States have elected city officials held the power—the sheer executive power—that they hold now. One hundred years ago, the officials could give out streetcar franchises and erect courthouses, appoint policemen and minor judges, but almost all of the physical changes in the city—the buildings, the transit systems, the piers—were wrought by private citizens, over whose work the city had only the most meager jurisdiction. Fifty years ago, the nation's first zoning laws gave city officials, for the first time, the right to control the size and kinds of buildings to be erected by private citizens. That was merely the beginning. Now the city's officials have, in most cities, the right and the duty to build low-rent housing, to build parks, to provide low-cost factory buildings to encourage industrial expansion. The city officials must own and run hospitals; must exercise responsibility for their share of the world's largest and by far its most expensive educational system. They must build schools for some people's children, demolishing the homes or livelihoods of other people before they can start. They may enter into contracts with the federal government for clearing slums, selling the land to private parties, or building their own improvements on it.

As they close their eyes, in figurative protection from the harangue, they can conjure up the changes they have already made in the shape and aspect of the city: the new hospitals, with red brick walls, and white lintels, where already the benches in the waiting rooms show signs of wear, and some of the floor tile is loose along the upstairs corridors; the new schools, largely glass and shiny preformed panels, built only three years before but already catering to a racial constituency different from the one they had planned it for. They can see the public housing developments, certainly an improvement over the slum buildings they replaced, but surrounded by grass turning brown, where people have cut across what was supposed to be a lawn. They can see the new highway, that slices ten minutes from the trip across town, but is already beginning to clog up at the Division Street exit at four-thirty in the afternoon; and they can see the new park, laid out splendidly with a nine-hole public pitch-and-putt course, while somewhere on a desk inside, a letter from the park commissioner complains that the greens need reseeding because the number of people using them has been twice the estimated total.

Never have American city officials held more executive power, and never have they had less political strength. In the face of the conflicting demands of the people in the hearing room, decisions must sometime be made.

Casting about for a safe course between the conflicting demands of their citizens, and the overwhelming needs of the city, as they themselves sense them, perhaps the officials will seek professional help. The specialization of the century has stimulated the growth of professional advisers, each with an area of competence: how to stay married; how to lose weight; how to pick a college for your child; how to run a city. If it is critical opinion your mayor wants, lots of it is available. Some is expensive, and involves hiring full-time consultants to come to town and study local problems in the field. Much more can be had for the price of a newspaper, or a book, or merely enough electricity to keep the television forum program going for half an hour on Saturday afternoon.

Alas for the poor patient; the doctors disagree in all respects but their assurance. The critics of the American city have been talking to it as a nagging wife addresses her drinking husband —in sublime confidence that the victim suffers from a simple disease, requiring only a simple remedy. If only, says the wife, you could stay away from that first highball when you leave the office. . . .

Similarly, Mrs. Jane Jacobs, whose *Death And Life Of Great American Cities* has been quoted as the final word on their plight by citizens suffering from an angry variety of afflictions, talks to the city on their behalf as though it were an erring husband brought to grief by bad company. *If only,* she tells the city, *you didn't hang out with those nasty city planners, and left yourself alone.* . . . You think too much, and always about yourself. You ought to take up a nice constructive hobby, like gardening, without artificial fertilizers.

Mr. Victor Gruen, not only a writer of books, but himself a city planner and designer, is similarly convinced that bad company has got the city in trouble. Mr. Gruen does not agree with Mrs. Jacobs that city planners are the cause of the trouble, however. He blames "auto-crats" and "traffickists." These are breeds of men who build automobiles, sell them, buy them, drive them, and, ultimately, want to use them everywhere. Stop listening to the traffickists, Mr. Gruen tells the city, and everything will turn out all right.

Miss Marya Mannes is most disturbed by the city's deplorable loss of *tone*. Things would certainly have remained very much better around here, she tells the city, if you hadn't let those awful people move in next door. Luckily, she does not feel compelled to explain how they could have been kept out.

Then, on a note of finality, comes Parson Lewis Mumford. He clears his throat, and, in oracular paragraphs, tells the patient that Salvation would be coming, if only the city hadn't put on all that weight.

This does not begin to complete the list of those who propose to tell what's wrong with the city; the full list includes not only editorial writers, but sociologists whose findings reflect deep thought and extensive research. The wife who uses a rolling pin has been joined by the lady armed with insights from her analyst. The journalist has picked up the urbanist, the cleric, the anthropologist.

Some of the criticisms contain new and startling leads; important, and previously obscure, facts. Many contain a measure of practical sense. Yet they fail to provide consistent help for the city official whose troubles feel more like a cerebral hemorrhage than a hangover. He is beset not merely by problems, but by demands of his constituents for specific, and often incompatible actions.

Perhaps it is true, as Mrs. Jacobs tells the world, that small old buildings are generally more interesting to the mind and eye than large buildings, built lately. But who can erect small old buildings to order? And who can satisfy the people who demand better houses right now, yet can't afford them?

It is also true, as Mr. Gruen says, that too many people bring their cars downtown, clog the streets, and demand new highways, bridges, parking lots. But how does calling them "traffick-ists," help the official to meet their demands? And what practical alternatives can he both find and afford?

It is true, as Miss Mannes has proclaimed, that New York, and many other older American cities have traded much of their dignity and grace for new buildings with new inhabitants. Does it help the official win the voters' silent acquiescence by telling them that they were born fifty years too late? Is his city like Vienna, whose citizens are proud to have always been fifty years too late?

Even if it is true, as Mr. Mumford insists, that medieval cities were clean, odorless, humane, and constrained from their pangs of growth by the walls outside, how does this information help the official who needs growth to provide the tax revenues for his groaning budget? In urging the values of city walls for the medieval city, Mr. Mumford neglects to explain how walls can be erected around the modern city without a return to the medieval theology and politics that made walls acceptable—at least until they were destroyed in battles, earthquakes, and revolutions. And who has wanted to rebuild them?

Then there are the more serious critics like Herbert Gans, Michael Harrington, and Nathan Glazer who appeal to the nagging conscience of the city official. Is your city doing enough for the poor? Are your clumsy attempts to stimulate growth in the downtown business section being carried, generally, on the shoulders or the bellies of those who happen to be getting in the way—the families living in the worst housing on the lowest incomes? What have you done lately about *de facto* racial integration?

If the official could work out a plan to conform to the suggestions made by any one of the critics, this mighty effort would throw him into conflict with the demands of the others. Concentrate on the urban crowding recommended by Mrs. Jacobs, and you fly in the face of the shrunken populations ordered by Lewis

Mumford; put low-income families into middle-class developments, to take the suggestion of Herbert Gans, and you confront
Marya Mannes with an even greater loss of the city's tone;
refuse to construct truck highways, in response to the pleas of
Victor Gruen, and you may be contributing to the very growth
of unemployment feared most by Michael Harrington.

The list of conflicts between the suggestions of the critics of
the city could be extended indefinitely. For his most depressed
moments, the city official can even find a set of critics, led
particularly by the members of the faculty of the Harvard-
M.I.T. Joint Center for Urban Studies, who will tell him that
the pain in his head is imaginary. There are no truly urban
problems at all. This conclusion, incidentally, has not led the
same gentlemen to recommend the closing of the institution
at which they teach.

Only an unimaginative city official could restrain himself
from asking, at least occasionally, why there is so much conflict
between the critics themselves. Is there nothing these people
agree about?

Here, the answer turns out to be quite simple. The critics
agree that nothing good has been done by private developers in
the American city in the past twenty-five years. The architectural
critics—like Ada Louise Huxtable and Allan Temko—report
that almost all the buildings which have been erected by private
commercial interests are ugly and when not positively ugly,
dreary in their repetitiousness. Worse, they have been built at
the price of destroying older buildings that were in many cases
greatly superior to them and far more humane (Jane Jacobs).
The prosperity caused by the postwar building boom has, in the
absence of effective government controls, caused the cities to
sprawl shamelessly over their adjacent green space (William S.
Whyte, Jr.); shoddy billboards and festering junkyards, the
result of private greed, have defaced the landscape (Peter
Blake); gross overpopulation, produced by lack of effective

planning controls, has destroyed the quality of urban man, and brought the modern city almost to the intolerable horrors of Imperial Rome (Lewis Mumford) ; children throwing stones through the windows of uncompleted new buildings express the hostility of Negroes to a ghetto that is worse than ever (James Baldwin); general prosperity in the city hides poor people whose plight is as terrible as any that the nation has known (Michael Harrington). And, in general, all agree that landmarks have been recklessly destroyed; human scale is lacking everywhere; architecture has rarely been so undistinguished; automobiles, structures, factories, profits, the almighty dollar, all have been placed ahead of the interest of the people.

The critics agree, too, that if private activities have made the city a mess, this mess remains unimproved by the public powers available to city officials. Subsidies to build government-owned homes for rent to low-income families, have produced only "sterility," "inhumanity," the creation of "economic ghettos." The power to control, through zoning laws, the use of urban land, has limited diversity, destroyed urbanity, stimulated monotony. The power to build highways with federal funds raised by a tax on gasoline has destroyed the center of the city, preferred automobiles to people, driven charm and diversity from the sidewalks. The power to condemn and replace properties that have been found to be deteriorated or substandard—urban renewal—has attracted the most biting criticism of all. It is state socialism for the rich (Charles Abrams); cataclysmic money (Jane Jacobs) ; and, to quote too many critics to list by name, it has thrown poor Negroes off valuable land, and replaced them with richer people who are subsidized at their expense.

When the specific criticisms of the city are so different, why are the attitudes that support them so similar? How can such divergent thinkers agree that private construction activities in our cities since World War I have been misguided? And reach similar agreement that public programs designed to shape or initiate private construction are as bad, or perhaps worse?

The city official might indeed wonder if there are some assumptions that his critics share about the city—but that he does not. Perhaps the perceptive official will agree that the critics share four assumptions about the modern city. Perhaps these assumptions have created, in their several ways, misunderstandings about the most serious problems that the modern city faces. Perhaps after one has looked at the four assumptions and the misunderstandings they have provoked, one can more fruitfully ask the same questions the official finds himself pondering at the public hearing: where does hope for the city lie; what is its future; what is its end?

II. | ROTISSERIES AND RETROGRESSION

The First Assumption: That cities have deteriorated for everyone who lives in them.

IT is accepted implicitly by most of the urban critics that cities are less pleasant to live in than they were before World War II. What does this really mean? No one, of course, can accurately recall the cities of thirty years ago, or reconstruct their urban pleasures. But perhaps we can weigh the extent and quality of the deterioration that troubles the critics by examining in detail one of the special urban pleasures which has clearly *not* deteriorated.

Consider the rotisserie chicken.

It's late on a winter Saturday afternoon in a large northern city. Assume that an urban critic (or any other city dweller of comfortable means) intended to eat at a restaurant with friends; but the friends have called to announce that *she* has a toothache, and *they* want to be excused. Assume also that the critic experiences a sudden desire to be excused from sitting in a room in which strangers are permitted to watch him eat. After carefully considering the lack of suitable nourishment in the refrigerator, the inertia of the stove, and the ominous silence of the cooking utensils, he decides on a brief sortie into the street. As he passes a nearby window, he observes five little chickens, their legs bound, their bodies pierced by spits attached to an endless chain that pulls them up and over a gas heating frame. An invisible but no less palpable force tans the skin of the chickens before his eyes. The fresh fat bubbles restlessly forth to drip into a tray at the base of the machine. Who, seeing those chickens on a wintry Saturday afternoon under the circumstances described, is not struck at one and the same time by an unexpected taste for rotisserie chicken, and a warm glow of satisfaction over his fellowship in a society which had prepared these chickens solely that they might be offered to his walking whim?

No premonitory telephone call, membership in any special club or brotherhood, status as good guy, social benefactor, patron of artists, or friend of friends is needed to procure for one's immediate use and enjoyment one rotisserie chicken. And no obligation! If one changed his mind, failed to appear, suddenly preferred canned Polish ham or a glass of papaya juice, no apologies are required of him, no excuses relevant. On the contrary, the very flexibility of the arrangement means, as well, that the storekeeper, at an unheralded order and then only, will jump to remove the chicken from its spit and nestle it into a foil-lined sack. Distant artisans have designed this sack and seen to its fabrication, solely for the purpose of ensuring that if anyone should take the cooked chicken home, it will arrive upstairs almost as warm as when it was removed from the spit.

The sense that all this has been foreseen—a long line of farmers, poultrymen, sack makers, gas appliance manufacturers, provision merchants, and store owners standing ready to ensure it—provokes the simple, ultimate pride of the city dweller. Each man may mark himself at the living end of the long chain of the world's work.

The rotisserie chicken is only a homely example of the city's continuing promise that the daily round of life may be so simplified that each man will have the more time to attend to the truly significant aspects of human experience, whatever, if any, they happen to be. It also suggests that in the city, the real city, the *big* city, not only barbecued chicken will be provided for his walking whim, but also *Béarnaise sauce,* people singing madrigals, rapid transit chess tournaments, homes in the section of the city one most admires, tickets for the theater, congenial company of the kind one happens to be interested in, and even a job. The terms of the city's promise vary, of course, from city to city, but the promise is there for those who have learned where to look for its fulfillment.

The city is a great bazaar for the initiate, and this constitutes the essential quality of urbanity. Stated or not, this appears to be the quality which the critics measure, a hypothesis which sug- gests the second important point about the rotisserie chicken. The critics may feel that the promise of ready availability of little cooked chickens with their legs trussed is one of the few which the city keeps more effectively for them today than it did thirty years ago. They seem to feel that in general, the ability of today's city to respond to the whim of the initiate has deteriorated. No amount of initiation can produce for the city dweller the satisfaction of what were commonplace whims thirty years ago: a restaurant that will make a *Béarnaise sauce* to his order; a theater where one can buy seats for the next performance; a park that looks clean enough to sit in; parking space; woodburning fireplaces; buildings with details that please the eye; clean buses; any taxicabs at all.

Because of these changes many have been willing to generalize that the city has deteriorated for everyone; but such an assumption is wholly unwarranted. The city's promises to its older initiates have deteriorated chiefly because the city and its purveyors have been encouraged to make so many more pledges to so many more people. Restaurants refuse to prepare *Béarnaise sauce* to order because the chef is paid too much to permit such frivolous use of his time. Theater tickets are harder to find on the spot because everyone who works in the theater is being paid much more money and only big hits survive; taxicabs are harder to find because more people are using them; and the parks, to touch lightly on a most complicated subject, are not so clean because the man who once speared waste paper with the nail on the end of a stick, is now a middle-class citizen who must be paid enough to afford his own car and possibly a motorboat as well. How many of him can the Parks Department afford?

The city seems less promising to the critics because more people are getting more of its services. In New York City, for example, where the population had scarcely increased in the thirty years between 1933 and 1963, automobile registrations had more than doubled. Per capita income in New York State increased more than three times in the twenty-year period between 1940 and 1960. So, of course, has the national income, and yet if one examines how the increase is divided among the families of the nation, one finds that the farm families, on the average, have received far less than the median increase, while the city families have received far more.

In talking about the deterioration of the cities, many critics emphasize the obvious fact that large numbers of families of above-average income have left to live in the suburbs. They fail to balance this with the more significant fact that an even larger number of city families who were poor thirty years ago have now become relatively affluent. They are in the marketplace demanding their share of the *Béarnaise sauce* and the taxi rides.

Furthermore, the spendable income of this new middle class has been increased by such devices as hospitalization insurance, the spread of pension and welfare plans, and in New York City by the rent control which still continues there. Incidentally, it reduces the median percentage of income spent on rent to (in 1960) 17.7 percent for the families living in apartments still under rent control, and thus augments the money they can spend in the Great Bazaar. The medical services offered by the hospitals grow geometrically more expensive, because more and more services are provided, while the people providing them are each being paid more money. Through the use of group insurance, hundreds of thousands of city dwellers who would, thirty years ago, have been in the public wards, are now lying in semiprivate rooms. There are voluntary hospitals in the cities whose public wards were once filled with patients but are now empty, a situation which, whatever its social blessings, creates a medical-teaching problem for the interns and residents on the staff. When the critic, or his friend, can't get a doctor to make a home call at night any more, this added load, and the doctor's added income, are probably the reason.

That one man's downswing may be the other man's upswing seems like a simple enough proposition to anyone who has observed a seesaw. But the sad loss of his own sense of initiation prevents the critic from seeing the other man's upswing. He notices only that he himself is going down. In order to satisfy the whims and tastes of a tremendously increased clientele, the suppliers of the city's pleasures have had to render them banal. And the prideful accomplishment of having learned one's way to the secret heart of the city is vitiated, because almost anyone else can find his way there, too.

I have no doubt that one of the most dismaying changes in the city is that the level of artistic taste—in literature, art, music, or dance—has risen so much faster than anyone would have expected thirty years ago. In the twenty years between 1937 and 1958, for example, the national expenditure on books increased five times. Esoterica that not so long ago could be found only in a special bookshop, patronized by the cognoscenti, are now being sold in paperback in a kiosk at the railroad station.

The very fact that more people are enjoying (or claiming to enjoy) the art that only the avant-garde once enjoyed (or claimed to) is, to that same avant-garde to which the critics

generally belong, a sign of the city's decline. If this seems an ungenerous attitude, it is nevertheless human. The sudden popularity of what had previously been branded arcane is particularly dismaying. It suggests either that one exaggerated the extent of one's real taste for it, or else that there is not so much
difference between oneself and a large part of the rest of the
world. In both cases, the result has been an extreme accelera-
tion in new discoveries in the cities, a constant race for new rites
of initiation: new schools of painting, new forms of theater, new
musical sensations. The esoteric is becoming banal with such
speed that it has seemed more practical to some initiates to render the banal esoteric, a process which has been described as
"camping." In any case, the constant smacking of lips over new
taste is one effect of the thunder of the spreading Ph.D. One
cannot attack it in principle, and yet it creates discomfort for
last year's initiates, a category that includes the critics.

A second reason for the sense of general deterioration is the
healthy emotional revulsion stimulated by change. A period of
social change may be a time for intoxicating enthusiasm, but
even with the enthusiasm, if there is any, sentient spirits feel an
air of sadness. Social change carries with it intimations of the
mortality of men and their institutions, of the physical world
itself. These are the overtones that pervade Mr. Robert Lowell's
poem about the Boston Common and the new garage beneath
it:

> ". . . Behind their cage,
> yellow dinosaur steamshovels were grunting
> as they cropped up tons of mush and grass
> to gouge their underworld garage." *

The same tones have been heard before, perhaps most famil-
iarly in Shakespeare's, "bare ruined quires, where late the sweet

* Reprinted from *For the Union Dead* by Robert Lowell, by permission of
Farrar, Straus & Giroux, Inc. Copyright © 1960 by Robert Lowell.

birds sang." Reminding us with brilliant economy that life cannot exist without change or death, they communicate an ironic melancholy which can easily be confused with a consideration of the merits of a specific alteration in the environment. Plato, perhaps thinking of this very confusion, warned of the danger of permitting poets to educate the young.

On another front, the same reaction to the implications of change is seen in the growing movement to preserve older buildings in the cities, setting them aside as historical or cultural landmarks. This is a complicated subject—but it does indicate that precisely at a time of change, its emotional implications lead to an attempt to mitigate it.

If the changes that have taken place in the city do not necessarily mean general deterioration, neither have they affected all the city dwellers equally. The large middle class in the cities has, despite all the outcries to the contrary, actually grown in size and in the income at its disposal. Yet there are at the bottom of the municipal heap many low-income families for whom change is urgently required, but for whom the last twenty or thirty years have meant that little has changed except their enticements.

Thanks in part to the wonders of television, these families now have a vision of how the world should be. The promise of equal rights, equal furniture, equal clothes, equal amusements, and equal tastes has never been more insistent. Yet contrast between the reality and the promise has never been greater. The low-income family, except to the extent that it has been moved into new quarters in publicly owned housing, is living in buildings that were designed originally for another use entirely or, if designed for occupancy by low-income families, at a period so different in time, at standards so different from those now proclaimed as "American," that the very contrast becomes a kind of pressure. It is interesting that so much of the criticism of the architectural style of low-income public houses comes from people who are not living in it: to whom it is a sign, not of other people's escape from drearier surroundings, but rather of the encroachment of the world on their own previous innocence. Thus Marya Mannes takes a boat ride around Manhattan and tells us that she hates the public housing projects she sees. "People [should] have light and air and plumbing," she says, but the public housing "obtrudes and spoils . . . the natural rhythm of a useful river."

Miss Mannes' somewhat grudging recognition that some changes are necessary for the city whose older form she greatly admired is occasioned by her sense that people lived in the old slum buildings. But change is needed also in the places where people work. The economy of the American city is largely imprisoned in multistory factory buildings with painfully slow elevators. Commerce, in the nation's older ports, is trapped on piers clustered too close to permit the use of modern barges; the older piers face marginal streets along the river's edge. They lack storage and freight assembly areas, a deficiency which produces a nightmare of tangled trucks when cargoes arrive. Truck highways are essential to bring freight access to factories, new and old, within the cities, if their raw materials and produce are to move, and their workers to be kept employed.

Because the city's structures are bony—city people live in buildings, not tents—the city itself resists these changes demanded of it. The very massiveness of its structures promises lack of adaptability. The solid buildings are so fireproof that city officials must plan conscious destruction as a preliminary to rebuilding. Catastrophic conflagrations can no longer be depended on to remove obsolescences even though these accidents served New York, Chicago, and San Francisco so effectively in the past. The European cities have been similarly served by wars, as well.

Every city was built by people who do not now live in it, and it fits its present population only like the borrowed shell the hermit crab inhabits. Yet, on the whole, it works; within the shell, the body grows and changes as it presses against its stony limits. Even while the rub of life against the shell raises blisters on the body politic, the body prefers present discomfort to the prospect of mortal change.

Change is painful in the city not only because it collides with a resisting physical structure, causing the movement, and perhaps the death, of other living organs attached to it. Forced change also contrasts with the sense of personal worth and dignity which is central to American doctrine and thought. Citizens may detest the area in which they are living. They may complain about the shortcomings of their working space. But they resist any sort of change when they are told they must accept it. Americans cannot develop an oriental fatalism about the forces which they might admit that they cannot control: population growth and the pressure exerted by it on one's neighborhood and one's city; the obsolescence of small stores because of the competing economies of mass purchasing and sales; the washing out of dozens of older crafts and skills by developing mechanization.

The critics sense the human tragedies implicit in these changes; and from them draw the general conclusion that all of the changes in the city constitute deterioration. Yet the city's problem is more subtle than this: to change the shape of the city's shell without breaking it; to tinker with the life inside yet not kill it.

But even this formulation conceals the basic fact of city life, the single fact most often ignored: within the city's shell there is not one life but many. The forces living in the city are in constant contention with each other, and not one of them is wholly right.

The critics of the city—from Mumford to Mannes to Jacobs —assume that there is a "we" in the city, which includes almost everybody. The "almost" takes care of the few exceptions whom each of these writers notes. Mrs. Jacobs' "we," for example, definitely includes her sister who lives in Stuyvesant Town, and excludes city planners and government officials generally. Mr. Mumford's "we" includes all his like-minded people, who have escaped the corruption of modern times, and most particularly have not succumbed to the automobile. Miss Mannes' "we" includes primarily the people who are on their way to Carnegie Hall for the evening, or perhaps, tonight, it's the opera. What none seems to recognize is that the "we's" are not identical; their differences cannot be reconciled by a single appeal to "we" against "they." The differences must be fought over to be reconciled. With luck, the fighting will be only political.

The contention of the colliding "we's" over the use of the physical space of cities—who shall live where, and how—is the central political fact in the present life of the cities. It would be pleasant to summarize the difference in the groups by a simple appeal to the elementary class differences that have become a part of folklore. But the fight for space in the cities—living space —swirls and eddies about the city's geography and class structure. It involves the same people in many different roles. There is the battle between the rich and the poor—or the middle class and the poor—for housing space. There is also the fight between the educational institutions and the people, often mostly Negro, who live near them. This has been as central an issue in Chicago, for example, as the continuing racial battle there.

While race is the most dramatic of the lines of cleavage between city groups, and shadows of race doubtless play on landscapes where it is not obviously the main issue, many other differences exist. Groups of citizens owning single family homes will fight, and force their elected representatives to fight, nearby construction of apartment houses and automobile service stations. Real estate groups will fight against measures that they consider dangerous to real estate values. Then they will split into two separate antagonistic camps on general zoning matters. Those real estate people who have invested heavily in vacant land will resist any new controls limiting the size of possible new buildings. The real estate investors who, on the other hand, own buildings may very well favor new and stricter controls, believing that they will tend to cut down new competition.

Just as the business interests see things differently from the tenant groups, so are there differences in point of view within the business community.

The industries that are faced with relocation almost always oppose new city-sponsored redevelopment programs. In New York, the taxicab companies, which traditionally occupy large garages on rundown land that is relatively close to the central business district, have had to move their garages so often since World War II that someone has described the taxicab garage as a favorable outcropping for bulldozer operations. Naturally, taxicab companies oppose such developments even though they well may be dues-paying members of the local Chamber of Commerce that enthusiastically supports the same development. Incidentally, the United States Chamber of Commerce opposes all federal activity in urban renewal, urging that local cities and private industry, hand-in-hand, should conduct urban renewal without help from the federal government. Many local Chambers of Commerce, on the other hand, not only support federal intervention, but urge that the federal government's share be increased from its present two thirds to three quarters or more, particularly in the smaller cities.

And there are equally important differences between different unions on matters of city policy and reconstruction. The construction trades unions, particularly when work is slack, will support almost all new construction projects; the unions representing the workers who are about to be displaced, frequently oppose a development which had the full-throated support of the construction trades unions, and perhaps even other unions more closely linked to the new *use* that will replace the present one.

This process of change must continue, perhaps at an even faster pace. The social critics will be hard to please as loved objects disappear with useless ones, good buildings crumble along with hovels. So long as men are able to criticize and comment, their words may modify the process, until ultimately new values will emerge from the change. Fifty years hence, a new generation of critics will be lamenting the passage of some of the values whose arrival is being lamented by the critics today.

III. LAMBS' DAY IN THE LIONS' CLUB

Second Assumption: That Americans live in communities.

CRITICS make a second misleading assumption about American cities, an assumption in which they are cheerfully joined by a host of well-intentioned amateurs. They assume that the word *community* can safely be used to describe any human settlement in which more than two people live without assaulting each other. If one wishes to keep the real world moving, however, *community* is a label to be used only when merited, like *Danger: Nitroglycerin.*

People talk blandly about the community, when they mean nothing more than a political jurisdiction that can be inscribed on a map, like Newark, New Jersey. Or, they talk of the community when they have in mind some vague geographical enclave, like the near North Side of Chicago. Or they talk of the community to mean a group of unrelated persons who share little of permanent importance but their latitude and longitude; for example, the commuters who board the Long Island Railroad at Rockville Center.

Yet, no matter how lightly the word is used, the overtones of *community* refuse to die out, lending to the place or persons referred to, a significance they never earned. The overtones of the word suggest that, in the area described, people have filed down their swords and spears; that they have created not only their own safety, but a web of love and kindness, understanding and mutual support, which it is sacrilege to tamper with. The careless abuse of the word *community* leads away from an understanding of the differences between the people occupying a geographical area, and towards a veneration for kinship that may not even exist. The unearned veneration blocks changes that may, on other counts, be highly desirable.

It can be demonstrated that Americans were not always so ready to talk loosely about communities as they are today. In the years before World War II, when structural engineers were lucky to find jobs in the shipping room, when interns were forbidden to marry, when attending a Major League baseball game involved an affront to one's sense of racial justice, all young people of sense and discernment knew that community was a distant goal. It was to be achieved only after an immense upheaval would have extracted the nasty differences between people, leaving the engineers talking economics with the shipping clerks, emancipating interns, and permitting black men to play ball with whites. As faith in the significance and inevitability of the coming immense upheaval has faded, even the young have sought to find the values of brotherhood in their immediate environment. It is probably a watermark of the change in mood that Greenwich Village, the section of New York City which most insistently looked beyond the here-and-now, is currently blessed with many spokesmen for the present Greenwich Village community. In the name of this legendary creation, they not only demand positive action to protect the streets against hucksters and the guitar players against the police (or sometimes vice versa). They also oppose the construction of new buildings that will bring into the area people who will be "unable to conform to the traditions of the community." This in the Mecca of the nonconformist!

In semisuburbia at the edge of the city, when the pressure of population growth means that apartment houses must now be built, home owners raise the cry that the community is being destroyed. Proposed actions must be measured not on their merits, but on what they do to the so-called community. The same cries are raised in other middle-class environs when new school patterns threaten a change in racial constituency, or when the suggestion is made that low-income families must be provided with a place to live nearby, or when someone proposes that well-planned industrial developments will benefit the tax rolls and provide employment. The so-called community may have been a potato farm five years ago; it may consist of old buildings whose inhabitants never spoke to each other before the new school was proposed; it may—as the last Census demonstrated in New York City—contain a population no more than 58 percent of which was living at the same address five years before. These facts matter not. What does seem to matter is the attachment of the portentous *community* label to the mild, spasmodic, and entirely particular kinship that might spring up about an ambulance service or a new school. The cry of *community* has overstressed the significance of roots, an invisible part of the human anatomy, and underrated the presence of feet. The American community which is being talked of so often, and so profoundly, is essentially superficial and highly mobile. Provided only that a certain homogeneity of social class and income can be maintained, American communities can be disassembled and reconstituted about as readily as freight trains.

Nor should it be imagined that the cry of "Don't touch our community" is raised only in the white, middle-class semisuburbs. Try to demolish dingy flats in an impoverished section of the city, and the city official finds himself opposed not only on the grounds of the individual hardships inflicted on the residents. The opposition claims also that the community is being destroyed. These are the very sections of the city in which disorganization and discouragement are so widespread that they may be thought to provoke the anxiety over one's own insignificance which, for example, David Riesman has described in *The Lonely Crowd.* It is no longer astonishing to find that Mr. Riesman himself has objected to planned urban redevelopment because it destroys the human relationships in the slums, relationships which he has been at pains to tell us eloquently do not exist.

A similar conclusion about the loss in community feeling suffered by people relocated from the site of a public improvement was reached by Marc Fried in Boston. Mr. Fried, who published his findings under the title "Grieving for a Lost Home," found that 26 percent of the women relocated were emotionally disturbed two years after the move. Were they not "emotionally disturbed" before moving? Those who have used Mr. Fried's work to attack urban renewal have inferred generally that people living in areas to be renewed—where home rents are low and physical deficiencies high—actually are well satisfied with their homes. With this assumption, I find myself in rather serious disagreement. It is my impression that what strikes observers of the poor as the "rejection of middle-class standards," or satisfaction with the low-income environment in which they are living, reflects primarily fear of what they do not know. This in turn reflects their sense that if the world in which they are living has done so poorly by them, it cannot reasonably be expected to do better.

To point out that the unknown is frightening, and perhaps less well arranged than it might be, does not change the inadequate home into something satisfactory. If nothing is done for the family living in the dark, cramped, dirty, neglected buildings, with vermin, rats, sleazy plumbing, and the unconquerable dirt, we may be postponing the fears engendered by proposed change, but we do nothing to mitigate the ever-present, grinding reminder of inferior status which a shoddy home represents. I am certain, but can't prove it, that especially for those whom sociologists sometimes describe as marginal people—those furthest removed from being able to impose their will on their environment—feelings about the inadequate home are complicated and ambiguous; its very inadequacy represents both a doleful confirmation of their low position in the world, and a hiding place against new experiences which the past has told them will only be worse. The object of these ambiguous feelings is hated at the same time and to the same pitch as its removal is feared.

For these marginal people, the "grief for a lost home" is an emotion with many roots; certainly one cannot derive from it the simple inference that if they had been left where they had been, all would have been well.

I sense also that society's own desire to demolish the inadequate house puts into the hands of a relocatee his first high card in an endless and hopelessly lost game with the hostile outer world. Knowing that this card can be played but once, its owner will not squander it. In the army, during World War II, many draftees became veterans before they had been soldiers. On the train to Camp Upton to get our uniforms, some of my fellow soldiers were already calculating their pension rights and veterans' preferences, not because they were especially greedy, but because they rather realistically saw that unlike many less meritorious people around them, they had never been dealt a hand to which the world assigned any value. But the fact that they had been required to serve in the army, however reluctantly, was such a hand. They intended to play it well. Our general romanticizing of people without money makes it sound a monstrous accusation, to suggest that some poor people have exaggerated the trauma of relocation in order to bargain best for new houses and cash. It would shock no one to hear that the owners of property, whose holdings are acquired by the state under eminent domain, characteristically overvalue their property. No one is shocked to hear that property owners actually hire people to represent them professionally in an effort to collect more than the property cost them, or than they would have been willing to sell it for privately. Everyone expects that of people with money. Something of the same technique is used by people who are forced to move in the course of the government's acquisition of land for whatever purpose, including urban renewal and public housing. Since they have no property, their only marketable asset is hardship in a society pledged to eliminate that hardship which it is unable to ignore. Because this hardship is described to social workers and community organizers who are constitutionally disposed to believe the people they are listening to, and whose luck it is to listen only to the downtrodden and disadvantaged, it seems an immoral suggestion that some of the people displaced by urban renewal might just possibly be exaggerating the sense of deprivation that they feel over their "lost homes."

A similar, if more natural misunderstanding, exists with regard to the mystical kinship shared by persons of another race or religion. Writers on urban problems are quick to tell their audience about the Negro community. This entity may indeed come into existence of a sort, like the Jewish community, when some central issue—perhaps remote in space, like Mississippi or the Sinai desert—is raised. But not otherwise. In matters less than citywide, there is not one Negro community; there are many in any large American city. The several Negro communities may even exist simultaneously in the same area. In Chicago, for example, it was widely held that the Negro community objected to an urban renewal plan in the Kenwood area adjacent to the University of Chicago. On closer examination, it turned out that at least two Negro communities occupied the same blocks. One, the vocal group, consisted of the owners of the houses in which the other community lived as roomers. The group that raised the objections could more accurately be described as the landlord community than as the Negro community, but for obvious reasons its members preferred the latter label.

A similar situation arose in the Bedford-Stuyvesant section of Brooklyn over a proposal to construct a middle-income housing cooperative with state and city subsidies. Although the middle-income development had originally been proposed by a group of Negro social workers and religious leaders, it was fought by the owners of the buildings that would be demolished. This group, also Negro, claimed to constitute the Negro community. The Board of Estimate, which decides such matters in New York City, abandoned the plans for the new housing after one of the landlords, a stout, and somewhat emotional lady, told the officials at a public hearing that the Negro people would defend their right to own houses in Brooklyn with the same vigor that Medgar Evers, the martyred NAACP worker in Mississippi, had stood for their voting rights. She threatened to lie in the streets in front of the bulldozers and give her life for the cause of her community. It was a formidable display, which the other Negroes—social workers, ministers, and tenants—could not begin to match. The Board of Estimate, apparently convinced that they had been watching the Negro community in action, figuratively tiptoed out of the room, and the new middle-income cooperative remained unbuilt.

The community mystique has prompted a number of social theorists to the pragmatic conclusion that if communities are desirable, and don't exist, it is necessary to create them. Community organization has become a highly regarded part of the effort to improve the conditions under which poor people live in the cities of America—although the subjects are not generally described as poor, but rather as disadvantaged or culturally deprived. I suggest that these words are used not merely because it seems impolite to call someone poor, but also because the social work profession tends to dampen the idea that the main difficulty faced by poor people is their lack of money. Such a suspicion would result in transferring a large part of the problem of the poor from the field of social work to that of economics. In any case, community organization has become such an important part of social work that the organization itself—not the physical improvement of the conditions in the life of the poor —is now often the major goal of the philanthropic work. Even with the stimulus of a practical goal, and lots of money, community organization is a terrible task. Without the stimulus and with less money, it requires the patience of Penelope: each day's work is unraveled every night.

To understand what life looks like to a community organizer one should accompany such a man on a mission, perhaps to the East Harlem section of New York City, once one of that city's highly flavored Italian areas, but now occupied largely by Puerto Ricans. Lacking a headquarters, a social worker who seeks to form a Boys' Club for the tenants in two adjoining tenement houses, must operate within the buildings themselves. Someone, no one remembers who, has agreed to hold a meeting at eight-thirty that night, in one of the tenants' apartments. The boys in the two buildings have been invited by the social worker, and, he hopes, one or two of the mothers who are interested.

When the social worker arrives, on time, only the tenants—a mother and daughter—are at home in the chosen apartment. The social worker sits on the very soft couch. The room is very hot. He notices its pink and blue walls, cannot keep his eyes from a lamp made of a conch shell. Was this the night for the meeting? One woman arrives, in tennis shoes, on her way home from the beauty parlor where she works three evenings a week (during the day, she has a full-time job). But she did not come to attend the meeting; in fact, she had forgotten about it. Nevertheless, she stays. She and the older woman then talk in Spanish with giggles and quick glances, half covert, at the social worker. The woman in sneakers, Mrs. Alvarez, talks like a leader: she has assumed command, but the social worker is not certain this is good. The door opens part way, and a small face briefly intrudes. The social worker greets the face by name— when are you coming to the meeting, Angel? Face disappears. Then Mrs. Lopez-Vega arrives from upstairs. She is the thin, nervous woman who started the idea for the Boys' Club (which the social worker really wants to start only because he thinks it will then be possible to organize the members' parents to form a Tenants' Association that will try to get the landlord to do something about the garbage collection, the leaky roof, and the undependable hot water system). Mrs. Lopez-Vega is surprised that the meeting appears about to take place; she insists on speaking English. There is nothing more important than a Boys' Club, she says, but isn't it already a bit late to start and where is Jaime, and what about the two Perez boys from downstairs who said last time they wanted to have a softball team and, two hours later, the social worker has decided to reschedule the meeting for the following week. He believes there is enough agreement about this to justify entering it into his report. The cold January wind is welcome after the heated apartment.

There are, it should be noted, community organizers who approach their task from a wholly different direction. Such a man is Saul Alinsky. Nicholas von Hoffman, one of Mr. Alinsky's associates in the Chicago Woodlawn Project, has described social reorganization in an article in *Social Progress*. Mr. von Hoffman explains his view that the only real opportunity offered to the community organizer is to make use of the natural leadership of the area he wishes to organize. The organizer, then, gives direction to the natural work of the local leader, often the kind of direction that it is impossible for the participant himself to see. Mr. von Hoffman very graphically compares the work of the professional organizer to the comments of a clever kibitzer in a chess game. He suggests that in the community chess game, the advice of the expert kibitzer is, or should be, of a generally revolutionary character.

It is not clear whether Mr. von Hoffman and Mr. Alinsky want to stimulate community organization because they seriously want revolutionary changes in American life, or whether they want to talk about revolution in order to stimulate community organization. If this latter is what they are doing, they certainly have stumbled on the tracks of a number of very practical politicians who have found that nothing is so exciting to people as the identification of a sinister enemy near at hand. The trouble comes later, when you try to control what you have started; Mr. von Hoffman's writing, which reads like a call for violent revolution penned by an astrologer, leaves open the question of whether Mr. Alinsky will be able to help the people he works with, and to limit what he has begun, any more than could the Sorcerer's Apprentice or Robespierre.

The difficulty in organizing communities would never be suspected merely from listening to the speeches of political leaders who, we may assume, have been reading newspaper editorials based on the books of the urban critics. Many of these leaders are elected to represent physical areas which contain groups of people so diverse in their point of view, their income, their religious affiliation and cultural interests, that they consist, in fact, of unrelated groups of people physically overlapping each other. But the leaders persist in speaking about the voters in their district as the community, and implying that their knowledge of what the community wants is as certain and as precise as the alleged fact that the community wants any one thing, or two things which are not mutually contradictory. I listened, once, to the leader of a Democratic Club on New York's West Side who addressed his organization at its annual luncheon, and told the members about the needs and wishes of their community. The community, in this case, is an area of the city with several hundred thousand inhabitants, over half of whom are Puerto Rican. There are also a large number of Negroes, together with the remnants of what was once a thriving colony of low-income Irish families overlooking what had once been an elevated railroad, and a considerable number of European refugees, most of them well on in years, and speaking a heavily accented English. At the luncheon at which he spoke so confidently about the community he represented, there was hardly a Puerto Rican; not one Negro except for a city official who did not live in the district; very few Irish names or faces, because the particular faction of the Democratic party to which the district leader's club belonged had started its political life in opposition to the older Irish politicians who had been in charge of the party previously. A clear majority at the luncheon were young, native-born lawyers and business people who were interested in getting into politics. The desires of those present, or their ideas of what is right, constituted the program that was being put forward in the name of the community. The community to which the speaker was referring consisted, for all practical purposes, of the people who were attending this lunch.

The stress on community is used not only to provide simple explanations for complicated phenomena, or to lend a gloss of independent authority to the desires of a group of people whom the speaker is attempting to flatter. It also serves to make a gross, and frequently unjustifiable, distinction between the urban dweller and his government and his institutions. "The community," says the leader of the local PTA, "is opposed to the idea of building the school where the Planning Commission wants to build it. The community knows its needs better than anyone else." This is a very convincing line of argument, until one realizes that it means only that a group of local residents are wrapping themselves up in the word *community*. The only persons able legitimately to speak in the name of the community in this sense are the members of the Planning Commission appointed by the Mayor who was elected by the voters. The PTA was not elected by anyone. Similarly, the community, as described by its self-appointed spokesmen, frequently finds itself opposed to the universities, the hospitals, the museums, and the other institutions which require space to live and fulfill the functions for which they were established. The *community* used in this sense means the city stripped of its government and its institutions; it resembles the whole living city about the way a filet of sole resembles a living flounder.

Of course if you are consistent about it, you can believe that human institutions are corrupting influences, and that in the perfect society governments are to be elected by some process other than political in which peoople would express their consensus by some wired-in communion of bloodstreams.

Surely people outside government, and their associations, have the right, indeed the duty, to shout at, complain to, criticize, and lampoon their elected officials. They also have the equally important right to refrain from electing them. Sometimes those outside government may be right on an issue, and their elected officials wrong. Indeed, those outside may be right on every issue—and those inside wrong. But it seems to me that the exalters of the community finally go further than this. Some of them, following their premises to their logical conclusions, suggest that elected officials must necessarily be wrong, because the act of assuming responsibility cuts one off from an understanding of what people need and want. This, I think, is nonsense, and it's the special kind of nonsense which, if listened to, would put the cities' problems beyond hope.

MONEY MADNESS

The Third Assumption: The temptations of money are so great that local governments will ride roughshod over the interests of the people to get it.

THE third assumption made by contemporary urban critics is that there is something at once indecent and dangerous about large sums of money, that mysterious and alluring subject of which it is never quite polite to speak. Most moderately well-brought-up Americans were told as children that only the vulgar discuss money; they did not know how much money their parents had or earned, an innocence that had the natural effect of making dollars as interesting as sex, and as little understood.

The ambiguities of money, like those of sex, have tended to make Americans exaggerate the healing qualities of the commodity. It has frequently been stated that middle-class Americans expect sex to accomplish miracles of happiness. Similarly, middle-class Americans have ascribed to money the miraculous power to prevail over most obstacles. It is generally held that the temptations of money are so momentous that only saints can resist them, and that money is so powerful that its use for the solution of problems entrains a weakening of moral fiber, much as does taking taxicabs instead of walking short distances.

Applied to the problems of the city, this sense of awe over money leads to curious conclusions. Mrs. Jane Jacobs, for example, tells her readers to beware of "cataclysmic money" in their attempts to rebuild, by private effort, worthwhile older buildings in the parts of the city that meet her idiosyncratic standards. Most private persons who actually rebuild older houses, partly for their own use, and partly to rent out, run short of money before they are finished. At some point in the proceedings, they lie awake at night wondering what part of their original plan must be abandoned or tearfully modified because of the dogged persistence with which costs of reconstruction outrun budgets. When they are warned by Mrs. Jacobs to beware of the "cataclysmic money" that would solve their immediate problem, she is playing on their middle-class guilt feelings about the mysterious and secret commodity. It is precisely money that they have been coveting: money in any form, honest, dishonest, theirs, or government's, but money. She has reminded them that money should properly be regarded by them as only a poor substitute for ingenuity and art; their lonely covetings are unworthy, and should be abandoned.

In a sense, Mrs. Jacobs has been using their awe of money to quicken their suspicions of something rather different—the intervention of government into the housing problem. She understands perfectly that without a flood of money, decent homes for the poor families of the cities—as well as a growing part of the middle-class families—are impossible. Yet she has no faith in government intervention because she feels it threatens the private reconstruction of neighborhoods like her own West Greenwich Village. Government intervention brings with it an irritating (to Mrs. Jacobs) predilection for separating soap factories from homes, a bias for reducing the cost of homes by high-volume construction, which, in the cities, means apartment houses. Mrs. Jacobs prefers her own economies: crowded land, simpler physical standards, and no money wasted on separating factories from homes, trucks from playstreets.

Yet even the Jacobs method—limited though its application may be to certain special sections of the older cities—requires money. Money rarely comes without strings. These are usually, in construction matters, the strings tied to their loans by mortgage officers who seek to protect their banks' investment standing and profits by demanding high construction standards and evidence of conventional neighborhood stability.

The federal government has sought to modify these restrictive standards by developing a system of mortgage insurance. The insurance is intended to stimulate construction—especially of a kind, or in areas, rejected by bankers—by removing the fear of risk from the queasy consciences of the bankers themselves. The risk then attaches to the consciences of the government servants who represent its insuring agency—the Federal Housing Administration, or FHA. FHA has helped to produce literally millions of homes, usually in places where the private bankers might *almost* have been willing to make loans insured only by their market judgment. In more difficult areas, or for less conventional construction, FHA has demonstrated an important human law: that the public servant's fear of being criticized is as great as the private citizen's fear of losing his own money. Since the government servants of the FHA are wary of being criticized for losing the taxpayers' money, they attach their own strings to their insurance policies. They have their standards, too; and so, indeed, have Mrs. Jacobs and the people who join her in admiring areas only if they meet her qualifications.

While Mrs. Jacobs warns of the "cataclysmic money" brought in by the government, she does not remind her readers that private money invested in rehabilitating small residence buildings—"unslumming" as she calls it—is equally "cataclysmic" for the tenants who happen to be living in them. These tenants—who must have been paying low rents if the entire enterprise is to be financially possible—must make way for Mrs. Jacobs and her "unslummers" just as surely as if a bulldozer knocked down their homes. In privately financed rehabilitation, the unsubsidized rise in rent is formidable. To be more precise, private rehabilitation is *more* "cataclysmic" to those affected by it than is public renewal, at least if the public activity is in a designated "urban renewal" area. In such areas, the government pays moving expenses for displaced tenants and provides assistance in finding new homes. And if the displaced tenants find their own homes—and if these meet normal community standards—they are paid a bonus. In New York, for example, the bonus for a five-person family may go as high as $500.

Faith in what Mrs. Jacobs is too sophisticated to believe in —floods of government money with no strings at all—has been expressed by a number of other critics of government housing programs, including such curious bedfellows as William Buckley, a right-wing Republican, and Charles Abrams. Both feel such awe of the power of money that they have written that the housing problem for low-income families can be solved simply by providing each family with the cash or credit to buy a good home on the private market. Mr. Abrams, two decades ago, in *The Future of Housing* discussed the snares of ill-considered home ownership by a family without regard to its ability to pay. Yet he now seems to be advocating a gross increase in home ownership produced by even more liberal mortgage terms than those of the past, with subsidized interest rates. The dream is compelling. With one hand full of money, the dreamer uses the other to lead people from the crowded, multifamily old houses of the city. He will spread them out in the semisuburbs, one family to a house.

In support of such a proposal, one might argue that an urban slum family—coming to the city from a rural farm—would understand a single-family house better than the demands of a multistory tenement. But what differences there are between the rural farm shack and the modern semisuburban house, which would be the home of the chosen family! Electricity, heat, refrigeration, stoves—all the problems of maintaining them, operating them, paying for replacements, and ordering repairs, dropped on the shoulders of a family made middle-class by a sudden shower of coin.

Mr. Abrams indicated the problems well enough twenty years ago: the problem of the deterioration of the building, and the setting aside of too large a part of the family budget in order to keep it up. This is augmented by uncertainty over rising local taxes, more difficult transportation, lack of skill in maintenance.

Nor does money, however precious, solve the planning problems involved in constructing subsidized one-family homes for low-income families in the outskirts of cities. If we build one-family homes, no more than twenty households can be fitted on to an acre; in multistory, multifamily construction, the norm may run from a comfortable 75 to a perilous 200. The low level of new development for single households means that the new homes must be placed on what was vacant land: the cost of acquiring existing buildings would be prohibitive. Such a scheme would mean assembling large new sections of vacant land near cities, serving them with new mass transit and new roads, new schools, new street-cleaning and garbage-collection services.

There are cities (Philadelphia is one) in which the typical low-income neighborhoods consist of endless rows of identical one-family homes. London's slums are similar. In Philadelphia, the local public housing authority has been buying and rehabilitating these for rent to low-income families. A number of houses can be acquired, with government powers, close enough together so that they can be efficiently maintained and managed.

If these can be rented to low-income families, it is presumably possible to sell the same families their houses, using cash grants, or subsidized mortgages. But what are the advantages? And what inspections and supervision would be needed to see that the houses do not, once again, slip back into their previous dilapidation? If the families begin to earn more money, and want to leave their houses, under what conditions can they sell them? And to whom? And who gets the money that went into the purchase? Perhaps a formula can be devised to cover this, but what purpose would be served by this complicated pattern of ownership? In the end, are these small, dark houses, with no windows along their sides because of the row construction, with almost useless front and rear yards, as satisfactory as the multi-family, multistory developments, covering a small portion of the land, which have been designed by good architects even on limited budgets? Money helps the form of the building, but its power to change the form of life remains uncertain.

One of the most significant difficulties in this use of money is the opposition of nearby home owners. They object strenuously to the construction of low-rent conventional public housing developments in their own neighborhoods, even when these developments look very different from their own homes. It seems fanciful to suggest that they would consent, not merely to be infiltrated, but to be surrounded and drowned in a sea of homes like their own, but belonging to people who are not really paying for them.

Failure to face this challenge to the power of money accounts for a general belief, often heard, that one day the cold war will end, releasing for the cure and feeding of cities vast sums of money no longer needed for armaments. This is a high hope, but one that ignores certain crucial facts. One of them is that it is difficult for the federal government to spend money in cities.

Money spent on arms is politically neutral as far as cities are concerned. It changes nothing important in any geographical area, because the government's direct spending is always concentrated in a place which by definition is unpopulated. In the old days when field artillery had ranges limited to twenty miles, it was possible to establish army camps within the country which did not displace a single person. When during World War II, the Army dropped such camps like confetti on the piney wastelands of the South, the money that accompanied them, however, benefitted the nearby villages, transforming Jeeter Lester into a taxicab driver, and Flem Snopes into a realtor. The scent of cash made wise the simple with a speed that good doctrine alone has never been able to achieve. I never heard of a Southern village which objected to the urban changes temporarily thrust upon its boggy suburbs by the United States Army; I am told that French villages competed equally strenuously for the privilege of having American military cemeteries (with the possibility of future tourism) located in their environs.

There is a further distinguishing mark to military expenditures: the federal government is permitted to make them directly. But this direct action is forbidden to the federal government inside the cities, except when it comes to putting up a courthouse, or, sometimes, a federal office building. Even United States post offices are now increasingly built by local businessmen and merely rented to the federal government. Low-rent public housing is subsidized by the federal government, but built and owned by local housing authorities, that are instruments of the cities or towns in which their projects are located. The federal highway program does not involve the construction of roads by the federal government, but rather the establishment of standards and the financing of the work of the states. The states and cities are not ready to roll over and let the federal government decide what to do within their borders.

Some accountants believe that it costs the United States four million dollars to shoot a single Atlas missile into space, where ultimately it disintegrates without causing any inconvenience to anyone. The same amount of money will pay for one elementary school in New York City where land and building costs are at least as high as they are anywhere in the United States. But what a difference there is in the ease of spending the money! While the missile bothers no one on earth, the school is certain to be controversial. At the public hearing on any big city's capital budget, *each* PTA president stands forth and explains why the school her children attend is the *worst* disgrace to the fair name of Buffalo, St. Paul, or Denver; that the cafeteria is *the* dingiest and most unsanitary; the library, the worst lit; and the building itself needs replacement most urgently. It remains for the officials to decide which PTA president is to be attended to first; whatever the decision, it will be unpopular with the others.

Let us assume that the funds survive the argument and the bitterness that flow from the need to defer five schools in order to erect one. A general area having been picked for the school, the officials must next delineate a precise site. Suddenly the field is reversed. Where, all too recently, the officials were faced with aggrieved mothers, each demanding that the school be placed in her district, now they are faced with angry property owners, storekeepers, residential tenants, demanding that the school not be placed on the site selected for it. They explain that the school should not cause the destruction of homes; that it should not be located near bars and grills; that its construction on what appears to be vacant land will cause the demolition of three tennis courts.

Finally comes the most difficult school question of all—how to select sites which will contribute to the breaking down of racial segregation. To achieve this end, city officials are told they should locate new schools only in "fringe areas," but this advice is more easily given than followed.

Plan a school in Manhattan's Upper East Side, for example,

where the nonwhite and white populations meet at 96th Street. It must be located near that boundary so that students can be drawn from both sides. But if it is located too far north, the white students' families will be reluctant to let them attend; if it's located too far south, the Puerto Rican families who, by and large, occupy the section of the city—East Harlem—directly above 96th Street, will be unwilling to let their children travel to it. The basic parental motivation is the same: in a strange part of the city, occupied by people of different race and different manners, the children will not be quite safe. This feeling is as strong among the Puerto Rican mothers as among the white mothers. As one explained to me, "If my child get sick, in the school here, someone come and he tell me. If he do something not right in the street, is okay where we live, but down there, where they not like us anyway, he only have to do one thing wrong, and who can say what happen to him?"

Another trouble with locating schools in the fringe areas is not only that they are more needed elsewhere—or more strongly demanded elsewhere—but also that the fringe areas are likely to be the very sections of the city most subject to change. In the northern cities, the nonwhite population has been growing with the result that the boundaries of the areas it occupies tend to bulge, and overflow. In practice, the laws banning racial segregation have developed only a few stable areas in which people of different races—but usually of similar economic background —live side by side. Without positive government subsidies to promote attractive, nonsegregated areas, the ban has turned many formerly all-white areas into all-Negro areas. This provides somewhat better housing for Negro families, but only rarely an interracial pattern of neighboring.

The educational effect has been that schools actually intended for fringe areas, where white and nonwhite neighborhoods meet, find themselves in wholly nonwhite areas once the sites have been approved, the architectural drawings made, the contracts let, and the land acquired. Racial geography changed during the progress of the work.

Throwing up their hands at these frustrations, some proponents of racially integrated education are talking now of a new idea—the educational park. Such a park would contain a combination of elementary, junior high schools, high schools, and perhaps junior colleges, constructed together on a large tract of land set aside exclusively for educational purposes. The tracts would be so large that, according to their advocates, they would create a world of their own, neither white, nor black, nor residential, nor commercial, but simply scholastic. Politically the scheme would appear to rest on a simple proposition: if white parents object to the busing of their children into Negro sections, and Negro parents object to the converse, a program of busing all children into a strange section may be politically marketable because each group's discomfiture is balanced by its appreciation of the other's.

No one familiar with the problems of site acquisition in the crowded cities can believe that it will be easy, or even perhaps possible, to assemble in any city the land needed for the construction of even a single educational park. If urban sites as large as fifty or one hundred acres are well served with transportation, they are likely to have been discovered by developers; if private developers are not attracted to a site in today's market, it is likely to be out in a desolate section of the city, near the flatlands or the dumps, where sea gulls wait to pick apart the edible shards of this prodigal civilization, and the smells of marsh and ordure combine to amuse the very young. Put my child's school out there? One can almost hear the anguished cry of the mother, visualizing her small progeny penned in his playground adjacent to the distant wasteland. If the federal government handed one city some $50,000,000 with which to erect an educational park, it might be possible to assemble the site, clear it, and proceed with the construction, but only after an extensive exercise in practical politics.

If it is so hard to accept money for education, a purpose which the world regards as almost holy, how much harder for the cities to accept and use money for purposes of which many important groups of citizens disapprove. Highway money, for example, was until recently acceptable in every city; now, public officials are hearing from those who happen to be living, or working in what will be the future roadbed. They also hear from those citizens who see a menace to cherished urban values in the clipping of central land space in the city to make room for automobiles.

Federal money for housing is not, like money for weather satellites, politically neutral in domestic politics. Housing money can't be spent in any of the cities until sites are approved by the local governing body, which must hold a public hearing. It is a rare housing proposal that does not land on someone's gouty toe. The money in it, the jobs, the pressures of the construction industry are too vague to drown out the complaints of those who will be relocated, or those whose middle-class neighborhood is threatened by change.

The long story of the Lower Manhattan Expressway indicates that federal money, even in large sums, is not so tempting that it can sweep everything before it. This Expressway, which would connect the Hudson River tunnel with the East River bridges, and provide direct truck access to and from Manhattan in the process, has been talked about by reputable planning bodies since 1928. The federal and state governments have agreed to pay practically all of the cost of constructing it. The Expressway remains unbuilt, at this writing.

To understand the magnitude of the financial temptation, one must understand that the Expressway would produce more than $100,000,000 in federal and state funds. Since the lion's share of construction money goes to labor, which spends it locally, the effect of approving the Expressway on the city's economy, merely during the period of construction, would be the same as though the city had succeeded in attracting $100,000,000 in convention business. To succeed in the latter, the city government, the Chamber of Commerce, and the Hotel Association would stop at very little short of fraud. Yet the Expressway remains unbuilt. The argument that it should be built because it will spur payrolls in the city is, when made, criticized as selfish, by those whose homes lie in the way of the Expressway. Somehow it is generally agreed that it is selfish to prefer your job to someone else's home, but that it is only human to prefer your home to someone else's job.

In spite of the financial difficulties in which most municipal governments find themselves, the simple money advantage to the city of accepting federal funds for redevelopment and reconstruction is seldom decisive.

The same is sometimes true for private funds. Even the state universities, which receive money from the state, from their alumni, and, under some circumstances, from the federal government, are unable to spend it as they wish, because, on the municipal scene, a new university building is no more important than the rundown residential buildings which it may replace. Indeed, it may be less important, because the people who attend universities rarely have much in common with the people who live in the seedy hotel, or the dilapidated tenement. For one thing, university students rarely vote; but this is not the full measure of the difference between the city's interest in the people displaced and its corresponding lack of interest in the institution. In Chicago, in New York, in Cambridge, and even in New Haven—to mention only a few of the cities where the Town and Gown conflict has lately sharpened—the university represents or symbolizes the marshaling of the strong conservative forces of the community. Whatever the social principles of the university, its faculties are white, by and large; whatever its dedication to the life of reason and the pursuit of truth, it has become a vast land-owning enterprise, whose annual budget and payroll rank it with the nation's largest businesses. The more enlightened of local politicians begin by asking the university to "be a good neighbor," meaning that although, in theory, they accept the notion that the university must expand to survive, they expect it to relocate those who must be displaced to make room for it (a reasonable demand), to develop social services to assist them, and to make some constructive contribution to the social problems of addiction, crime, and prostitution that all too often are concentrated in the areas immediately surrounding some of the nation's larger urban universities. The university pledges itself to all of these goals.

Ultimately, it turns out that neither the enlightened politician nor the university spokesman has been telling the whole truth. The president of the university, knowing that he has no answer to the social problems of the neighborhood, is willing to spend some money for what amounts to good public relations, but in the end, when he wants to demolish a building, or take it over for faculty or student housing, his first obligation is to the university. He is paid by the trustees to get the building demolished when the university needs it; to clean up the crime in the area as quickly as possible; and to conserve the university's money for the purposes for which it was originally given, the teaching of its enrolled students and the advancement of scholarship.

The local politician claims to want only that the university adhere to more humane methods in dealings with the local people in the course of relocating them. In his heart, he has hoped that the cost of such procedures—and the delays involved —will so exceed the university's capacity and patience that it will give up and ultimately find some way to keep the local people and their votes where they have been. Obviously these two basic positions cannot be reconciled; it becomes increasingly difficult for the universities to spend their money even on physical reconstruction and development in the cities.

It is perhaps a consequence of the resistance to money that it is now common to hear challenges of the value of money in any case.

It has become fashionable to believe that because money cannot provide help for all of the problems of the city, that therefore it can provide help for none of them. Indeed, some are now claiming that providing money for the cure of human ills imposes a sort of tyranny on the recipient: he is, in the recent phrasing of the social worker, being victimized in that we (the social workers and their backers) are imposing middle-class standards where they are, in fact, irrelevant. Those who claim this—who urge that the emphasis on cleanliness, order, regular work habits, and nonviolent behavior in personal relations, imposes middle-class virtues on lower-class people—have forgotten that they are simply echoing the Victorian notion that the Lower Orders behave as they do because they want to, and that any interference with their pattern of life is misguided and even cruel.

Money cannot provide in our cities what nothing else has provided on order: the human miracle of liberation. It is equally futile to believe that money alone makes beauty, cures drug addiction, or itself magically manufactures human happiness, or stops hatred. But the absence of money may certainly provoke the evils which its presence does not cure.

Lack of money produces welfare budgets in which human needs are weighed out with an apothecary's balance, and human desires in an eyedropper. Lack of money means excommunication from an urban world which exists primarily for the exchange of goods and services conveniently, in which the wonders of the marketplace are thrown in our faces day and night from billboards, television sets, supermarket windows, signs on trucks, billboards in buses, subway trains, over the radio and even hung from the skies. It is hard to believe that a human spirit will flourish generally in a state of excommunication.

Money can save life. In the cities it can produce fireproof buildings, important in an America which has made extensive use of wood even in its dense cities. Money can redeem the natural resources of the nation from wastage and pollution. Money can, in the cities, provide privacy as well as safety, a basic physical prerequisite to a life of dignity and purpose. Money, spent by national intent, is simply a national decision to devote resources and manpower to the achievement of a specific goal.

The cities must develop a strategy for the use of money, a program which will make possible serious federal programs for dealing with the urgent problems of the cities. There is no work before the cities requiring so much imagination and care. Yet their uneasiness about money keeps the urban critics from collaborating with the elected municipal officials in the development of programs. Without firm support for important programs for the city, the federal government's surplus income will go into tax reduction instead of public improvements and the social programs that the cities need.

V. GOOD NIGHT, LINCOLN STEFFENS

The Fourth Assumption: That newspaper writing about local government is by and large, accurate; and that the more startling the account, the more accurate it is likely to be.

THE urban critics have been schooled in a variety of disciplines—architecture, journalism, sociology, literature. (Who remembers, for example, that Lewis Mumford wrote avant-garde fiction in the 1920's?) Noticeably, however, they have not come from the ranks of former government officials: few estranged mayors are explaining what is wrong with cities, or entertaining the public with gaudy reminiscences of how life looked from City Hall. Whatever may have caused this, it has meant that the critics, as a whole, know little more about the workings of a city government than what they read in the newspapers. Next after mimeographed broadsides put out by plaintive taxpayers, serious journalistic essays about municipal government may well be Gutenberg's least valuable bequest to the American city. Serious journalism does not mean the reports turned out daily by the competent reporters covering the regular City Hall beat; it does mean the profound "think" pieces assigned to the working newsmen by the managing editor with an idea, or the special essays sometimes written by otherwise responsible newsmen during their vacations, or for sale to a market other than their regular employers.

I suggest that nothing could serve American city government better than putting the works of Lincoln Steffens on specially restricted shelves in the journalism schools of the nation. *The Shame of the Cities* continues to haunt the city rooms of the country's major newspapers.

Reading serious journalism about the city, and noting the baleful eyes with which its writers perceive municipal events, one realizes that, just as the French soldier was supposed to carry a Marshal's baton in his knapsack, so the modern reporter carries an unused copy of *The Shame of the Cities* in the top of his portable typewriter—the one he uses at home for serious work. Has anyone bothered to read this book lately? It turns out to be bland, vague, and repetitious. Journeying from city to city, and devoting one chapter to each, Mr. Steffens discovered that each city suffered from the same problem: there was gross collusion between politicians and crass businessmen in the award of highly profitable municipal contracts or franchises. Nevertheless Steffens finds that some businessmen of good family remained honest and incorruptible. If these could be lured from the wing chairs in their clubrooms, honesty might triumph over wickedness and sin, returning good government to St. Louis, Minneapolis, San Francisco, or Camelot. In the hands of Perry Mason, Mr. Steffens' evidence of specific wrongdoing committed by specific people might have convinced a television jury, but the cities described by him in 1902-1904 seem no more real today than that beachless version of Atlantic City on a Monopoly board.

I do not quarrel with Mr. Steffens' view that honesty is a good policy for those who can afford it, but I do quarrel with the writers who feel that this issue—collusion between government and business—is simple, and that Lincoln Steffens has defined it. The relations between private industry and municipal government have become exceedingly complicated. In any city, jobs for people living and working there, and thus education, health, and welfare funds for the city government, depend on the answers given by businessmen to their own questions: Shall we stay here? Can we expand here? Or had we better move elsewhere? Urban governments seek to elicit the answers they desperately need by offering inducements in the form of special tax benefits, and plant construction credits. In the case of the older cities, the municipal officials hope to sway the businessman to stay and grow, preserving jobs and taxes for the city involved. This is collusion of a sort between city official and business executives, using public powers to increase the profits of the latter. It is an attempt to make a public virtue out of a process which Lincoln Steffens described as a shameful crime; the act is the same—the granting of public favors to private interests—but new circumstances have changed its meaning.

Lincoln Steffens' suggestion that municipal problems are related to a single cause—dishonesty as he defines it—confirms the cheerful notion that a personal culprit is responsible for municipal mischances and disappointments. The attractions of this theory are persuasive to most journalists, who, carrying with them the rest of the population, customarily blame their mayor for whatever may be unsatisfactory, on the theory that he combines the resources of the federal treasury with the authority of a commanding general in the field.

Several years ago, *The Nation* published a special edition dealing with New York City problems and titled, in frank salute to Lincoln Steffens, "The Shame of New York." The edition was a splendid specimen of the Steffens effect. When it appeared, the reader discovered it to be crowded with facts—names, dates, and allegations of wrongdoing much more precise than anything the master himself had set down in *The Shame of the Cities*. Subsequent researchers testified that a number of facts had been incorrectly reported by Fred Cook

and Gene Gleason, the authors of "The Shame of New York."
Corrections notwithstanding, misstated facts and unjustified assumptions had done their damage. They had confused housing,
one of the city's most troublesome problems, in a flood of moral
oversimplification. I suggest that much of the discussion of the
housing problem by the critics reveals a similar misunderstanding.

What Americans call housing—more particularly, decent
homes—constitutes a major trouble in the cities of the nation.
Nothing else is quite so unsatisfactory to so many people. Particularly unsatisfactory are the homes for families of limited
income, especially when these families are unable to flex their
limited strength in a market distorted by race and religion,
prejudice and restrictions.

A city family needs a home that must be heated in winter,
and well ventilated in summer. The dwelling must be strong
enough to keep out the winds and the rain, the snow and perhaps an earthquake, to say nothing of wild beasts and burglars.
If the city is large, the house must be so designed that it can be
put alongside, or even over or under, another house, without
danger to both. The modern city house must be so well
served by water and other utilities that the neighborhood will
not be swept again, as so often in the past, by plague and fire.
If several homes are piled on top of each other, mere human
muscles will not provide the power to take people from the
street to the upper stories. A 140-pound housewife carrying ten
pounds of groceries up three flights of stairs has done the same
work as raising half a ton almost five feet. She therefore demands an elevator, which is, in effect, a vertical electric trolley
car that must be paid for by the tenants in the building. Any
product made to these specifications must be the most expensive
single product, by far, put at the exclusive use of a single
consumer. In New York, Chicago, San Francisco, such a home,
including land, costs $20,000 today. It should be obvious, even

to the man on the subway, that if a new barely minimum en-
closed place for him and his family costs more than a new Rolls-
Royce Silver Cloud saloon with whitewall tires and a builtin
walnut bar, he will have a problem buying or renting it for
his personal and exclusive use.

Government housing policy is, in effect, directed toward closing this "Silver Cloud gap."

Nor is the original cost of construction the whole story. Heating requires fuel; elevators require electricity. Someone must
gather the garbage and wash the public halls; someone must
mow the grass, if there is grass, or pick up the scraps of paper
that have been dropped around the building. Someone must
collect the rents, and pay the janitor, find new tenants when
one moves out, repair the stove that breaks down, and clear the
stoppage in the waste line under the kitchen sink. Someone
must repaint apartments, fix holes in the wall, deal with damages that appear mysteriously, accompany city inspectors on
their occasional rounds. Anyone who has ever owned his own
home knows the work that maintaining it involves; the extent
of the work increases more than arithmetically when a number
of unrelated families share the same building. All these costs
widen the Silver Cloud gap.

And its width ultimately depends on the number of systems
that have been installed to reduce the tenant's own work load.
If, as in Viennese low-cost apartments, each tenant must heat
his own space, the management not only saves the cost of the
heating system and the fuel, but the cost of the man who would
tend the boilers, inspect the equipment, issue specifications
for fuel, examine bids, check quantities and pay the fuel company's bill. Central heating, elevators, air-conditioning—the
maintenance of each one of these systems has widened the Silver
Cloud gap beyond its earlier limits.

And this is precisely the point at which the Lincoln Steffens
view has intervened to obscure the housing problem. The gov-

ernment's attempt to close the Silver Cloud gap must depend
in part upon assisting private enterprise, or at least certain private enterprises, with favors never before given by governments
in this country to purely private enterprise in the cities except
corruptly. This bit of history affects especially the journalistic
view of the government program known as the Title I program.
The Nation's issue on "The Shame of New York" specifically
attacked this Title I program. In Mr. Steffens' footsteps, the
writers of "The Shame of New York" condemned that city's
Title I activities because, they claimed, it put too *large* a public
subsidy at the disposal of private developers. I think it can be
shown that the trouble was exactly the opposite: that the Title I
program failed to achieve all its objectives because it put too
small a public subsidy at the disposal of private developers.

The Title I program was adopted by Congress in 1949. Its
passage was the Congressional answer to a plain and disturbing
fact: the cities of the United States, taken as a whole, were challenged by new and formidable competition. The competitors
were the vacant land areas around the city, to which many well-
off families were moving. Similar empty spaces attracted
branches of downtown stores, factories, and sometimes even
office buildings. Families gave many reasons for wanting to
move, but the reasons had remained impractical until FHA
mortgage insurance simplified the financing of new, single-
family houses. Escaping families left the poor behind to over-
crowd the inadequate structures in which they were living, has-
tening their deterioration. Fleeing industrialists abandoned
factory buildings that were substantially underused, or perhaps
vacant altogether.

Congress recognized the danger to the cities in this flight
from their centers. It chose not to ignore the problem—for
many reasons, perhaps. Humane concern over the overcrowded
and deteriorating slums was surely one of them. Another was
the recognition that unless the decay at the center was arrested,

the movement outward would accelerate, because there would be less to keep other well-off families and factories. Fear that this erosion of their tax base would send cities to the federal government for more help, probably constituted a third reason. A growing recognition that federal housing policies had stimulated the competition was a fourth.

Perhaps more important than any of these, Congress was moved to stem the tide primarily because it acknowledged that the cities were a *fact*, that they existed. The cities represented a tremendous investment of private and public money, in homes, schools, streets, mass transit systems, hospitals. They represented also a human fact that radiated moral as well as political power. It was inconceivable that even conservative members of the national Congress could simply allow the wastage of these assets.

Congress decided in 1949, in effect, that hope for the cities rested on making them more competitive in their continuing battle with the suburbs. Since the primary attraction of the suburbs was this vacant land, Congress decided that to prevent further urban wastage, the cities would have to be given enough help to get rid of some of their undesirable and unsound buildings, thus making the land beneath them vacant, and relatively no more costly than the vacant land outside the city itself. Undesirable or not, the existing city structures generally proved expensive to buy, so expensive that private city builders operating on their own could not buy them, demolish them, and then compete with suburban builders who started with vacant land. Anyone who bought these buildings would have to charge rents high enough to give him a satisfactory return on an investment that would have covered the total cost of the land itself plus the buildings that were on it when he started.

In New York City, and a few other places in the world, some sections of the city had become so fashionable that residential tenants have been willing to pay enough rent to cover such acquisition and demolition cost in their rents, together with all the costs of the new building. New office buildings have been characteristically built on the sites of older ones. But despite great popular misunderstanding, these reusable sites constitute only a tiny, highly desirable part of the entire city. Congressmen felt that if government—federal and city government in partnership—paid for the cost of acquiring the buildings that had been on less desirable city sites, a private developer could then afford to build on the land which might otherwise lie festering forever in the heart of the city. There was some happy talk at the time to the effect that this contribution to the builders' acquisition costs of badly used land—a contribution which came to be known as a write-down—would enable the new private owners to build housing for moderate-income citizens on such sites.

Anyone who bothered to look carefully at this thought, would soon see that in cities where builders could build on vacant land cheaply enough to cater to middle-income families, Title I would produce middle-income housing; in cities where builders could not build cheaply enough for this purpose, Title I would not produce it without further subsidies. In practice, Title I land acquisition subsidies made the builder's attempt to construct moderate-cost housing somewhat harder than it would have been on vacant land he acquired himself elsewhere. The government, not unnaturally, having invested money in getting rid of what had previously been on the site, wanted to be sure it wasn't contributing to development of a wholly new set of undesirable buildings. It insisted that the city as a whole adopt a "workable plan" including a housing code, and that any development under Title I must meet standards of light and air, fireproof construction, open space, and other structural characteristics which, whatever their esthetic qualities, were surely more expensive to build than the wood-joist, brick-wall apartment houses decorated with fire escapes that private builders construct on vacant land on the outskirts of many of our cities. Until recently, the federal government provided no special financing for the investor who was to build on Title I land; he had to work this out for himself.

Finally, there was basic difficulty with Title I from the building investor's point of view: by definition it did not give him a site on Fifth Avenue or the Avenue Foch for which there was a ready demand, but rather a site in a section of the city that was already notorious for its lack of desirability. Thus, without giving the developer the financial assistance and subsidy that would have made moderate-cost housing possible, the Title I program facilitated his buying land only in a part of the city where the tenants who could afford it did not wish to live.

Even a careful, unbiased reader could read "The Shame of New York" all day without learning that this is the real set of conditions governing Title I. The burden of that story is that the program was simply a pointless bonanza for private speculators; and that eager developers, so avid for the profits in Title I that they were prepared to bribe and cheat in order to obtain "sponsorship" of projects, doomed the Title I program to perpetual corruption and failure.

As it was originally designed by Congress, the Title I program seemed like the answer to the problems of a great many cities. Only a few of the cities, however—San Francisco, Washington, Philadelphia, and New York—found that prospective private developers were as interested in the cities as the cities were in them. To attract developers on the terms which the federal government enabled them to offer, the cities had to turn their attention to areas distinguished more by their potential appeal to the high-priced end of the private market than by their strategic significance for the city as a whole. Ultimately, under the pressure of the planners and the practical politicians, who were themselves under pressure from citizens and private organizations, the states and the federal government modified some of the ground rules. These changes made moderate rentals possible in urban renewal areas, and even encouraged cities to place low-rent, publicly owned projects in them. Since the urban renewal area was now more of a bargain to the ultimate consumer, whose income was to be subject to maximum limits before he could get an apartment, the city was able to select renewal areas with less attention to the market attractions and more attention to its own total needs.

Also in response to the same presssures, the federal and local governments encouraged the use of Title I for the expansion of universities and other cultural enterprises, and for the construction of commercial or industrial facilities. The rehabilitation of existing buildings was encouraged, instead of demolition and replacement, at least in those infrequent slum areas where the older buildings were once good enough to justify rejuvenation. Finally, more attention was paid to relocating families who were living on the sites to be redeveloped. The fate of very small retail businesses remains bleak, however, in the cities of the nation, and it must frankly be said that those which must be relocated from urban renewal sites sometimes fail to survive the move, although it might be conjectured of those that failed that their survival was problematical under the best of circumstances.

All of these changes were wrought by the use of money, subsidies which in one form and another were made available by federal, state, and local governments to urban renewal developers. In exchange for the subsidies, the developers had to agree to limit their possible profits, and to permit minute examination of their books and records, and approval of their expenditures in advance. In practice, the apartment houses produced with these additional governmental aids on Title I land have increasingly been owned by cooperatives, sponsored largely by labor unions or local community groups. Controlled profits have surely been made by some if not all of the contractors erecting the buildings—financed either by state- or city-subsidized mortgages, or by the federal government's subsidized mortgage plan. But the ultimate ownership of the property rests in the hands of the people who live in it, and whose income is below maximums established by federal or local laws.

None of these changes and developments, and none of the reasons motivating the original Title I program have in any way mitigated the bulk of the basic journalistic indictment, nor can it be fairly said that these changes were made in response to newspaper criticism. The Title I program fails to meet the Lincoln Steffens test because it provides for special favors from the municipality (with the added complicity of the federal government) for the apparent benefit of a private person or a group of private people. The acceptance of this indictment by the critics underlies most of their resistance to Title I. The resistance will continue, I believe, even if the federal government's new plan for rent subsidies becomes practical, and such subsidies are used in the future development of Title I areas. The critics' conviction that there is something morally wrong in such government-private relations attracts far more attention to the relocation from Title I housing sites than to the relocation from the sites of future government-owned improvements like schools and highways. It is the injustice of relocation that one hears about from the critics, not its successes. And it is Title I relocation that one hears about, not the relocations caused by private industry, operating alone, or school construction, or highway construction, or public housing construction, although these have, in almost every city in the nation, caused much more dislocation than has Title I.

The gravamen of the charge made by Cook and Gleason against the Manhattantown project typified the Steffens suspicion that favored developers, once they had been permitted to purchase the site at a written-down price, refused to proceed with the development, in the hope that they "might try to keep an old slum going as long as possible while they skimmed off a fortune in rents." * Another assumption basic to almost all journalistic exploration of the slums is that they are highly profitable to somebody, and that if this person can only be found, and forced to reinvest his swollen profits in his starving buildings, the Silver Cloud gap, at least in older buildings, can be closed. To this assumption is added the implication that municipal government corruptly protects the profits of the slum owner by not enforcing the laws controlling conditions in such buildings.

That slums are profitable appears to be a proposition readily capable of proof or refutation. Unfortunately, it is not.

In the first place, no one requires the owners of most slum buildings to keep public records of their operation. Only a few cities require that the owners of rental housing be licensed. When owners of rental buildings submit financial reports to protest their taxes, or to demand increases in controlled rents, they naturally tend to understate their income; when they ask banks for mortgage money, or offer their buildings for sale, they are inclined to overstate it.

Even if accurate figures on rents collected and operating disbursements were available, it would be surprisingly difficult to decide what constitutes the dollar profit on a particular building. These are not clean and neat enterprises, with inventory controls, maintenance budgets, and reserves against the possibility of not being able to collect all the accounts receivable. The amounts of money involved in the rent roll of a single tenement house or low-rent older apartment house are small; a single unbudgeted major repair can change an annual profit to a loss. The families living in the slum buildings, by definition, include the workmen most likely to be laid off, and rent arrears are common. As if these difficulties were not enough,

---

* Even if slums were ordinarily profitable, the emptying of the buildings during staged demolition means a rapid decline in rental income, while the fall in operating costs is much slower.

we must also consider that low-rent tenement houses often fail to meet the legal standards they are required to meet. Would there be any cash left for the owner if he did meet the requirements of law? My own experience in the management of experimental non-profit slum rehabilitation leads me to think that legal operation is financially impossible.

Finally, the profit received by the owner of this kind of property is very different from the profit collected by the owner of stock in General Motors. No one knows how much of the owner's time was involved in operating the property, nor how to calculate the value of that time. The low-rent buildings that are generally in the best condition are those whose owners live in them, and do not only the managerial work, but even the carpentry and the minor plumbing themselves.

Nor is this the end of the difficulty in determining the profit of old buildings. Let us assume that we have operating and rent collection figures from tenement houses, and that we have the experience necessary to correct them for their inevitable biases. Let us assume also that we have decided to neglect the depreciation in value as the building ages and to make an arbitrary management charge, no matter who does the work of managing. What we have is the net income of a building, or an average net income of buildings, expressed in dollars. But to compare this income with that returned by other investments, we must determine the profitability, that is, the ratio between the annual dollar profit and the value of the investment—a difficult value to determine.*

The real estate investor uses this ratio to gauge his profitability. He is interested in knowing how much profit he can make on his own funds, so that he can decide whether his money could be working better elsewhere. However, such a calculation of the return on the investor's money depends on something

---

* The most lucid study of tenement-house profitability is Chester Rapkin's *The Real Estate Market in an Urban Renewal Area,* New York City Planning Commission, 1959.

more than the simple profit-and-loss accounting of the operations of the building. It depends, rather, on how much of his
own money he must invest in order to receive the profits from
a certain piece of property, and on the terms he is able to ne-
gotiate for the money he borrows.

It is characteristic of slum property that normal mortgage
institutions are reluctant to lend money on it. The reasons are
many: the risk is high; more intensive supervision is required
for loans of this kind than for loans on new, substantial properties; the individual loan amount is relatively small, meaning
that the overhead in mortgaging is higher; mortgage insurance
from the federal government is unavailable. The banks know
in any case that the world takes a dim view of people who own
and operate slum properties: banks are reluctant to buck popular trends unless their daring can win unusually high rewards.
All of this points to the conclusion that a relatively low proportion of reasonably priced money can be found for a slum
property. On mortgages that may be obtained, the rate of interest is likely to be high, and the amortization period short. The
result is that the monthly cost of mortgage service is likely to
be high. All these factors combine to limit the profit-expanding
magic of the mortgage. Specialists like Chester Rapkin have
analyzed the effect of possible mortgage terms on the profitability of the tenement houses he investigated. Rapkin discovered that the owner was earning about 13 percent on his own
money each year but that to purchase a tenement house, he had
to put up 30 percent of the purchase price in cash. The high
cash margin means that the owner's capital can buy him control
over only a limited number of buildings unless he pays high
mortgage costs, or forms exploitive syndicates that simply do
not intend to maintain minimal physical decency. For the honorable owner, limited in his funds, the risk of loss in any one
of his buildings may endanger his profits on the whole lot.

Thus, it is clear that large real estate operators have little interest in owning low-rent old buildings. Their owners tend to be small investors of several different types. Some will make some kinds of repairs, but not others; some would like to maintain properties, but cannot afford to; some inherited properties, and cannot get rid of them (real estate cannot be abandoned because the owner continues liable for its dangers and shortcomings); some rent to tenants who abuse and destroy their property; some demonstrate a callous indifference to the housing codes and the humanity of their tenants that glares through endless rationalizations; some are retired couples who try to derive a retirement income from a single building; some simply buy and sell properties and sometimes repurchase them like stock traders, forming and dissolving syndicates as confidence men are reported to establish and collapse bucket shops.

None of these differences is apparent to the newspaper pundit for whom all real estate owners are alike.

Revising a public policy for the improvement of existing buildings—when their ownership is in such diverse hands in our major cities—seems an almost impossible legislative task. How can government funds be risked in such a market? How can senior, extortionist mortgages be evaded? The difficulty of these tasks has hardly been glimpsed by the critics, who, believing in the journalistic myth of the profitable slum, seem unwilling to understand why rehabilitation programs are difficult to plan. Just take the profit out of the slums, they say. A better slogan might be: put profit into slums for decent owners so that they will have the means and the incentive to fix them up and keep them fixed. How can this be accomplished without raising rents exorbitantly?

A program for refurbishing existing slums must provide financial help for the owner who will use it successfully, and expropriation for the owner who will not. No law can successfully require an owner to continue losing money indefinitely. A government administration capable of dealing with the

shades of difference in real, live landlords must be extraordinarily sensitive, extraordinarily complex, and extraordinarily
expensive. It will, perforce, be engaged in favoritism, partiality,
and public assistance for private profit-making interests—all
of the acts which, on other grounds and in another epoch, Lincoln Steffens condemned. Perhaps the critics, in their denunciation of the bulldozer, look forward to such city programs with
cheers and happy anticipation. But if such programs ever become a reality, the journalists will need only a week to find out
that they favor some owners over other owners, that they provide public assistance at great public risk for private gain, and
that they depend on expediency instead of principle. The restless movement of Mr. Steffens in his catafalque will crack the
plaster; it is hard to believe that the officials will not prefer life
in the quiet old permanent slum.

Even if the city administration decided to let Mr. Steffens
sleep undisturbed, by postponing indefinitely the development of a risky and inequitable policy toward the owners of
frail and weary homes for the poor, he would probably be
roused by rumblings from another quarter, rumblings about
public housing.

The very words, public housing, still stir the emotions of
many Americans, possibly because this is the nation's boldest
venture into state ownership. Public housing means government ownership of that holiest of private domains, the home
and hearth. It is therefore socialism in a sense in which the
postal service and the TVA—both public utilities—are not.
The socialism of public housing naturally offends many staunch
believers in the primacy of private enterprise. It also offends
many former and current socialists because the results indicate
that public ownership is not itself a wonder drug for the cure of
human ills.

To explain the gap between what they believe public housing is, and what they believe it might be, the journalists rely

on lavish use of the word *bureaucracy*. This probably returns us to Lincoln Steffens, even though the poor man never used the word and probably never even heard of it. If bureaucracy is a specific accusation, not merely a shapeless epithet hurled in the direction of any institutional growth which happens to be governmental, it must refer to that narrow view of his office that inclines the officeholder to grudging fulfillment of its forms, with total indifference to their human implications.

Officeholders with this view of their work may be simply incompetent, or they may be victims of the difficulty all administrative systems find in devising rewards for imagination and daring that are as convincing as the punishments for deviation and error. But it can also be surmised that many bureaucratic systems grew in response to the fear of newspaper criticism. "Accuse me of graft, will you?" the bureaucrat rhetorically asks the press. "Okay, I'll run my shop according to the book." The book has been written by state and federal legislators who also fear newspaper criticism and have concluded that it is better that a hundred hungry people be humiliated than that a single lazy villain gull the taxpayers.

Applied to public housing, the epithet *bureaucracy* is especially convenient for the journalists because it lends a gloss of unanimity to widely divergent and even contradictory criticisms. One journalist criticizes public housing because he sees it as simply a depository for families on welfare, unwilling or unable to fend for themselves; another journalist attacks it because it fails to provide decent housing for the very lowest income levels. Since both blame the defect they see on bureaucracy, neither sees that their criticisms contradict each other. The fact, incidentally, is that, in New York City, for example, some 18 percent of the families in public housing receive welfare allotments to supplement their incomes from other sources. No family is turned down because of its inability to pay rents, because welfare supplemental assistance is presumably available for that purpose, although many of the families receiving welfare are ineligible for public housing for other reasons.

Public housing is criticized by some newspaper writers because they think it is deteriorating physically into new slums; by others because they believe that public housing administrators consider the physical condition of their buildings more important than the state of mind of their occupants. This basic difference does not keep both parties from agreeing that the troubles are caused by bureaucracy. Similarly, some newspapers describe the public housing developments as extravagant or inordinately expensive; others criticize them as mean and inhuman. Whatever the fault may be, both agree that bureaucrats are responsible. Finally, some newspapers criticize public housing on the grounds that people who could afford their own homes are living in it; others attack it for precisely the opposite reason: because its tenants are limited entirely to the poor.

One of the more interesting of the journalistic accounts stressing this last point was written by Harrison Salisbury, the present assistant managing editor of the New York *Times*. Mr. Salisbury had represented his newspaper in Moscow for five years; in 1958, four years after returning to the United States, he wrote a series of articles for the *Times* in which he discussed youth problems in the city with special reference to public housing. He concluded that the limits imposed on the incomes of public housing tenants were responsible for many of the social problems which he found in the projects. He quoted Kenneth Clark, apparently with favor, as suggesting that the bureaucrats are responsible for the shortcomings of public housing.

Mr. Salisbury's view of income limitations has widespread support among people who might otherwise be counted among the friends of public housing. The denunciation of income limits has been echoed by a number of urban critics, who have drawn from the existence of limits the suggestion that homes for low-income families should be provided without public ownership. Many of the critics seem to have forgotten how the public ownership came into existence.

The federal government authorized a public housing program for the first time in 1937. There was nothing particularly new about the ownership of at least some homes by the national government. The White House, say, is public housing; so are the quarters in the vanishing manned lighthouses along the nation's coasts; so is the Commandant's house in the Brooklyn Navy Yard, built in 1807 and perhaps soon to be designated a New York City landmark. But in a constitutional government with limited powers, these homes were traditionally built only for people who, like presidents and lighthouse keepers, already were involved in a special relationship to the government. New in 1937 was the notion that the government should build, own, and maintain homes for people who bore no special relationship to it, whose claim to its attention lay in the fact that without substantial government help they had no hope of getting decent homes in their lifetimes.

It is important to remember that almost no private interests ever built homes deliberately for people in the lowest income brackets. In cities, the poor huddled together in homes built and abandoned by wealthier people. Only by huddling could they afford even the shoddy quarters they were living in. The attempt to reduce the huddling and lighten the shoddiness by passing laws requiring higher standards brought higher rentals as well. Local efforts to provide lower-cost homes through limited profits and philanthropy dwindled away. In 1937, as the construction industry lay paralyzed by the Great Depression, Congress decided that along with a program of public works, low-rent housing construction might help to revive it, and employment with it. The congressmen who reached this conclusion had to find a program that could be fitted into the American system of government.

The program they ultimately devised—one which has stood the tests of the constitutional lawyers and the buyers of municipal bonds—rested on three axioms of public policy and economics. First, it was widely understood that the neediest people in the country couldn't afford decent homes if they had to pay any part of the cost of building them. They would be lucky to be able to pay for upkeep, heat, and management. Second, it was assumed that government should not be permitted to pay for the whole cost of constructing homes if private people would ultimately own them. Third, no public program for housing low-income families could be permitted to compete with the efforts of private industry to provide homes for people who could afford them.

The first axiom was satisfied when Congress decided that the federal government would pay for the whole cost of new houses to be rented to poor people. Even as you and I, the federal government preferred to pay this cost a little bit at a time, over a fifty-year period. The government's fifty-year promise to pay encouraged bond buyers to advance the cash with which the carpenters and bricklayers were paid. The second axiom was met when Congress decided that the homes built with its money could belong only to local government institutions, called Housing Authorities, which would actually erect, own, and operate the buildings. To meet the third stipulation, Congress decreed that such publicly owned housing could be rented only to individuals and families of low-income as defined by local law, and that no government money could be used in any city or town for low-rent housing if there were vacancies in existing good housing that rented at or near the prospective rentals for public housing.

While it is clear that many new governmental forms are now

possible in this field—for example, that the government itself might now lease, rather than build, the houses for low-rent families; and that some of the housing could and should be provided through rehabilitating existing buildings rather than constructing new ones—I don't believe that congressional or public attitudes have changed enough to make any one of the three axioms now obsolete as public policy or as economics.

Putting aside for the moment the question of the relevance of Mr. Salisbury's attack on the third of these requirements as the reason for his dissatisfaction with public housing, one must admit that some of the defects described by him exist. He looked at the public housing projects and found that a number of them contained juvenile gangs very like the gangs that had flourished in the old slums. He found that some of the buildings had deteriorated physically. He talked with parish priests and police officers, social workers and storekeepers, who had spent their lives dealing with and observing the poor. They told him that many public housing developments failed to develop the community spirit which, they claimed, existed in some neighborhoods where poor people lived. As observations, these can be accurate, yet lead to faulty inferences. Mr. Salisbury also heard the same people say that in the first years of the existence of public housing, its neighborhood spirit had been better, and the physical deterioration less marked. Mr. Salisbury recognized that many people who had been living in public housing left it after World War II. He inferred that they had left when their incomes rose. From this he drew the further inference that they were forced out because their incomes had passed the permitted limits. Then he concluded that if there were no income limits, conditions in public housing would be much improved.

The indictment against public housing can be made even stronger without becoming unfair. The ceilings in the projects are low; the corridors are narrow; the tiles that form their wainscoting are ugly. There is a smell in the projects, or in many of them: a smell of food cooking, and sometimes in the elevators, a smell of urine. Even in the best of the projects, the disinfectants that are used to clean the halls leave behind them a powerful smell which cannot be called agreeable. But these impressions should be projected against the smells and dirt, the decay and airlessness, of the buildings in which the poor who do not live in public housing projects are still living. The impressions of public housing's public spaces—its corridors, elevators, lobbies, and courtyards which are by far its least successful achievements—should be projected also against the impression of its private spaces, the individual apartments, the great majority of which are well kept. The basic facilities are there: the view, the air, the sunlight, the stove, refrigerator, and tiled bathroom. The apartment was designed so that it can be kept clean, and it frequently glows with a pride that one has only to see in order to understand. The air and sunlight which no amount of tinkering can introduce into the row tenement without tearing down its outside walls are brought to every room in the public housing apartment; the necessary consequence is that the public corridors are internal and lit only artificially. Unfortunately, the public space can be ruined by one slovenly tenant; a hundred well-kept private spaces make no impression on it.

Mr. Salisbury saw and smelled, like any other observer in a public housing project, the almost ineradicable stigmata of the poor. To suggest that income limits should be different in public housing projects is to suggest, in effect, that the developments should cater to a different, a less poor, clientele.

Most of the people who left low-rent housing after a rise in income, left because they wanted to; they were not forced out. They left to move to a building or an area where higher incomes were the general rule. They would not be attracted back to public housing, nor if still there, can they be persuaded to stay, unless assured that the project will be substantially filled with a higher-income tenancy. This certainly might improve the appearance of the projects, perhaps even diminish the cooking smells of cheap greens, but it would leave the problem of housing low-income families more desperate than before. It is these families—not the better-off families—who most need the degree of subsidy provided in public housing.

Even the most loyal friends of public housing have trouble deciding what they want it to accomplish. On the one hand, they expect the buildings to be neat and trim, beautiful and permanent; they want to avoid new slums. On the other hand, they want the families who need housing most to have first preference as tenants, without considering the social and physical maintenance problems that some of the neediest families bring with them. When the consequences of these two wishes visibly collide, a compromise is too often sought in some superficial tinkering with the pattern of ownership or admission. Mr. Salisbury suggested that administrative income limits were to blame; other writers, exploring the problems of public housing in the new light of the respectability provided by his criticism in the *Times,* have suggested that the whole ownership pattern should be changed. Replace public ownership with private ownership: this is the cry of those who believe (perhaps because they have not examined their own statements) that Congress, the people, and the press, would support a program of providing privately owned homes entirely at government expense. Mingle income groups in a single development so that you will supply leadership: this is the cry of those who have not noticed that families with higher incomes are simply unwilling to live under circumstances that stifle their pride in their own position. Make personal entrance requirements less strict so that anybody of low income can live in public housing: this is the cry of those who have seldom seen a problem family, or talked to the neighbors of such a family, neighbors who are themselves trying to fight their way up in a hugely competitive world.

The human discouragement sensed by Mr. Salisbury in the projects is not really a housing problem, but rather the result of job discrimination that affects many of the Puerto Rican and Negro families now living in public housing. Since many among them will have more difficulty in raising their incomes than did their white predecessors, Mr. Salisbury seems to hope that raised income ceilings will keep in the projects those few families who do succeed, and that they will serve to give the added stimulus and example needed by their less fortunate neighbors. But this hope fails to provide for the standard pattern of American mobility, a pattern expressed by the families who, having begun to earn more money, move into a neighborhood compatible with their new means.

The issue behind the issue seen by Mr. Salisbury is the role of class in American life, an embarrassing issue to a government founded on the asserted equality of man. Will the public housing projects become the permanent homes of the permanently poor, or will they provide the staging area for traditional American advancement? There is no reason why they should not simultaneously provide both, but they will never provide what American cities have scarcely provided anywhere: neighborhoods in which poor and well-off families live side-by-side, and enjoy a social relationship as intimate as their physical propinquity.

The prospects for providing decent homes for those who cannot buy or rent them privately is a difficult and complicated problem, made more so by those who fail to recognize class issues, or who are somehow ashamed of them. If there were no class issues in American life, however, there would be no social mobility, on which Americans pride themselves. Progress in this difficult housing area requires meticulous attention to the facts of individual projects, and a public willingness to support attitudes that the press is suspicious of: to be tough in the face of disturbing tenants; realistic in the assessment of class attitudes in a world that prefers platitudinous unguents; generous in a world that considers itself already overtaxed.

It is ironic that the shade of Lincoln Steffens, of all people, should have encouraged reporters to skimp the patient attention required to comment intelligently on the problem of housing the poor. Even sadder is the extent to which journalistic slapdash has been picked up and echoed by serious critics who have perhaps never entered public housing developments, or bothered to search out the successful ones, or analyzed the qualities of architecture, site selection, management, and size that have made some more successful than others. By failing to distinguish which of these elements are intrinsic to government ownership, and which are merely produced by local politics in which both journalists and critics might play a vitally constructive role, the journalists have contributed to an almost total rejection of public housing by Congress.

Without federally subsidized, publicly owned low-rent housing, there is simply no way of providing widespread decent homes for the American urban poor in their own lifetime, a statement provoked by a hundred years' history of practical experimentation with such hybrid alternatives as nonprofit ownership, highly subsidized cooperatives, or limited-dividend sponsorship. Housing the poor requires community facilities, meeting rooms, playspaces (indoors and out), day care nurseries, and old age centers, which cannot be provided by private sponsors; it involves social services as well as dedicated property management which, performed humanely, has exhausted every private interest that has attempted to provide it. Of course, the managers of public housing need encouragement to do a better job, but the problems of public housing turn on vital decisions by the electorate and its representatives, not by bureaucrats.

Between the fear of graft and corruption on the one hand, and the detestation of bureaucracy on the other, the followers of Lincoln Steffens leave very little road room for either the elected official or the private builder.

Part II | HARD CHOICES

VI. | ON WITH THE DIG

THE excavation is now complete. Was the digging worth the effort? It remains for us to look at the problems of the American city, at least at those which arouse the most prolonged attention of the critics. How have their assumptions obscured their view of them? And, with the assumptions at least made clear, is it possible to glimpse lines of action that may be of greater help? Finally we might even be able to suggest an order of priority, a way of looking at the city and its problems that will give some clue to unscrambling the citizens' voices in the rooms at City Hall.

Several observers, each one looking at the city and finding his attention attracted by something individual, might well come up with different descriptions or different lists. But over a long period of time, the problems of the American city that most agitate its citizens, its critics, and its public officials are, I believe, five.

First, is race, and the physical distribution of people through the city on the basis of their skin color. If I did not distrust the word because of its gross and frequent misuse, I would call this the problem of the continuing ghetto.

Second, and almost as important, judged by the attention

given to it by the critics, the newspapers, and, most recently, the national administration, is the new architecture and urban beauty.

Third, and of growing importance, is the question of technology and the city, which includes the subject of urban transportation and the conservation of the natural resources surrounding the city.

Fourth, there is the most compelling of the city's problems, the endless problems of its poor.

Finally comes the question of politics in the city, the means of resolving the conflicting interests.

VII. | THE HOLES IN THE WALL

THIRTY years ago, the foreign visitor to American cities was fascinated by a singular view unseen at home: the skyline of the downtown business district. Today, in much the same way, he wants to marvel at, and shake his head over, the segregated living quarters of the Negro in the American city.

So do many of the urban critics, including not only such students of race as Nathan Glazer and Bayard Rustin, but even the conservative Martin Anderson and James Q. Wilson. An invisible wall has been described as penning the Negro population within restricted sections of the Northern city. Educational segregation results from the residential segregation, ensuring that Negroes will attend inferior schools. Inferior training means employment handicaps. Poorer employment opportunities mean lower income, the lower income means less buying power for homes, and so the cycle is unbreakable.

Despite its familiarity, this is not wholly an accurate description. A wall, felt if invisible, does surround the Negro sections of the northern American cities. Yet there are holes in the wall that pass undetected by any of the senses. We can explain the obscurity of these holes by reference to the assumptions of the critics. Lewis Mumford perhaps ignores the holes in the wall

because of his basic assumption that cities are necessarily deteriorating; perhaps Mrs. Jacobs overlooks the holes because they
can be widened only by a tremendous use of money, of whose
side effects she is afraid.

Putting these assumptions aside, we may be able to see both
walls and holes a little better in a closer look.

In the city where I live, it is difficult to come to any physical
planning decision—to locate a housing project or a school, a
highway or a park—without somehow involving the question
of race. To indicate the intricacy of racial affairs, to demonstrate that we must deal with something far more complicated
than a white community on one side of the wall and a Negro
community on the other, let me merely chronicle some of the
references to race to which I have lately listened.

Not long ago, in New York City, the Board of Estimate,
which has been loosely described as the elected governing body
of the city, held a hearing on the subject of the Lower Manhattan Expressway, a proposed highway link cutting across the
island. Opponents of the proposal attacked it because, they
claimed, it would destroy a racially integrated neighborhood
for the benefit of discriminating construction unions. Proponents countered by presenting as the spokesman on behalf of
the International Brotherhood of Carpenters, a mechanic who
happened to be black. He stated that to protect vicious landlords who discriminate, the opponents were blocking an urgent
public necessity. As a matter of fact, both sides were exaggerating their virtues. The area that would be crossed by the highway contains a considerable number of Chinese, but very few
Negroes. Certainly, on the other hand, a Negro delegate of the
Brotherhood of Carpenters is hardly representative of most of
his union brothers. Is building a highway, then, a racial issue?
Is it part of the ghetto wall?

In Washington, D.C., as in a number of other cities, a voluntary group of citizens has been founded for the purpose of preventing "blockbusting." When a Negro family buys a house in a section of the city where only white families had previously been living, the antiblockbusting group tries to encourage white owners to remain, keeping their homes off the market so that the neighborhood will not become all-black. Painted signs, expressing a similar objective, have appeared in many of the semisuburban sections that ring New York City, Detroit, Cleveland. These pro-integration workers measure their success by the number of white families who can be persuaded to buy in the section threatened by panic selling to Negroes. I have heard representatives of such an organization say that they hope to accumulate money for a special mortgage supplementation fund, that will make cheaper mortgage terms available to white families. In other words, the believers in racial integration hope that it can be advanced by favoring white families. Is this pro-white favoritism less discriminatory against the Negro family which is seeking a good home than the discrimination practiced by those developers who refuse to sell to Negroes in the first place?

For a number of years, New York State law has forbidden landlords to consider race, religion, or national origin in selecting tenants for multifamily apartment houses financed by state or federal subsidies. In projects where it is conceivable that a significant number of white families may wish to live, the New York City Housing Authority has been holding some of its publicly owned apartments vacant although Negro applicants have tried to rent them. The Authority intends, with the tacit support of civil rights agencies, to save these vacancies for white tenants who have not yet applied. Under such circumstances, the Negro applicants are not denied apartments, but they are urged to apply for a project which either has a shortage of Negro families, or else is already so overwhelmingly Negro that no one expects racial constituents to be balanced.

The projects that are likely to be integrated are those located in the most pleasant surroundings. Thus, this policy discourages Negroes from moving into the projects in the nicest surroundings, in order to encourage white families, who presumably have a wider choice of housing in the first place, to move into them.

Mrs. Jane Jacobs, in her book *Death And Life Of Great American Cities,* urges high densities of human habitation in order to preserve the urbanity of cities. According to Mrs. Jacobs, the presence of large numbers of people on the street at different times during the day—not merely at the fixed hours representing the ebb and flow of office and factory employment —ensures safety.

Mrs. Jacobs to the contrary, in predominantly Negro residential sections of the city, overcrowding has been the one characteristic most often blamed for unsatisfactory housing. Overcrowding means bedrooms occupied by children and parents together, sometimes with more distant relatives and strangers. Overcrowding means toilets shared by several families, with none responsible for keeping them clean. Overcrowding means dirty hallways, overwhelmed garbage collection facilities; overcrowding means small rooms, insufficient natural light or ventilation. Children, for these objective physical reasons and because of the general distastefulness of the places in which they live, are unwilling to stay home to do their schoolwork, unable, frequently, to see what they are doing if they do stay home, unable to achieve a moment's privacy, unable to gather about themselves confidence that the conditions of life can be changed by even a mighty application of their own efforts. Overcrowding means a lack of playspace, means airshafts into which garbage is dropped because there are no incinerators. (Who wants to walk down five flights of stairs at night?) Overcrowding to the Negro means shabbiness, broken fixtures, slovenliness, means paying too much for too little, means the end result of exclusion. The fact that human energy survives these conditions, that children do play in the streets, and that, on summer nights, men gather on the stoops of old buildings to talk, drink beer, laugh, quarrel, make love, gamble, buy and sell, means to some people that the juice of human life is richer in overcrowded areas. To me, the significance of what you see is only that you see it: there is room only on the street. Nevertheless, I watched a stout Negro lady, her black coat held together with a big blanket pin, as she arrived at City Hall to protest against a city proposal to demolish such an overcrowded area. She carried under her arm, as the rationale for her opposition, a copy of Mrs. Jacobs' book. "We don't live in no slum," she said, "and we don't want to live in no project. We want to stay where we is, but we want it fixed up the way she says." While Mrs. Jacobs has no doubt indicated what families with means can accomplish in rehabilitating those older buildings which lend themselves to such an investment, what does her praise of high residential densities offer to the woman who was carrying her book?

Under the sponsorship of the New York Life Insurance Company, a remarkable development of apartment houses has been built in what had been an overcrowded, wholly Negro area on the near South Side of Chicago. The Lake Meadows development was originally planned as an interracial development. When the buildings were first finished, however, white families disdained them because of their location. When the apartments were fully rented, less than one percent of the tenants were white. Over the past five years, attracted, perhaps, by the pleasant architecture and site planning, and the relatively low rental price of the apartments in Lake Meadows, white families have come to Lake Meadows. The white population has risen to more than 30 percent. Should the management encourage more white occupancy, but discourage Negroes from moving in?

In New York City, a housing development for so-called middle-income families (earning roughly from $6,000 to $9,000 per year) was erected in East Harlem by the New York City Housing Authority. East Harlem was formerly dominated by its Italian population; Italian-Americans still own its bakeries, funeral homes, and restaurants, but they comprise less than one-quarter of a population which has become largely Puerto Rican. Before the development was completed, the Housing Authority contracted to sell it to a private nonprofit organization. The original members of this organization pledged themselves to put up $5,000 each, so that the the buildings could be sold cooperatively. Interracial occupancy was the objective of the entire proposal, and, in its early stages, great emphasis was placed on attracting white families to the development. Many people who speak with confidence about housing and housing markets (including this writer), felt that it would be impossible to induce white families to move into East Harlem. We were wrong. The first section of this 1,635-family development was filled with a well-balanced interracial constituency that was approximately 50 percent white. The entire development has now been taken over by cooperators; despite the relatively high white occupancy of its first half, the second half has been more difficult to sell to white families. The project has been occupied in part for almost four years and some families are moving out in the natural course of events. A cooperative corporation, unlike the public housing agency, cannot afford to keep apartments vacant while it waits for a white family to apply. Any delay in filling the apartments means that the expenses allocated to the other tenants rise. If apartments are not promptly filled, rents may have to rise with them. Does the cooperative ownership of this project imperil its racial balance in such a location? It's a hard question.

In Harlem—a section of New York City which everyone knows is almost entirely occupied by Negro familes—stood the Polo Grounds, the baseball stadium in which the New York Giants played for many years. The Giants now play in San Francisco, and New York City has built a new stadium on vacant land in Long Island for the Mets. This left the Polo Grounds vacant and available for the construction of housing. The New York City Housing Authority has taken over the site and is preparing to construct on it a low-rent housing development. This decision stimulated the vigorous opposition of a number of Harlem organizations, including one called the Harlem Neighborhoods Association. The Harlem Neighborhoods Association has stated its belief that Harlem should not be identified in the public mind as a primarily low-income neighborhood, and that, in the interests of racial integration, the Polo Grounds should be improved with a project that would be available to people of a higher income than those eligible for public housing. It has been estimated that the land value is so high that middle-income apartments on that site would require a family income in excess of $10,000. The city government does not believe that many families with such an income would wish to live in Harlem.

In any case, last winter there was a series of rent strikes in Harlem; these protests developed in some of the older buildings in the area, those riddled with serious violations of the housing codes. The violations, according to the leader of the rent strikes, included rats, lack of heat, broken plaster, no water. One need not himself have verified the conditions by climbing through the chilly, reeking buildings, with their dank, damp corners and decaying wood, echoing with the blast of radios, laughter, fighting, children's cries. The fact that tenants, in order to force improvements, were willing to risk the dangers of eviction—where else can they find space they can afford?—indicates that the description contains a measure of accuracy. These people are in the economic group for whom public low-rent housing is built. How can the Harlem Neighborhoods Association believe that there is any other economic group more urgently in need of the new homes on the Polo Grounds site?

These random anecdotes yield no simple and precise picture, the picture one would have expected to develop, believing in a white community separated from a Negro community by the invisible wall. One may be able, however, to make out two recurrent themes. One is that while it is possible to open to Negro occupants apartment houses or neighborhoods that had been closed to them, it is far more difficult to keep white families from leaving, or induce them to move in later. The second, equally important implication is that to refer to a Negro community is only a loose and irrelevant way of discussing a complex of people, groups, and institutions whose differences are as important as their similarities.

These differences play a crucial role for the official who seeks to define the wall of segregation in order to enlarge the holes in it. There is not a single race segregation problem: there are several. Loose assumptions about the community and cloudy wishes about the ultimate goal of race relations have obscured the divisibility of the several problems. The official who is searching for improvements in this critical area of the city had best begin by distinguishing at least three.

First, the officials might separate from the rest the problem of how to provide a decent home for the low-income Negro family that would make an acceptable neighbor and tenant in a reasonably decent apartment house, but that cannot find such a place to live. This is typical of the majority of Negro families. The task of providing them with decent homes is largely a matter of getting the money needed to provide decent homes for *all* low-income families, of both races. The amount of money will surely be "cataclysmic."

Second, the officials must find homes for those low-income families who do not know how to live as acceptable neighbors and tenants, or who suffer from personality problems that prevent them from becoming acceptable. Looked at as the official looks at them, these families present a terrible problem, but it is hardly different from that presented by the white families who are similarly "ineligible" for publicly owned housing.

Third, the officials have the problem of the moderately prosperous Negro families, earning between $5,000 and $15,000 per year. There were in 1959 about 1,100,000 nonwhite families in this income range in the United States. What shall be done to accommodate them in the cities or suburbs as they wish to be accommodated?

Since the first problem falls largely in the backyards of the economists, and the second in the dense jungles of the psychiatrists, it is the third which lands with singular force in the laps of those concerned with Negro-white relationships. What shall they do in the American city to make it habitable for the Negro middle class? How shall they enable the members of that group to exercise their power to choose a home, demonstrating that the intense effort put into the achievement of their income was justified by what it could buy?

Giving the Negro middle class the freedom to spend its money on housing as it wishes, is, perhaps regrettably, a political assignment. Left to itself, the machinery of the private market has been too corroded by prejudice and fear. In accepting the assignment, the city official must be ready to put aside temporarily other Negro-white housing problems. Perhaps he will even, temporarily, make them worse. This is politically tough, but justifiable. If the Negro middle-class family cannot demonstrably enjoy its income, what is the use of urging the poorer Negro to forswear the meager compensations of life on the bottom and drag himself painfully up the economic ladder?

Accepting the implications of this order of priority will put the official into conflict with urban critics like Herbert Gans. Mr. Gans (in *Commentary* magazine) views with equanimity the departure of middle-income families from the city. Ultimately, he believes that municipal governments would attend adequately to the needs of the Negro poor only when the Negro poor control them. Any governmental program which displaces low-income families to make room for high-income families is poisoned, in Mr. Gans's view, by its essential immorality.

To explain why I assign first priority to the situation of the Negro middle class, I find myself having to discuss as a whole Negro-white relations in the United States. The outsider could approach no other subject with greater diffidence. One's shyness is increased by the tones of conviction that are used by almost everyone else writing on the subject. Many wise people believe (wrongly, I think) that it is itself a mark of bigotry to divide the problem of race and residence into subproblems, of which one comes first. They believe that the justice of racial integration is so great that one becomes impious in proposing an order of business.

If the moral absolutists are right, we might as well start turning the mimeograph machines into bobbie pins. Of all the world's social problems, none is less likely to be cured all at once than anti-Negro discrimination and its consequences in America. Its elements will, in changed form, perhaps, but ponderous substance, survive even any revolutionary change in American government or American institutions. Can one define American anti-Negro discrimination as a whole in a way that adequately describes the differences between Philadelphia, Mississippi, and Philadelphia, Pennsylvania?

The very question offends those who claim that between North and South there is no real difference in the race question. They explain that since Northern whites merely satisfy their need for primacy and exclusivity with greater subtlety than do Southern whites, the two groups are ethically identical. I am interested less in ethical identities than in the clear fact that a law exists in Philadelphia, Pennsylvania, requiring equal access by all races to jobs and homes, while a law in Philadelphia, Mississippi, requires the opposite.

Another strange comparison is sometimes made between North and South. People assert that Negroes in the South are likely to be happier, or less troubled than Negroes in the North. When crooned by Southern gentlemen, over a banjo accompaniment, this proposition would merely hide the voting booth behind the magnolia blossoms. The steady flood of Negroes leaving the South is ample refutation. Yet, the claim that Negroes in the South are happier is made not only by Southern whites; Northern Negroes also put it forward. And a closer look at the migrating Negroes indicates that they are almost all poor. They are coming North not to enjoy the nearer approach to full citizenship on which conscientious white people sometimes vaunt themselves. They are coming for jobs. They are not so much embracing the North's accomplishment of human liberty. They are being pushed off the Southern farms by rural automation.

If the Northern "equality" were indeed so significant, if the North beckoned to the Southern Negro with the same promise that lured millions of Europeans to the American shore, at least some Southern Negro families of means would be liquidating their savings and coming North to play their roles on the larger, freer stage. Unfortunately, the North does not beckon philosophically to the Southern Negro. When he wants freedom, he goes to France. The well-off Southern Negro ignores the North because he senses that his position would not be more challenging there. It would simply become more difficult.

In the South, the middle-class Negro lives under well-defined conditions. He is expected to live in the Negro world, but his white peers recognize his existence. In the North, it is not clear what world he is expected to live in; and nobody recognizes his existence. In the North also, as Dr. Robert Weaver has frequently pointed out, the physical conditions of the Negro middle class are likely to be worse than in the South.

Yet, unless American history is to take a wholly different turn, it is this invisible Negro middle class which will provide hope and leadership for the other millions of the same ethnic group. In comparing the Negro middle class to other American ethnic groups, the outsider is handicapped by complexities.

Several aspects of Negro life in the United States are familiar. Other peoples in other climes have faced them. The total circumstances of the Negro situation in the United States, however, form a unique combination, one whose impact on those who have had to experience it can hardly be summarized by those who have not. Other nations have had human slavery; other peoples have been captured and subjected to forced migration. Other countries contain a multiracial population, of which one race enjoys superior status. Other immigrant peoples, brought to their new homes by force, have suffered the systematic extinction of their own cultural heritage. Others have been forbidden to acquire the culture of the superior race in the land in which they were brought to live. Castes or race groups within many societies have been prevented from attaining the economic and cultural level of the rest of the population, so that they concentrated within their numbers an extraordinarily high ratio of the untrained and the poor.

The unique aspect of the Negro situation in America is not only that all of these occur at one and the same time. It is that these conditions have been inflicted and maintained by the leaders of a society which called these deeds injustices, and suggested that their infliction was morally wrong. American society subscribes to the doctrine of human equality; it has proclaimed individual liberty to be the highest law of the land, and insists that each man has the "inalienable" right to seek happiness in his own way, merely so long as this does not interfere with the rights of others, similarly circumscribed. The American Negro's strange plight has been that in the midst of this ideological plenty, he is required to starve.

Nor can it seriously be argued that in the past one hundred years the American promises of freedom and equality were hypocritically intended, for propaganda only. The tenets were embodied and codified, parsed, discussed, and analyzed by our highest courts, which almost systematically applied the principles to an ever-broadening area of human activity. Until very lately, however, they hardly broadened at all the racial constituency which was affected by the decisions of the court. Even when the Supreme Court, in the past, handed down decisions that deprived Negro Americans of their equal sharing of the bounties of the country, these very decisions were formulated by reference to the freedom, equality, and human dignity which were assumed in the Constitution. The freedom of other Americans to deprive the Negro of his rights was established far more readily than the Negro's right to enjoy his freedom. The state of California recently passed, in the name of freedom, a constitutional amendment depriving the state government of the power to adopt a law ensuring Negroes equal access to residences throughout the state. The ban, incidentally, has had an interesting consequence which we shall examine later.

Other oppressed minorities escaped this final indignity. The essential principles of the Hindu religion did not conflict with the treatment of the Untouchables, by proclaiming the eternal validity of treating all men equally. The slave in Ethiopia might accept his life as the only life possible, and make the best of it without reflection; he might, on the other hand, dream of overthrowing his masters, winning his freedom, and perhaps making his master his slave. He might dream of a new world in which there would be neither slave nor master.

For the Negro in the United States, any one of these positions has been difficult. Once chattel slavery was overthrown, the elemental victory had been won. Gaining acceptance by the masters—and sharing one's guaranteed entitlement to their rights and privileges—seemed more relevant than overthrowing them. If one fled to another part of the world, it might be difficult merely to gain even verbal acceptance of the same basic principles that distinguished America. How could the cause of human freedom be better stated, or where would it be more generally meant, than in the Constitution of the United States?

This question snaps with special vigor at the Negro who has organized his family in the pattern of white America (a pattern which slavery deliberately extinguished); it hits the Negro who has managed, usually with considerable hardship, to win himself an education; it troubles the Negro who has attained business ownership, professional status, or a well-paid, responsible white-collar job. His achievements are notably greater than those he might have attained in a poorer country, even though it might be wholly free from anti-Negro prejudice. To the extent that he has earned the money by accepting the responsibilities of the middle-class American, he is, of course, living testament to the validity of the American promise. To the extent that he is not permitted to live where he can afford to live, or is discouraged from mingling socially with the people with whom he works, or is wholly unrecognized as anything but another Negro, and therefore assumed to be of meager education and little money, he is of course, living testimony of the total, and probably almost permanent inadequacy of the American promises. The conflict between these two propositions vitiates the achievement of the Negro middle-class citizen. He feels that American society is peculiarly determined to undermine his position, and weaken his ability to serve as a model for those who might be ready to make a similar effort.

The North has made the middle-class Negro a bitter joke. Nobody senses it so much as the middle-class Negro himself, and nobody laughs at it harder than the Negro who has not achieved that status.

A recent set of events dramatized for me the problem of the middle-class Negro. The events started some five or six years ago, when the New York Racing Association decided to abandon its racing at the Jamaica Race Track. The large acreage of the track was surrounded by the homes of an almost entirely Negro population. With the help of mortgages granted by the New York State Division of Housing and Community Renewal and the New York State Housing Finance Agency, the United Housing Foundation, an organization that is devoted to the construction of middle-income housing cooperatives, bought the site of the track. The Foundation built on it a moderate-cost cooperative apartment development, intended for use by families with incomes in the $5,000-$10,000 class. The development ultimately contained some 6,000 apartments, which, despite the surrounding population, were purchased by a gratifying number of white cooperators. At completion, the project was occupied by an integrated clientele, with approximately 5,000 white families, and 1,000 nonwhite tenants.

About one year after completion, the New York City Housing Authority announced plans to build a small, low-rent public housing project across the street from the cooperative. This proposal aroused tremendous excitement in the area, in response to which the president of the borough of Queens conducted an informal hearing at his office.

About fifty people came to the hearing. The majority were

Negro owners of homes in the vicinity of the cooperative. Every one of them opposed the construction of low-rent housing near his home, an opposition in which they were joined by the local chapter of the NAACP. "Many of us used to live in public housing, because we couldn't afford better," one of the Negro home owners told the borough president. "Now we own our own homes, and they're good homes too; we've got one of the nicest areas you'd want to see. We've got an integrated community now, with the cooperative there, and why does the city want to spoil what we've got by bringing in those low-income families? Put them somewhere else, why don't you? Doesn't the city of New York want us to get up in the world, that you should do this and try to tear us down again?"

Whatever the merits of the argument as to the effect of the low-rent housing project on his area, the meaning of this man's objection was clear: he needed confirmation in his role as a middle-class citizen, and he knew, or suspected, that the city was more likely to put a public housing project near his home, because he was a Negro middle-class citizen, than to put it near the home of a white middle-class citizen similarly located. He sensed that the low-income Negro citizen would be well aware of this. He understood that despite all its promises to the contrary the city was once again making him invisible.

In his case, what the city will not see, does hurt it.

Americanization of any group of new urban arrivals has always required the emergence of models—those initially successful and self-supporting members of the recently arrived group who established a pattern of success. The later arrivals, or the children of the less successful, emulate the models. But the only Negroes whom white America has encouraged the Negroes to establish as models are the unusual talents who have come forward in sports and the theater, and a few political figures who have skillfully exploited the vacuum. Plenty of young Negroes want to become Willie Mays, or Louis Arm-

strong, and perhaps Adam Clayton Powell. Until Negro lawyers, businessmen, and doctors can, without fanfare or fuss, find
themselves free to live where they want to live in the cities, the
Negro child has a better chance to achieve status by snatching
a lottery ticket in the great Willie Mays raffle, than he has by
sending himself through school and college, at tremendous
pain and great sacrifice, once having exposed himself to the
grating humiliations of hope.

Yet, quite unseen by white America, a Negro society emerged
long before the civil rights movement—shadowy, gentle, perhaps closer in spirit to the ante-bellum South than anything
the white South has since produced. A Negro middle class is
emerging today. It is true that 48 percent of the nonwhite population earns less than enough income to avoid penury. (Only
19 percent of the white population is similarly situated.) But
this leaves 52 percent of the Negro population above the
poverty line, and a very significant number of those earn incomes that would put them into the middle-class bracket of the
entire population, provided only that they were permitted to
spend this money as they wish, and were not penalized by extra-
high rents for their bad luck in being born black. In addition,
growing numbers of Negroes are getting professional training;
the long, hard, and undramatic work of the Urban League in
opening employment opportunities has been remarkably
successful. Ironically, discrimination against Negroes by private
industry has turned to their advantage in one respect. For
many years, the government was the Negro's only fair employer.
As the role of government has grown in American life, some
Negroes were peculiarly well situated to take advantage of its
growth. In the New York City Civil Service, the percentage
of supervisors who are Negro is higher than the percentage of
Negroes in the general population. And young Negro professional and semiprofessional families are moving upward, taking advantage of opportunities offered them under federal and

some state laws. A woman I know told me that her parents, veterans of the Jewish labor movement, recently became co-operators in a labor-union-sponsored apartment development. Firm believers in racial equality, they were delighted that a number of Negro families had taken apartments as well. Several months later, my friend told me that her parents, queried about their neighbors, had lost some of their enthusiasm, but for an interesting reason. Oh, the Negro families were lovely people, charming, young, and well educated, but they didn't seem to want to spend one evening a week singing "Joe Hill" and "Solidarity Forever." They were all college graduates, and on Thursday evening they played duplicate bridge, or took graduate work. My friend's parents were just a tiny bit chagrined at being outclassed.

But for every Negro middle-class family that is able to find a decent home of its choice, a dozen more are trapped, excluded from the suburbs, and unable to find a suitable apartment within the city. I will suggest strategies for finding new integrated homes. My program, however, depends on giving the Negro middle class priority over the Negro poor.

I say this despite the fact that mere numbers would indicate that most of the Negro families needing help, as well as those needing the most help, are poor. Forty-eight percent of America's nonwhite families live on incomes too low to provide an acceptable standard of living. Surely, my critics are correct in assuming that Lincoln Steffens would say that those who need the most help should be helped first. I am not suggesting that nothing be done about the housing accommodations of low-income Negro families. Quite the contrary. I advocate a large increase in the construction or remodeling of decent homes for the poor. But I do not believe that these will, for years to come, be anything but racially segregated.

The present facts of American life are against the integration of low-rent housing. The applications for apartments in the low-rent projects operated by the New York City Housing Authority are symptomatic of the national trend. The applications from Negro families—or families assumed (by virtue of their present address) to be Negro (the applications bear no notation as to race, as a matter of law)—far outnumber the applications from families assumed to be white.

On the other hand, most of the families who leave public housing do so because their incomes have increased and they wish to move elsewhere. Most of these are white families, because their economic opportunities are better.

Obviously, if the public housing intake is mostly nonwhite, and the public housing outflow is largely white, one needs no credentials as a social scientist to foresee that its population will inevitably become largely if not exclusively Negro.

Two points might be added. Social scientists do feel that when the percentage of Negroes in a development exceeds a certain point (the point varies from development to development) additional white families move out simply because of the number of Negroes. This makes it worse, of course. On the other hand, none of these racial generalizations applies to housing projects for the aged. Age reduces the difference in earning capacity between American Negroes and whites. Whereas Negroes of every age tend to be handicapped in the job market, all aged people are in fact handicapped, irrespective of race. Thus the intake in projects for the aged tends to be better balanced, and there is little voluntary outflow.

Those critics who, like Herbert Gans, wish to solve Negro-white relations as a whole, have suggested that if it is impossible to integrate low-rent developments without a truly nondiscriminatory job market, the solution is to abandon low-rent developments. Instead, officials should attempt to achieve racial integration by enclosing people of very different economic means in a single building. In other words, if a majority of Negroes earn low incomes and a majority of whites enjoy higher incomes, combine low- and higher-income families in a single building and you will have racial integration.

The simplicity of this syllogism has seduced even the United States Congress. Congress adopted legislation in 1965 to provide rent subsidies so that families who formerly could find good homes only in public housing projects would be able to live in apartments owned by limited-profit or nonprofit landlords (or in cooperatives). Here, the poor, presumably Negro, tenants will live with others, presumably white, who will be paying considerably higher, unsubsidized rents. There will be no gentle gradation from one income group to the other, but a sharp break.

If it is intended to promote racial integration, this legislation rests on the theory that higher-income white families are willing to pay higher rents in order to share an apartment house with lower-income Negro families who are paying lower rents.

Although I cannot claim to have met such white families, I will not be dogmatic and say that there are none in the United States. I will say that they are too few to carry a national housing program on their heads. Incidentally, I disbelieve even more firmly that middle-class Negro families would pay higher rent in order to live in the same building with low-income white families. Somehow no one ever thinks of that possibility, perhaps because of the near-invisibility of Negro middle-class families. I did hear a Negro woman insurance broker complain to the New York City Planning Commission that other citizens were demanding low-rent public housing in a Title I area down the street from where she owned a private house. The demanders had claimed that low-rent housing would bring in Negro families, and integrate the area. "What's the matter with me and my husband?" she asked. "And Dr. Warner down the street? Don't we count? Can't you see us? Is the only good Negro a poor Negro?"

Dr. Weaver, the Secretary of the Department of Housing and

Urban Development, initially had proposed a very different use of subsidies from the use finally approved by the Congress. He suggested that rent subsidies be used to provide better homes for the families whose incomes exceed the limits for low-rent housing, yet are too low to find homes on the private market. Congress changed the emphasis with the approval of a number of urban critics, including James Q. Wilson, Herbert Gans, and the editorial board of the New York *Times*.

Its advocates have labeled the attempt to mingle people of different income in a single building, economic integration. But, experience with the partly subsidized middle-income developments already occupied, shows that unless the site is very carefully selected, and the construction values extraordinary, white families will not move into a development which has a high percentage of Negro families, even when all of them share the same income level and class status. Precisely how high a percentage is too high depends on the values offered. The New York Life development at Lake Meadows, mentioned earlier in this chapter, is a striking example of the difficulty of working out this kind of arrangement, and a brilliantly successful exception to a general rule. Again, it is a development in which all tenants have substantially the same income.

For economic integration to "work"—to produce developments in which people significantly different live together, paying substantially different rents for the same kinds of apartments—extraordinary and as yet unknown pressures would have to be brought on the higher-income white families, or extraordinary values given them. I cannot imagine what either the values or the pressures would be, and I suspect that its advocates have not either.

But the impractical quality of this idea is not its only disadvantage. It also, I believe, gives wide currency to a wholly inadequate notion of the facts of life for a family of very low income in America. Supporters of economic integration assume that the major difference between a middle- and low-income family is its address. If the addresses can be changed, so runs the theory, the stigma of lower-class status will be erased, and lower-class life will then be easier to bear.

But the trouble with the lives of low-income families is not any stigma that they feel. It's their hard lack of money. This means not only too little money to buy (or rent) decent homes, but too little to buy good food, handsome clothing, good liquor, first-class cosmetics, distant recreation. It means too little money to hire lawyers to protect their rights and too little to finance political campaigns. Put the impoverished family in a building filled with people who can afford a higher level of these expenditures, and you increase, not lighten, the burdens of poverty. When I was a young believer in the peaceable kingdom, it was assumed that men's incomes would some day be made equal, or at least that gross discrepancies would be ironed out. This, it seems to me, is more sensible than assuming that the differences in income will remain, but that somehow their bite can be painlessly extracted.

Like it or not, differences in income reflect, or cause, differences in the habits of life. These differences may be extremely important to the conduct of housing affairs, particularly in the management of cooperative houses, in which the tenant-owners must decide what to spend their corporate money for. I suggest that in the American culture the difference between the low-income and the middle-income family is related to the way in which future income is conceived. The middle-income family is more likely to be able to postpone present for future gratification; its fears are not so immediate—it is in the habit of worrying about problems further off—it is accustomed to weighing alternative pleasures before choosing one. This, alas, is a practice that the low-income family cannot follow. While it is true that some low-income families in whom are found middle-income habits and straitened circumstances could live in middle-income cooperatives, like the sons of missionaries attending prep school on scholarships, I suggest that for most of them the experience would be uncomfortable. That the differences are not visible differences and therefore hard to define makes them no less real, though it does make the social mobility with which a family moves from class to class much simpler in the American culture than elsewhere.

Finally the suggestion of economic integration would complete the humiliation of the Negro middle class. Those who praise economic integration assume that almost all Negroes are poor. This is based in turn on a misunderstanding of the significance of the Negro ghetto—a misunderstanding which has been aided and abetted by a number of critics of urban affairs, including Wolf von Eckardt and Peter Blake.

The ghetto itself is a magnificent example of the economic integration of an area—rich Negroes, poor Negroes, middle-class Negroes, proletarian Negroes—all crowded in together because they cannot live elsewhere. "Don't tell me what it's like to live with poor people," a prominent Negro woman politician said to me. "They wouldn't let us live anywhere else."

To insist that Negroes will be able to share housing with whites only if class differences are obliterated uncovers the main argument in support of economic integration as the key to residential racial desegregation. Most of its supporters advocate it simply because it sounds more progressive, more daring, more revolutionary. Conversely, the suggestion that residential desegregation in the North involves, in the first instance, middle-class families only, seems hardly worthy of the "Freedom Now" demands by CORE and SNCC. Who should tell the young people chaining themselves to courthouse doors in the North, and in the South risking their lives for equal access to the ballot box by all, that "Integration Now" is for the middle class only? I suggest that sometime they will find it out by themselves.

Those whose energy and devotion to justice provide the cities with their best hope for the future, will learn also that the slogan "Freedom Now" is itself practically meaningless. If such a slogan impedes the execution of policies that will effectively mitigate racial segregation, and enable Negroes to participate fully in American life, then the slogan will have to be abandoned. Simple slogans are suitable for simple issues—equal access to the vote, for example. But what does "Freedom Now" mean in the North, when applied to the question of racial segregation in residences? That one must be free to live where he wants to? Choosing a place to live is an economic decision, not the exercise of an abstract human right. Laws mandating non-discrimination have been in force for a number of years. Does their enactment mean that the demand of the slogan has been met? Hardly. If people are free to live where they want, the rights of those who want to move in are no different from those who merely want to move away. Calls for freedom, like the rumble of Egyptian chariots, may simply accelerate the exodus. It may be tiresome but it is a fact of human maturation that at some point or other in the course of social change, full-throated emotion must be replaced by dreary thought. I recently spoke at a meeting of a CORE chapter in New York City called to develop a program for de-ghettoizing Harlem. In the midst of the discussion of the strategies of desegregation, one impatient young woman finally broke in. "I'm disgusted with CORE," she told us. "You're sitting around discussing what ought to be done, instead of just going out and doing something."

God knows I share her impatience with panel discussions and meetings—the allegedly democratic way of canvassing Truth by encouraging the simultaneous expression of seven different points of view and labeling Babel a workshop. I suggest, however, that just "going out and doing something" on the street may be even less entertaining to its involuntary audience. The revolutionary ardor that has opened the polling booths and the places of public accommodation only helps to convince wary and undecided middle-class whites in the North that Negroes have dubious friends and make strange neighbors. There are times when, and subject matters on which, sensibilities must be flouted to achieve an objective; but so long as white families are relatively free to choose their own housing, residential desegregation is not one of them.

Recognizing the perils of agitation in this area and yet being unwilling to formulate strategems that will work in a free market, one New York organization has urged that no families in the city should be permitted to choose their own homes. Instead, any dwelling units which become vacant should be centrally registered and assigned by the municipal government to those whose presence will facilitate racial integration. All this in the name of freedom. This suggestion is but one of many made by people and groups who believe that a revolutionary change in American life is necessary and desirable, and that it will be pulled on stage by poor Negroes and white college students, chanting "Freedom Now." Theirs is a religious belief, immune from rational examination.

If I must have a religious belief of my own, it is that, given international peace and an amply prosperous economy (two rather large blessings), the expanding strength of the Negro middle class, and the desire by many other urban groups for peaceful development, will combine to muffle the sometimes irrelevant ardors and confusing demonstrations in the North. Then it may become possible to work out a reasonably propitious program of residential racial integration, largely consistent with the existing forms of American life. It will then be popular, or at least socially acceptable, to say that housing integration begins as a strategy for middle-class families.

Assuming that this is so, what weapons are there?

Most interested people think first of Fair Housing laws, passed by the separate states or cities, and forbidding discrimination in the sale or leasing of at least certain classes of homes. The passage of such laws is important, but their achievements have been largely psychological. They give the endorsement of government to the idea of racial integration in residences, and this may in turn affect programs in which the government itself is directly involved in housing construction. The Fair Housing laws provide an excuse (it is sad that such an excuse is needed) for the owner of property who does not wish to discriminate against prospective tenants or purchasers on racial grounds. He can defend his fairness by telling his other tenants, or his neighbors, that he is merely following the law in renting and selling to Negroes.

The advocates of Fair Housing laws often tell the public that the proposed laws will make very little real difference, if passed. The ineffectuality is stressed in order to calm the opposition. Unfortunately the strategic claim turns out to be factually impeccable. The laws make little practical difference. In New York City, which contains almost three million homes or apartments, only 1,200 complaints of racial discrimination in housing have been brought to the Commission on Human Rights since 1958. Approximately one-half were regarded by the commission as unsubstantiated, or were withdrawn. Six hundred and thirteen cases were "satisfactorily" resolved in seven years, but this does not mean that the applicants got the apartments they wanted; it usually meant that the landlord agreed to offer his next comparable vacancy to them, whenever that might happen to become available.

It is difficult to believe that the existence of the law has greatly changed the customary pattern of New York City, a pattern in which some private apartment houses are rented entirely to Negro tenants, and the rest entirely to white tenants, and that the houses rented to each race tend to be clustered together in a pattern of segregated neighborhoods.

New York law provides that complaints must be made by

people who consider themselves aggrieved; but a private person making a complaint has no right to sue for damages. His cure is only that he will be allowed to rent the apartment or buy the house previously denied him, unless that apartment or house has been already disposed of. In the latter cases, which constitute the great majority, he is made whole by a promise that he may acquire the next similar accommodation owned by the same landlord. It has been suggested that these cumbersome procedures have discouraged people from making complaints, and that the number of complaints would more accurately reflect the condition of the housing market if people had the right to sue for money (although it is hard to develop a legal theory which would set a value on the damage done by the discriminating landlord), or if there were some way to keep the apartment from being rented, or the house from being sold, until the Commission decides the complaint.

Yet these suggestions still fail to meet a major difficulty; that most people are reluctant to force their way into a house or a neighborhood where they understand that they are not wanted. Privately sponsored Fair Housing committees have been established in a number of cities. Where they are active, these committees try to pinpoint discriminatory landlords by sending a white applicant to a building which has advertised a vacant apartment. If the white applicant is offered and refuses the apartment, a Negro applicant is immediately afterwards sent to look at the same apartment. If the Negro applicant is told there are no vacancies, a presumption of discrimination appears reasonable. This device has helped to provide apartments for Negro applicants in previously segregated buildings. But most of the applicants are single people or young couples who are free from the responsibilities of raising children in an unfriendly neighborhood. Appeals for volunteers to break down racial barriers in Alabama and Mississippi involve only a brief commitment, though a dangerous one. But the appeals to Negro families to settle in white areas involve a permanent commitment in which the comfort and safety of one's children are risked.

The practical hope for the development of racially integrated housing lies in another direction entirely. It lies in the frank recognition of the unsatisfactory quality of much of the older urban housing, and in the willingness of both federal and local government to invest large sums of money to replace or improve it. The best hope for practical residential integration of middle-class families lies in urban renewal programs. In fact, the most significant accomplishments in integrated living in the cities of the North have been made through clever use of federal government grants for urban renewal, coupled with further subsidies for the construction of middle-income housing. This combination has produced new or rehabilitated homes for families of both races, living together normally, without special brotherhood programs, preferential mortgage treatment for one race or another, or any of the other artificial and uncomfortable mechanisms that are simply incapable of being projected on a national scale by any administration that anyone has been able to devise.

Urban renewal not only can be but has been the most effective path to Negro-white middle-class integration. I say this in full knowledge of the fact that the critics have damned urban renewal as "Negro removal." I say this in spite of the fact that some cities have actually used urban renewal, or tried to use it, to block racial integration.

And I say it despite the fact that even the most conscientious of the urban critics have damned urban renewal, largely, as I believe, because they have not looked behind the moral strictures in the Lincoln Steffens tradition in the newspapers. They have looked at the displacements that are part of any urban renewal program, and not examined the results carefully enough.

Urban renewal, a federal program to assist cities with money for land redevelopment, is neither "good" nor "bad" race relations; racial integration will be achieved only when the political leadership of a city resolves to achieve it. Given these favorable auspices, its achievements are practically unique. New York has achieved interracial middle-income developments at Morningside Gardens, the first middle-income Title I development in the city. Opened in 1957, Morningside Gardens drew an exceptionally well-educated group of co-operators. No one knows the precise racial characteristics of the development, but a good guess is that the percentage of Negro families is approximately the same as the percentage of Negro families in the total population of New York City. This was merely the trailblazing project. Similar cooperatives, built on land made reasonable through Title I (Lindsay Park in Williamsburg; ILGWU Houses in Chelsea; Seward Park, on the Lower East Side), now stand on sites in New York City that were made available only through demolition; they are now occupied by families earning between $6,000 and $15,000 per year. All of them are racially integrated. Individually, their populations are in no recognizable way different from other middle-income families throughout the city. The same has been accomplished in San Francisco; Paterson, New Jersey; Madison, Wisconsin; Cincinnati, which is almost a southern city in its social patterns; and Minneapolis, according to Dr. Weaver, Administrator of the Housing and Home Finance Agency. Dr. Weaver has also remarked that biracial residential buildings may soon exist in urban renewal areas in Los Angeles, New Haven, Chicago, Boston, Detroit, and more than twenty other cities.

Although many vocal critics of the modern American city have inveighed against the Title I program, and the high-rise buildings typical of its results—high-rise usually because the designers were trying to keep ground space open for family use, as playgrounds, green space, swimming pools, and automobile parking—few indeed have bothered to look inside the structures which were specially financed to provide cooperative (rarely rental) apartments for families of regular but modest income.

Those who are familiar with urban redevelopments of this kind sometimes sense that the critics have been victims of the sleight-of-hand of a monster magician. They have been so distracted by the big bangs set off by James Baldwin and LeRoi Jones, and simultaneously by the flashes from Watts and Bogalusa, that they could not notice what was happening in another direction. Within those Title I developments dedicated to the production of racially integrated, moderate-cost housing, remarkable social and psychological changes have been taking place.

A new social class, perhaps a new middle class, has been emerging. For the first time in American life, this new class is neither white nor Negro, but interracial. Because of the external similarities of the large buildings, the outside observer assumes that their inhabitants are crushed into conformity; on the contrary, their diverse individuality expresses itself in the cooperative decoration of the internal public spaces; in the style and furnishing of the individual apartments; and most of all in the varied life styles, tastes, and the sometimes maddeningly disorganized internal politics of the cooperative.

Interestingly enough, the internal politics of the cooperatives do not seem markedly racial or religious; the fruits of unionization and the benefits of the civil service have meant that tenant cooperators in the same general income range reflect a wide variety of intellectual and social backgrounds. The people living in these new developments, usually constructed on the sites of the worst of the centrally located old slums, share two basic qualities: incomes in the $6,000 to $12,000 bracket; and the fact that they came from dingy, inadequate apartments in segregated neighborhoods where, without government intervention, they might have continued to live forever. Whatever may be the difficulties in maintaining the racial mixture in these new developments, it is hard to avoid the feeling that children raised in such an atmosphere will have a wholly new attitude toward racial difference, a more casual, natural attitude that will be as different from that of today's college youth as the latter differs from the attitudes in American colleges thirty or forty years ago.

Although Title I does not by itself, as we have seen, produce racially integrated living for middle-income families, it provides the raw material—land—and provides it in a place which would not otherwise be available for families of this income range—areas near the heart of the city. To make this land serve the purpose of middle-income families of all races, special low-cost mortgages must be provided for developers willing to work on a limited-profit basis. The advantages to the city in using the Title I land for this purpose are many. It stops the deterioration which, otherwise, is almost impossible to stop; it provides added tax revenue, even when the city is able and willing to grant partial, temporary exemption from real estate taxes for the new middle-income developments; it uses existing facilities (transit lines, hospitals, libraries, commercial developments), and minimizes the difficulties of transportation to the suburbs. Successful middle-income development in a Title I area may also facilitate the construction of low-rent public housing nearby without causing the concentration of low-rent housing in a single area that has, for example, proved so disturbing a feature of Chicago's recent efforts to produce a public housing program.

Finally, many cities desire Title I redevelopment so strongly that they are even willing to correct their principles to earn it. Buffalo, New York, for example, is one of the cities which adopted housing codes regulating conditions in residential buildings solely to qualify for federal Title I aid. More significant even than this is California's position on race prejudice. The constitutional amendment adopted by the Californians in 1964 bars, as we have said, the adoption of any law which mandates nondiscrimination in housing. This puts it in conflict with federal regulations requiring nondiscrimination as a condition of federal aid to housing. The most effective pressure on the state of California to modify or change its ban will come from the cities in the state which have been cut off from federal urban renewal subsidies as a result of the amendment.

This example of the power of Title I to influence the race relations of local communities could probably be echoed dozens of times across the nation.

Yet there are difficulties in working out this program in practice. The subsidized mortgages which the federal government developed for this very purpose must be made more readily available. They cannot be replaced, as we have seen, by a system of individual subsidies available only to low-income tenants, based on a wholly fanciful theory of class attachments. In any case, state and municipal programs can furnish the subsidies necessary to make middle-income developments possible on Title I land, with no apparent direct cost to the taxpayers, through the establishment of local government mortgage funds. There will be opposition to this by the owners of older apartment structures, until they understand that these mortgages offer great opportunities for them.

Another problem arises from the very nature of Title I operations: because they are concerned with land that is already in use, something, or more important, someone, must be moved to make the land available for a new use. Relocation, as we shall see, is painful for everyone, even if, in many cases, it merely substitutes an identifiable scapegoat for the vague but persistent dissatisfactions of the slums. In any case, satisfactory relocation requires a low-rent housing program for the people moved, and this must be added to the low-rent rehousing program needed to improve the conditions in the urban slums, that would be intolerable even if there were no Title I program. As if this were not enough of a burden for local government officials, whatever their financial assistance from Washington, they must also bear the political consequence of moving poor people to make room for wealthier ones, a difficult assignment for a city government, especially when the poor people being moved are represented by ward or district leaders who, usually, are happy to attack the central city officials who are preparing to remove their constituents. To postpone action in a carefully selected site may avoid this attack, but it defers the solution of a problem about which something can be done, in order to lament the existence of another problem which no one quite knows how to solve.

The selection of the proper sites for Title I middle-income housing is all-important if they are to provide models for interracial living patterns. Although the buildings on the site may be decrepit and dilapidated before the redevelopment begins, the site itself must attract new families who have something of a choice of residence, and who are probably living in homes that meet the government's minimal standards even if they are inadequate for the family needs. As Dr. Weaver described it, "If favorably located (from the point of view of attractiveness to white families) moderate-income housing is well-designed, it will be bi-racial in many sections of the Nation."

Usually, a site is attractive because it has absorbed prestige from the institutions near it (the environs of a world-famous university, for example), or because it has a favorable view. The more propitious the circumstances, the harder the present occupants of the site will resist its redevelopment, naturally; and the more biting will be the sense of injustice in the city that the poor are being evicted for the benefit of the better-off. The more likely the critics are to concentrate on the problem of relocation, the less likely they are to notice the values after reconstruction. A bitter argument has been raging about the environs of Columbia University in Manhattan, which stands in an area in which there are a number of shoddy so-called hotels containing a distillate of all the urban social problems: addiction, prostitution, thievery, and violence. There are also a much larger number of old, inadequate, and dilapidated buildings containing poor families who want the social pathology cleaned up, want their own homes to be improved, and want to be able to stay in the same prestigious areas. "The people around here don't want to leave Manhattan, because the theaters are here," one of their leaders told me. I was not told how many of them had actually attended a theater.

On the other side, one must not select any area for Title I middle-income development which is *too* good; one such project in a city leads middle-income families, particularly white families, to resist taking apartments in "second-best" locations. In New York, which has had more experience of this kind than any other city, all the middle-income projects in Manhattan outside Central Harlem have filled readily with a mixture of white and Negro families. Projects in certain relatively unfashionable sections of the Bronx—not originally Negro sections—attract white families only very slowly. The Negro families, though of the same income group, are under greater pressure to find decent homes. They take apartments as soon as these come on the market, which only heightens the resistance of white middle-income families who look at vacancies and find that the building already contains a Negro majority. Finding sites that are good but not too good is obviously a job for an artist; which indicates that the strategy of racial integration cannot be summarized in neat mathematical rules.

A further difficulty in this use of Title I is the architectural one: many of the most persistent urban critics hate apartment houses, especially those built with government subsidies. These buildings not only look alike, but they look alike on a big scale. Whatever the merits of the criticisms, it is a fact that the builders most likely to proceed with middle-income development on a limited-profit basis, are more interested in costs than beauty; and so, perhaps regrettably, their tenants have been people more interested in convenience than style. As a result the critics in practice, find themselves opposing what they merely mean to improve.

For the biggest obstacle to the use of Title I for interracial housing for the middle-income group lies precisely in the area of politics. How many cities' officials really want to construct interracial housing in the heart of town? The forces opposing this use of governmental power can rely on all the obstacles we have noted; and they do. Against this opposition, the official who wants to use his powers for this end must rely on the united support of all those people who believe residential racial integration is vital to the future of the American city. The trouble is that all those good people fail to agree; the assumptions they have made about money, about government and private collaboration, about the community, have kept the critics from seeing that in urban renewal the cities have an instrument with which all can take the vital first step toward residential racial integration. And while they carp, the instrument may be rusting away.

VIII. THEY DON'T BUILD PALACES LIKE VERSAILLES ANY MORE

W HEN the European trade association for hereditary ruling monarchs holds its decennial conventions, the delegates must divide themselves into workshops to discuss how to improve the conditions under which the membership lives and works. The session attracting the greatest interest is surely that in which gentlemen and dowagers discuss their basic housing accommodations; there is a special pleasure in cataloguing the deprivations that have been inflicted by the thoughtlessness of outside agencies. The ruling monarchs have a just complaint: they don't build palaces like Versailles any more.

A squad of critical volunteers waits to thrill the convention of ruling monarchs with tales of what the century of the common man means to the style of cities. Each contemporary monarch understands very well that he has dropped from the attentuated upper limb of his family tree into the age of standardization. His social conscience was pruned until he can readily recite the spreading comforts conferred on his subjects by mass production. It is easy enough to concede the blessings of corn flakes, canned soup, shoe laces, and homogenized pasteurized milk. On any given shelf these familiar and repetitious objects demand only a small arc of the eye's orbit. It is not easy at all, on the other hand, to concede the blessing of boredom in the urban landscape which surrounds and enfolds urban man as completely as his air. Under the twin pressures of high development costs and growing population, the heterogeneous urban landscape of the past is being chopped down; in its place grow large, simpleminded cubes of glass and metal, esthetically inspired by cereal boxes, and, according to the critics, foreshadowing the time when each city will resemble a vast temporary army camp, built in a morning, and keeping within its boundaries only those who have been unable to get leave to go elsewhere.

The critics, treasuring their sense of the inevitable deterioration of the modern city, are eloquent in describing architectural doom. An observer who does not share their conviction of predestined catastrophe might be persuaded to search for some mitigating influences which, with intelligence and luck, might be strengthened. A closer look at the urban landscape may reveal four influences which make the army camp simile a century or two premature, or perhaps irrelevant altogether. The first of these mitigating influences is the possibility that, with a rational application of effort, older buildings may be fruitfully saved alongside the new. The second is that municipal governments themselves may be encouraged to produce interesting and distinguished public structures. The third is that purely private owners of commercial structures may be led to erect handsome and diverting new buildings, and to keep alive some of those built in an earlier day. The fourth is the possibility that by determined effort someone somewhere will make progress in meeting the severest esthetic challenge to the modern city: how to provide interest and variety in the vast residential construction that cities need now for their less affluent inhabitants, and the even vaster construction that will be needed to meet the predictable requirements of the future.

Saving the Old

No single subject stimulates the adrenal glands and the tear ducts of the urban critics more than the demolition of the older buildings in the American city. Mrs. Ada Louise Huxtable, the architectural critic of the New York *Times,* and Mr. Wolf von Eckardt, who performs similar chores for the Washington *Post,* will be happy to tell the assembled monarchs that democratic visigoths are busy tearing down the precious heritage of the American past.

This news may be somewhat puzzling to the Europeans, who were raised on the notion that America hadn't any. Certainly the American architectural heritage lacks chefs-d'oeuvre which have won unquestioned world renown: many of its newer buildings are far better known abroad than are its older ones. There are few buildings noted for having been the scene of important or even of dubious historical events (buildings which sometimes sprout on the European tundra to the bemusement of tourists), like "Anne Hathaway's cottage" at Stratford. Pre-Revolutionary America was largely agricultural; the stately homes of the Washingtons, the Lees, the Madisons, the Roosevelts, and, most especially, the Jeffersons, stand in the countryside, safe from the menace of urban bridges, tunnels, and office buildings.

The architectural heritage threatened by American city changes is more special, but no less real. It includes town houses, churches, and a few rare public buildings, erected during the Federalist period of the 1790's and the early 1800's. There remain also American adaptations of European styles, the modernized Greek and the romanticized Gothic, for example, dating back to the 1820's, 30's, and 40's. The heritage includes regional treasures, sometimes comprising whole groups or districts of similarly sized buildings of congenial styles, perhaps distinguished less for their lines than their artifacts, like the wrought-iron balconies of New Orleans, or the hardware products of the Northeast, manifested in railings, lamps, and door ornaments to complement the fan-shaped fenestration over rectangular doors and windows. The American inheritance includes commercial structures noted for their technical innovations, like the earthquake-resistant Montgomery Block in San Francisco, designed by "Old Brains," General Henry W. Halleck, Civil War predecessor of the contemporary Chief of Staff of the nation, or the prefabricated cast-iron fronts of the commercial buildings on New York's Worth Street, or the beginnings of the skyscraper, as in Louis Sullivan's Schiller (Garrick Theatre) Building in Chicago.

The American architectural heritage includes also the stately Romanesque and Renaissance villas of the post-Civil-War industrialists, erected between 1870 and 1910 on the broad avenue of the American Belgravias. The same tycoons also saw to the construction of very large public and commercial buildings, in their roles as trustees or business managers. Finally, the heritage includes a number of public, commercial, or eleemosynary institutions of Victorian aspect in which, like the Jefferson Market Courthouse or the Company 15 Firehouse in San Francisco, enthusiastic eclecticism made a virtue of ugliness, stimulating sentimental loyalty in the unlikeliest bosoms.

The menace to this heritage is real also. In New York, the palaces of all the Vanderbilts have gone; so has Mrs. Astor's house, and Charles Schwab's. The Montgomery Block has gone from San Francisco, and the firehouse of Engine Company 15 has gone too. In Bridgeport, Connecticut, a rare treasure of the Gothic Revival, the Harral Wheeler House, designed in 1843 by Alexander Jackson Davis, vanished as hastily as a gypsy tearoom. In Chicago, the Garrick Theatre building is down; so is the Rush Street house of Cyrus McCormick, with its heavy French accent; so, too, Marshall Field's house, designed by Richard Morris Hunt, the first home in Chicago to include

electric light. Where not actually leveled, some older buildings are threatened with crucial changes in their settings that
may reduce their significance. Thus, the citizens of New Orleans
may be forced to choose between an interstate highway, vital
to the city's heavy commerce, and an undisturbed vista of the
city's Vieux Carré, vital to its personality and to its tourist
trade as well.

These isolated evidences of the demolition of the architectural heritage of the nation are only a few random examples of
a situation that is widespread in all the cities. The federal government, during the Depression years, established a painstak-
ing study, state-by-state, of the historic buildings of the nation.
In the course of it, over 20,000 buildings were considered
worthy of note. It is estimated that between 1940 and 1966,
more than 20 percent of the buildings identified by HABS
(Historical American Buildings Survey) were destroyed. In
some individual cities things are even worse than the national
average. The HABS survey covered 145 San Francisco buildings. Ninety-five of these have been demolished; twenty-seven
are still standing but in a form that is so changed that they are
described as "ruined" architecturally; only twenty-three survive
as recognizable historic buildings. As cities respond to the human needs of people now living in them, they continue to out-
strip their past at an accelerating rate. The Historic Alexandria
Foundation was established in Alexandria, Virginia, in 1962.
Its specialists identified 773 historic buildings. Within three
years, by December 1965, 11 percent of these had been destroyed or desecrated, and an additional 17 percent threatened.

In some cases, buildings of this type were saved by accident
or conscious effort. In the smaller towns a few outstanding mansions were converted into funeral homes; and in the large cities,
the first to be given up as residences became museums. But the
limit on the number of useful museums is set by the number of
the worthwhile objects, not by the availability of structures in

which to place them. And now, when museums are needed in Los Angeles, New York, or Chicago, it is clear that new structures are more efficient than converted mansions with curved walls and inconvenient room arrangements, buildings in which the creators' enthusiasm bubbled out over the top of the facade in a flood of friezes, pilasters, balustrades, lunettes, and statuary. Years ago, when functionalism was flooding the architectural schools and the left-wing weeklies, these ornaments struck the young observer as insincere. But insincerity is an offense which age tends to mitigate, especially if one must examine instead the Frank Lloyd Wright-designed Guggenheim Museum, a machine for viewing, in which the observer is treated like a loose ball bearing, or the new Senate Office Building—as sincere as a bathroom, the tiled inside of which its gleaming stone somewhat resembles.

Much of the attachment to the buildings of the recent past, expressed so poignantly by Huxtable and Eckardt, can be understood far more reasonably as an attachment to the social order of that period's upper-class life, of which the buildings are merely a manifestation chilled into stone and brick. Some law of social reaction makes that order all the more cherished when it is clear that its physical forms cannot withstand the pressures of the present, and when enough time has passed to obscure the cold mornings and long stairways, the smelly closet privies and the damp sheets that were on the other side of the elaborate facade of Versailles.

No one builds like Versailles today because no single cause in American life can, like the Sun King, command the concentration of such vast economic force on a single objective. Not even the military could accumulate its stock of A- and H-bombs, unless the process of accumulation stimulated the employment of millions of Americans, and contributed to production and exchange of quantities of other goods. If the employment at the same cost of millions of Congolese in digging a trench in their own country were the only guarantee of America's military safety, but the residents of the Congo used their wages only to gamble with each other, and continued to resist the purchase of American toothpaste, this nation might manage with a smaller margin of military security. Louis XIV was not bound to consider the standard of living of his constituents. He made a gesture toward the French economy by deliberately employing French painters, gardeners, architects, and artisans in the construction of Versailles, but no one challenged him in an editorial to justify his choice of the artists who pleased him most.

Architectural critics have stressed the esthetic qualities of structures. They have distinguished the importance of the general form of a building, and the desirability of deriving this form in harmony with the function that the building is intended to fill. They have explained the sensuous importance, not only of the solids of the structure itself, but of the patterned space which it encloses. They have called attention to the building's manipulation of the surrounding environment, and its recomposition of that environment into new planes of light and shade in which the textures of the building's surface play an important part. But they have not, perhaps because they assume it is harmful, paid very much attention to the artistic effects of money in architecture. Yet, to the observer's eye, architecture is unique among the arts in its power of economic concentration; it pulls together all of the riches of the world that built it, and it is this quality of architecture as a monument to wealth that is important to the common observer.

Follow a troupe of tourists through Versailles or Schönbrunn, through Saint Peter's or the temples at Agrigento, through the stately homes of England—Woburn or Blenheim—and notice that the oohs and ahs are extracted by the incidental ornamentation, by the immensity of the structure, and by its overwhelming impression of wealth. Can all this have been the home of a single family? How did the simple Greek mechanics raise these monstrous columns? How did the church, a spiritual body, acquire so much temporal wealth, and why was it willing to spend it thus?

When European men found that kings possessed no special divinity, when all churches attained equal access to the truth, and when the belief that government was the servant of people rather than their master gained currency, no one was left with the power to decree such concentrated effort. Architecture of celebration—art as a monument, if you will—lies outside the power of a government which has agreed to rule by consent of the governed. It can be said that the better the government in this sense—the worse, or, at least, the less interesting, its architecture. The most important, interesting, and lavish buildings of the past hundred years have been constructed not by governments, to celebrate themselves, but by private, nonreligious institutions.*

Because the needs and uses of profit-making institutions change rapidly, it is difficult to maintain their buildings as part of the permanent urban landscape. Sometimes, the good citizens find they are about to lose on these practical grounds, a building they like for which no one can find a current use, its economic base having wasted away. Architectural critics, like Mr. Blake, sometimes seem to have ignored the difference between the cultural impulse which built Mont St. Michel, and that which built a department store. Mr. Blake's assumption of the general deterioration of the urban environment leads him to decry the modern need to replace stores which can no longer be used effectively, and to contrast this with the ability of older civilizations to maintain their churches or palaces over long spans of centuries. In scornful terms he criticizes New York for the demolition (sometimes by private effort, sometimes by public effort) of commercial buildings with historically interesting cast-

* The religious institutions are making a comeback but since they cannot spare the funds for land acquisition, their most exciting works are rural.

iron fronts, even though he cannot suggest what should be done with them.

A good example of this kind of situation was Pennsylvania Station in New York City. Whether or not one admired its style (I did not) , it was one of the city's most impressive structures. But what does one do with an impressive railroad station which has ceased to be of value as a railroad station? In a dying city one boards it up, and watches it become ruins; ultimately shepherds sit on its eroded columns and goats graze between the tracks. In a living city one first prostitutes it into a more efficient machine for selling commuter and race track tickets, and then into an architectural billboard, hanging signs, kiosks, and booths from its Roman vaults. Finally, the day is reached when someone decides it is worth more as land than as structure, and down it comes to be replaced by an office building or a sports arena, or both.

On the other hand, government and religious activities being less dependent on technology, change less over the years. The structures built originally to contain them demonstrate greater adaptability. One of the more beautiful structures in New York City, its City Hall, was completed in 1812 by a government whose scope and size have since changed almost beyond imagination; yet it is still in use.

Whereas New York's City Hall once contained all of the city's offices, it now holds but a few, including that of the Mayor. The city itself has increased its population sixty-five-fold since 1812. Other buildings have been added to the city's own holdings to contain new services. But the city has still one Mayor only, and the City Hall can still contain him.

This is a tribute, not only to the slow change in the forms of government, but also to the style and gracious dignity of the City Hall itself. These gentle characteristics do not reflect the stormy conditions under which it was built. In 1803 the city of New York offered a prize of $350 for the best design for its City

Hall. This was not a handsome prize, even in 1803 dollars, but architectural contests are a losing proposition even for the winner, unless he badly needs public notice. Despite the modest architectural fee, the later construction costs of New York's City Hall mounted so high (in comparison with the balance in the City Treasury) that the building was not finished for nine years. During all of that time, contemporary citizens were happy to suggest to the administration how their taxes could have been better used. Before a modern New Yorker views this infant democracy disparagingly through the lorgnettes made to cure a 150-year-old case of municipal myopia, let him at least admit that some of the uses to which the city's money have been put—hygiene, for example; schools; street paving—might have been even more beneficial than the lovely City Hall New York ultimately got.

The hereditary ruling monarchs, and their American guest lecturers, assume that the community (that word again) shares their view that the esthetic and cultural value of a landmark building is supreme. It follows, therefore, that a decision to demolish such a building must be simple vandalism. The critics accuse American cities of the systematic destruction of their past. As an accusation, this is somewhat milder than the charge that the cities are systematically destroying their future, but the critics, once again, assume that all urban values deteriorate, and that the best part of the cities lies behind them. Destroy the cities' past, the critics feel, and one's hope for their future dies with it.

Even if one is gloomy about the future, the facts do not generally support the accusation of vandalism leveled against the destruction of an older building. No one, I believe, has suggested that New York's City Hall be touched. Saving less singular older buildings may, depending on the circumstances, be a difficult assignment, even when the buildings possess qualities cherished by respected cataloguers as well as the vocal public.

Saving such a building is difficult in the first instance because the question would not arise if the owner had not already entertained the notion of demolishing it. Its owner customarily decides to demolish an older building only in the expectation of erecting something new on its site. To calculate which is socially more valuable—the present building or its future replacement—is not so simple as it seems to those who believe that the value of a landmark, any landmark, however defined, is supreme. The rest of us may believe that if the values of the future building are understated in favor of an overestimation of the past, vandalism of another kind may be committed: vandalism against the future, carrying the name of unreasonable obstruction of desirable change.

Why should its owner wish to demolish a landmark building to make room for something new? To make a quick buck, of course, the critics hiss, with that happy smugness with which one criticizes those who have succumbed to a temptation to which one has not been exposed. It turns out, however, that, even if all agree that the ownership of a landmark building ought to be a far more restricted property right than ownership of an El Greco or a Gutenberg Bible, many landmark buildings are owned not by speculators at all, but by nonprofit institutions which are not intrinsically interested in the quick buck. Those landmark buildings in the United States which are not owned by government, are most likely to be owned by foundations, societies, museums, schools, and churches (except in landmark districts, of which more later).

For the most part, these agencies have acquired the buildings by gift from their previous or original owners, or as the result of someone else's generosity. The institutions use the landmark buildings for their operations, or, in some cases, they may finance their own corporate purposes with the income derived from rental of the landmark property, precisely as the benefactor intended. If they outgrow the building they use themselves, or if their corporate purposes require additional funds, shall they refuse to sell the landmark for as much money as may be offered? May not the sale fulfill the purposes for which the original donor gave them either the landmark itself, or the money to buy it? Shall New York's Society of Friends not sell its second, redundant Meeting House, even if it is one of the City's rare Italianate (1860) relics, so that the Society's school may be expanded to include about a quarter of the worthy children on its waiting list? Are the leaders of the Society true to their corporate trust, in refusing such an offer?

And if one says that this is a mere financial problem, a matter of raising money from some other source to make good only a paper loss, one reaches then the second difficulty. How does the owner keep alive a building for which he has no further use, and in which he cannot interest any other occupant? A building is not an inert object of fine art to be hung on an empty wall, or placed on a pedestal. A building needs care, maintenance, use. Without these it rots. And all the invocations to imagination, the pleas that someone else think of a "creative" use for a landmark, echo emptily if the building is not adaptable to contemporary use.

The survival potential of any landmark in any city can be estimated very simply by reference to two factors. One is the adaptability of its original use. Least adaptable, for example, are the large structures like railroad stations whose function is closely connected with a specific technological use, subject to obsolescence.

The second factor (inversely) determining survival potential is the economic redevelopment value of the site on which the landmark stands. A railroad station in the center of a large city has a high economic redevelopment value. This, combined with its low adaptability, means that its survival potential is almost nil. One should not be astonished, therefore, to see that Philadelphia's urban redevelopment began with the demolition of the Broad Street Station; and, as we have seen, that New York's Pennsylvania Station fell to the steel balls of the wreckers' cranes. It should also occasion no surprise that wholly unused, small suburban stations remain undisturbed for years. Their adaptability is practically nil, but so is the economic redevelopment value of their sites. As a result, no one either takes care of these structures, or bothers to demolish them, and their sometimes fascinating, quaint architecture is hidden in their dusty deterioration.

Logically, landmarks can be saved from demolition either by increasing their adaptability, or by reducing the economic redevelopment value of their site. Most of the people who fret about the disappearance of landmarks, exhort their owners to increase the adaptability of their buildings. Those who would like to prevent the demolition of the Savoy Plaza Hotel in New York, which cannot profitably be operated as a hotel, urge that it be adapted to some new use—apartments, perhaps, or physicians' offices. But the land value of its Fifth Avenue site is so high that it is far more profitable to take down the existing building and erect in its place a new, much larger office building. Those who want to prevent this from happening could effectively reduce the economic redevelopment value of the land by restricting its future use by zoning limits on the size of the building that could be built on it. Unless the new building can be very much larger than the old, remodeling of the present hotel would be more profitable than demolition and redevelopment.

Anyone who has struggled to pass a more restrictive zoning resolution in a city, whose great construction activity threatens ever-higher human densities and makes higher standards imperative, must know how hard it is to persuade the city government to impose limits on what can be done with the most expensive land in the city. The construction industry—uniting labor and management—opposes restrictions which mean less work. The city treasurer objects because these limits in the development of expensive land also impair the tax increases the city might expect from larger improvements. A new zoning law, at least, offers general advantages to the city; but narrowly conceived landmark legislation, which would merely prevent the reconstruction of certain historic sites, seems to offer the city treasurer—at least when applied to sites with a high economic redevelopment value—a choice between landmarks and schools. If you had to listen to the demands of the city's mothers, you would not blame the treasurer for not taking the landmark lovers so seriously.

If the most difficult landmarks to save are railroad stations in valuable central locations, the next hardest are the mansions erected by wealthy families, fifty or eighty years ago. This is particularly true of mansions erected near the center of the city, on an avenue which has become legally available and commercially desirable for apartment house or office building construction. These old mansions are far too big for one-family occupancy under current conditions. The tax burden of the underlying land is so heavy that it cannot be borne simply by dividing the mansion into several small apartments, even if that should not conflict with the city's housing codes and neighborhood sensibilities.

High inheritance taxes and other economic problems have often placed these buildings in institutional hands. If the tax-free institutions cannot use them, who can? Mr. Giorgio Cavaglieri, formerly president of the Municipal Art Society of New York, has suggested that large corporations make their headquarters in the ersatz *palazzi* of the older American cities. He thinks that the prestige of being identified with Mr. Carnegie's copy of a Georgian palace would compensate its commercial occupants for any loss of efficiency due to the palace's tiny slow elevator. Mr. Cavaglieri explains that, in Europe, the large entrepreneur and his stockholders accept the reality of the value that their company assimilates from locating in some notable Parisian *hôtel particulier,* or on a fabled locale, like the Piazza di San Marco. Yet, economics are banging on the door. There is a dollar difference between a location in a real *hôtel particulier,* and location in an imitation—a difference similar to that between Rembrandt's painting of the Town Council, and the lithographed copy you can find on the top of your cigar box. No amount of invocation and ballyhoo will cause the industrialist's bankers to confuse the one with the other. Its doom was written on the walls of the circa-1890 Chenonceaux that Mr. Brokaw built on Fifth Avenue land, once the land it was built on could legally be used for an apartment house.

The case is very different for older single-family homes that occupy sites for which there is less current demand (and which are therefore better protected by zoning restrictions). This is particularly true if, as is often the case, the land was of relatively low value when the houses on it were built. Hence, these houses were built by families of less spectacular fortunes than those who built on the broad avenues of the central city. The smaller houses on less treasured land tend, for the same reason, to be of a size more compatible with modern pocketbooks and modern servants, or the lack of them. And where zoning restricts this land to residential use, an entire historic district can be preserved, especially with the help of legal restrictions on remodeling that might change the character of buildings. Such legal restrictions use a public sanction to enforce private covenants that frequently have helped to preserve the character of such districts as Georgetown, in Washington; Brooklyn Heights, in New York; and Society Hill, in Philadelphia. But it is nonsense to confuse the conditions that apply in such areas with the low adaptability and high economic redevelopment value of the big houses on Upper Fifth Avenue, in Manhattan. Here the wealthiest families in the nation were unable to preserve the character of a happy little neighborhood designed for billionaires and butlers.

Nor am I impressed with the possibility of turning such a home into a memorial of the particular family that lived in it, having watched the struggle waged to keep alive the so-called Old Merchant's House in New York City. This was an early nineteenth-century, upper-middle-class home-and-office, carefully preserved by a foundation with the cultural artifacts of the contemporary world. Not enough visitors come to the Old Merchant's House to meet its operating expenses. This is a melancholy demonstration of a fact that seems obscure to many people: the streets of a city are not its attic.

Quite different is the case of religious architecture, which has demonstrated an adaptability that beggars the survival, not only of the New York City Hall, but of the Tower of London. Many a Roman temple became a Christian church; the Pantheon in Rome, which was first a temple, then a church, and now a monument, is said to have contributed the bronze from its portico to St. Peter's. Melted down, the bronze provided the magnificent twisted baroque columns holding up the baldachino or canopy over the Papal altar. That's real economy—one can almost hear an irate citizen citing the Pantheon to the city fathers as a reproach for the carelessness with which they propose to dissipate on architecture the funds he would have them use for schools.

Civic Virtue—Civic Beauty

Competition for funds—a basic birthmark of a government dependent upon elections—is only one of the disadvantages confronting contemporary city officials when they try to build a new Versailles. Architects refuse to bid against each other for city work; their selection is a matter of judgment. Judgment unsupported by a record is open to the attacks of the modern Lincoln Steffens. If a public building is to be constructed, there will be a budget appropriation; and a specific city department will have charge of its construction. The department will be filled with worthy gentlemen who have survived a Civil Service system which was, in turn, established by believers in good government. Job descriptions are the order of the day; and the slots are filled by competitive examinations. Anyone who has ever sat on an examining board for Civil Service vacancies in the higher ranks has listened to the ritualistic incantations which have replaced the restless search for merit. Will you please define the difference between a Supervisor and an Administrator? Under what heading in the files do you find the specifications for doors? What happens if one of the draughtsmen you are supervising presents a drawing which does not meet the requirements established under Regulation F26797-J? It is true that the Civil Service was established to raise the quality of government by eliminating corrupt hiring and guaranteeing tenure; it is true that disbanding the Civil Service would not necessarily produce good buildings, and might produce very much worse buildings than those the cities are already building. Yet it does seem likely that extraordinary energy is required on the part of the consultant architect, and extraordinary courage on the part of a city official, if the Civil Service is not, under the prodding of the press, to prevent the very good with the same zeal with which it prevents the very bad.

I suggest that interesting architecture is not arrived at reasonably, and that the system of public letting to rigid specifications is calculated to produce honesty ahead of beauty. That there are good reasons for preferring moral qualities to esthetic ones, I do not deny. Yet it must be said that the good is often interred with a public servant's bones, while his descendants must live with the buildings he put up. The public-letting system requires an architect to draw plans for construction firms to bid on; a budget figure is established, and the architect knows that to come within that figure, he must avoid, as though it were diseased, any type of construction with which the prospective bidders may be unfamiliar. The concern with fair treatment of bidders extends now to the point where the basic contract for new public buildings must be divided into four separate contracts, each of which must be publicly awarded to the lowest bidder. In some jurisdictions, every bidder on the general contract must list the subcontracting firm that gave him his low bid. Certainly all this is fair, but one wonders if Lorenzo the Magnificent could have surrendered his majesty to the forms of virtue, and still built his library. If Americans want great public buildings they must elect officials willing to run risks to build them. They must also, and this is even harder, support the right of these officials to make mistakes, even while reserving their own right to comment on them.

Several years ago, the City Club of New York, by local standards an ancient body which has dedicated itself to the cause of better government, offered a prize to the designer of the best public building erected in the city of New York. After earnest scrutiny, the judges of the contest announced that they had found no building worthy of the prize. When asked by the club to comment on this singular development, I remarked that its members should have awarded themselves a special prize for doing so much to make outstanding public buildings impossible. Throughout its life, the club had insisted on equitable specifications, democratic review of proposals, objective criteria, and promotions in accordance with a merit system. A lobby for good municipal architecture might well support the official who flouts these very accomplishments.

There is no reason why such a lobby should not become an important factor in every American city. It might be led by the local chapter of the American Institute of Architects and it would serve as a committee for architectural integrity. It would come to the defense of the public official who engages a reputable architect, and gives him his head. All too often those who wish to stimulate good municipal architecture begin by criticizing the public official for his past failures and mediocrities. This may be more fun, but it merely stimulates caution on the part of the official, precisely the opposite of the daring that is needed.

Many younger architects have been urging a wider use of competition for the selection of designers. The trouble with architectural competition is that it should begin with a competition to select judges. If the judges are chosen poorly, the competition may easily result in even more mediocrity than the selection methods ordinarily used. If some committee for integrity in architecture would come to the defense of an individual architect whose ideas are being unreasonably restricted because of official fear of criticism, if such a committee would be willing to fight for more generous architectural fees on public work of all kinds, if such a committee would be willing to support not merely a modest addition to the cost of buildings for decorative vases and outdoor sculpture, but generosity or even extravagance in the basic design, if such a committee would be willing to forego professional courtesy and professional rivalry in its dealings with the public, the press, and the official government, the city would then have created a countervailing force to the good government demands for economy.

This active force is needed to protect good municipal design. The trouble is that once such a committee gets started its responsibilities broaden and the point begins to dull. It takes on new responsibilities, like landmark conservation, and tends to become only another vaguely motivated, heart-in-the-right-place civic agency.

Good municipal architecture is a political demand, a demand that money be spent on this instead of other worthy causes. Political also is the demand that public officials expose themselves to criticism to achieve good architecture. Let no one think that this is an easy position for an official to take, or that he will not be roundly criticized for its consequences. Even if those who believe in fiscal generosity are a minority, they can remember that political battles can be won by small groups willing to make their impact intense and specific. But such battles will not be won by those who feel they must be on the virtuous side of every argument. It has become fashionable to believe that beauty can be achieved by adding a 5 percent allowance to the basic cost of the structure. But the eye cannot be seduced by an agent's fee. Interesting municipal architecture may mean the use of several different architects to design structures that are part of the same complex. This sounds easy enough. But it means different specifications, different contracts. These mean that the economies of repetition must be abandoned, and the cost of the individual contracts may rise drastically as a result. Intelligent variety in new municipal structures springs not from the conscious striving for something different, but rather from the natural differences between different minds. Its unwelcome consequences may include delays, uncertainties, waste. The delays mean not only higher costs and higher taxes, they mean that people may suffer inconvenience and hardship, dislocation and uncertainty, all in the name of civic beauty. If the advocates of beauty are unwilling to stand up for these essential preconditions when the going heats up, how can they blame the officials, whose livelihood is at stake, for preferring the sober virtues of law and order to the wild music of the arts?

Private Money, Private Taste.

The relative freedom from criticism enjoyed by private entrepreneurs, both profit-making and institutional, gives them a somewhat easier time in designing buildings, especially if people do not live in them. The enterprise, of whatever nature, that erects a structure to celebrate itself deserves general thanks. The Seagram's building on Park Avenue in New York City is magnificent; so are the CBS building, and a smaller gem put up by Corning Glass. The National Geographic Society building in Washington, D.C., is splendid. One may be somewhat skeptical of the esthetic impulse that convinced the National Maritime Union that because its members work on ships, their concrete headquarters should suggest one. Yet the citizen may still prefer its tasteless unconventionality to the grinding boredom of more dignified structures.

Yale University—which, thirty years ago, vacillated between imitation Georgian and imitation Tudor—now has built a hockey rink and an art gallery that, far from resembling a retouched postcard photo of Cambridge University, dares to suggest that a private American university has a significance of its own.

Increasingly, however, the ostensible headquarters of national profit-making organizations are being built, not by those enterprises at all, but by investors who merely lease them to their tenants. This means that the true owner of the building is interested solely in how much rentable space he can construct on the given lot. Once New Yorkers worried that, since the Seagram's building had achieved a perfect form like the final tonic chord at the resolution of a symphony, the city would be faced with the prospect of a dozen Seagram-style buildings, striking together a series of final chords without the preceding development. This worry has been replaced by another: that instead of the harmonics of the Van der Rohe structure, the more important business thoroughfares of the city will be lined with a series of structures that simply ape the Seagram's building.

The basic trouble with the leased headquarters is that the owner of the building is interested primarily in pleasing his tenant. He has had the building designed primarily from the inside out, rather than from the outside in. This in itself means crowding to the legal limit, because the owner realizes that to attract the tenant, he must make the rents as low as he can per square foot, spreading the land cost over the largest possible number of office square feet.

From a distance, the modern commercial office structural machine, its glass sparkling in the sunlight, provides something of the artistic splendor of a new automobile. Yet the automobile, poised to conquer and control the world, is more magnetic. From the nearby street, the transparent and refulgent sheath of the structural machine is altogether sealed against the observer. Its refusal to respond either to him or to its surroundings merely indicates that its interior is so shallow that any penetration by the outside air conquers the building itself. There are, of course, exceptions. The Lever building, a magnificent structure owned by the company whose name it bears, astonishes the observer with what is almost a Japanese garden within its recesses, suggesting that the glass of the building is meant more to tantalize than to reveal.

Inside even the most commercial of these structures, however, one has the better of it. On the upper floors, one floats freely in the sky; the eradication of the boundary between interior and exterior, disturbing from the outside, is a triumph from within. Does the abolition of the boundary raise office efficiency? Is the glass office building an efficient machine? Certainly the vista from one of the glass structures is best when one can look out and see structures made of stone and brick. A glass machine is at its worst when its occupants find themselves looking at the reflection of their building on the outside wall of another building exactly like it across the street. Behold, one can make out the inhabitants of that second structure, peering from *its* windows at *its* form reflected on the first building's shiny skin. If unbacked glass were a better reflector, this echo of a visual echo could be bounced back and forth forever.

Contrast this with the limestone and granite that composed the opaque skins of older buildings. There is pleasure over the years in watching the relationship develop between space and structure. The slow change of the color of the stone symbolizes the maturing life of a building reacting to its own environment. One of the major objections to the new public housing construction of the postwar years—the endless use of red brick—may be a reaction not so much to the brick itself, but rather to the fact of its newness, the flat, pink, unfledged color of its youth. Over the years the brick will soften and darken, until it absorbs the very dirt and smudge of the world around it. The buildings will seem less insistent to the observer. Then some day they must be cleaned again and the cycle of life in the city recommences.

It seems possible that under the pressure of land value, the central business districts of a number of American cities will be fully developed (in the absence of effective zoning controls, they will be overdeveloped) with one or more avenues of these new buildings standing beside each other in gleaming splendor. If glass is to be the universal coating (there is some cheering evidence that the vogue for glass is receding), this prospect seems horrifying, but the contemporary judgment of a new cityscape is not necessarily reliable. As an example of a contemporary judgment subsequently gone awry, one might consider this description of a growing city:

"The rage of building has laid hold on such a number of adventurers, that one sees new houses starting up in every outlet and every corner of [the city] contrived without judgment, executed without solidarity, and stuck together with so little regard to plan and propriety, that the different lines of the new rows and buildings interfere with, and intersect one another in every different angle of conjunction. They look like the wreck of streets and squares disjointed by an earthquake, which hath broken the ground into a variety of holes and hillocks; or as if some Gothic devil had stuffed them altogether in a bag, and left them to stand higgledy piggledy, just as chance directed. What sort of a monster (the city) will become in a few years, with those growing excrescences, may be easily conceived; but the want of beauty and proportion is not the worst effect of these new mansions; they are built so slight, with the soft, crumbling stone found in this neighborhood, that I shall never sleep quietly in one of them . . ."

These strictures were written in 1771 by Tobias Smollett, and they represent either his own view or that of a considerable body of Englishmen of conservative temperament. The point is that the city whose design so appalled Mr. Smollett, or his contemporaries, was not Gary, Indiana, or Calcutta, but *Bath.*

Almost 200 years later, Lewis Mumford wrote about the very same city,

"Even now, after a century and a half of change, the heart of Bath has qualities of design that even the best examples in Paris, Nancy, London, or Edinburgh do not surpass. The excellence of Bath shows the advantage of a strict discipline, when it is supple enough to adapt itself to challenging realities, geographic and historic. The placing of the Royal Crescent on a height that commands the whole valley, protected by the park that spreads below, shows that it was no mere application of an arbitrary geometric figure; and while nothing in the rest of the eighteenth century city reaches this level of planning, the further building of Bath, right through the Regency, never fell too short of its standard."

Whether or not we can judge accurately the ultimate esthetic value of the new downtowns of the American city, it seems reasonable to believe that the structures which are owned by occupant builders are likely to be more handsome than those merely leased. Is there any way to encourage owner occupancy? If there is, it is less apparent than the ways in which it is actively *discouraged* by local real estate taxes. The laws by which municipalities are authorized by their state governments to tax real property almost invariably include the proviso that the *fair value* of the property is to be subject to tax. The cities employ tax appraisers who determine the fair value of each parcel of land and buildings within the city. One measure of the fair value of a building and its land is the annual rental income derived from it. If the appraiser multiplies the annual rental income by a fixed number—large, in the case of new prime property, and low in the case of old, poorly located property—he derives a standard appraisal of the value of the property.

In the case of the Seagram's building in New York City, however, which is owned by one of several interlocking companies, and which is obviously the kind of building and ownership which one seeks to encourage, the value derived in this formula was remarkably low in relation to the actual cost of development of the structure. The tax appraisers, therefore, decided that the company that owned the building was charging its affiliates arbitrarily low rentals. They therefore disregarded the rent-multiple as an indication of the real value of the building, and based their valuation on its actual cost. This resulted in a remarkably high ratio of taxes to rental income, naturally. The owning company appealed this expensive result, but the highest court in the state supported the appraisers. Certainly this decision discourages owner occupancy of office buildings, because it subjects to taxes the extra investment that an owner may put into a structure in order to beautify it in connection with his own name.

The construction of new commercial buildings is so dramatic in the city that many people believe that no older structure is safe. This fear is exaggerated. Older commercial buildings are not disappearing from American cities, except perhaps along one or two major business arteries of the city. And when the contrast between old and new can be maintained, it is both piquant and beautiful, two qualities which are magnified by the random, accidental nature of the combination. I prefer the improvisation that occurs in those commercial sections of the city where land values have not risen to the highest levels. And where the difference in age is highlighted by a difference in occupancy and use, the structures form a garden of stone, brick and glass, growing so slowly that the pace defies notice. The unfolding gives a certain visual truth to the airy metaphor in which a city is described as an organic whole with a life of its own.

Looking across the small park behind the New York Public Library at 42nd Street and Fifth Avenue, one can enjoy precisely this observation. Opposite one corner of the park, stands a ten-story building, built for artists' studios some fifty years ago, and therefore marked by high ceilings, that can be perceived from outside the building, through the large horizontal windows, emphasized by decorative white lintels and keystones. Evidently, the original owners of the building were proud of their investment, and both willing and able to use for the exterior walls a light-brown brick that contrasts with the white window lintels in a somewhat antique idiom. Across the street, a new, small textile showroom building constructed of white limestone or marble, presents a low facade consisting entirely of vertical pilasters, in grid form. To the right of this structure, a small clump of older yellow brick store buildings occupies the corner of the street. Behind them a new, moderately tall office building has risen, consisting mainly of dark glass horizontal bands, forming a contrast, though a muted one, with the buildings that stand before it. Behind this new structure, one glimpses the spiny roof turrets of older, loft-and-office buildings, in stone and brick. Across the street, on the right side of the vista, stands a new, very high bank building composed of setbacks that narrow as they rise, as simple in form as a stepladder, that adds an almost humorous touch to the whole scene. The whole is precisely the kind of unregimented harmony that characterizes the most beautiful of cities. How can the development of such a vista be encouraged and preserved?

Zoning—by limiting the profits to be made by tearing down older buildings and replacing them with new ones—helps. It encourages the continued use of the structures that already exist. But negative controls are not the whole story. The corner we have looked at continues to exist because commercial and industrial activities still thrive in it; this is a part of the garment-manufacturing and sales center of the city. The artists' studios are now showrooms and advertising photographic studios; the loft-and-office buildings are busy parts of the manufacturing train that includes all phases of the production of women's clothing. If manufacturing or wholesale trade cannot survive in the city, architectural variety is doomed with it. Manufacturing and wholesale trade cannot survive without efficient truck transportation, and this, to be efficient, requires special highways, bridges, and tunnels. It requires off-street unloading berths, all of which can be provided only if existing structures are torn down to make room for them. There is, therefore, in the real city, no single team for which all those who favor these varied structurescapes can play—the man who seeks to keep alive one structurescape may be conniving to destroy another in the process, so that truck traffic will nourish the corner he wishes to preserve. A program for conserving the rich contrasts of commercial buildings in the city depends, like rural conservation, on intelligence and selectivity. It depends more on an appraisal of the uses of technology, than on scathing denunciation of money and its uses. The flow of trade is as important to the commercial building as people are to the residential structure; it is as fruitless to rail against the one, as against the other.

Variety and Spice

The case is somewhat different when we consider residential structures, however, because the homes needed by the American people (at least those not oppressed by poverty) are remarkably similar, one to the other, and they become more so constantly. Electric machines and higher wages have removed the strings of servants' rooms that once distinguished the homes of the wealthy from those of the merely comfortable. Concrete highways and gasoline motors have excised the stables, some with weathercocks and some with haylofts, from the estates of the rich, who must now share with the merely employed, garages that are as alike as matchboxes. It is commonplace architectural criticism to remark on the similarity of all new apartment houses, whatever their rental level. There are no stonecutters, and no one today can afford the cartouches, scrolls, urchins, totemistic emblems that for the next hundred years will continue to disappear, bit by bit, into the stone columns and arches of sixty-year-old apartment houses on which they were carved. The status of the modern apartment house is expressed in the color of its brick. Since the public housing developments have concentrated on red brick—in most areas of the nation a cheap, satisfactory, and long-lived material—the luxury development is likely to be a house of another color. Any other color. Yellow, white, or water-color. It is difficult for the builder now to brag about the height of his ceilings, because all have become so low that they are dwarfed beside floor heights of even the old tenement house.

The absence of decoration is not only a mark of economy, or rather a mark of *the* economy—the good society having so developed that the skilled, on-site journeyman insists that he be paid wages high enough to purchase for himself a new home similar in its amenities to the home he is building for the wealthy. The absence of ornamentation is also one corollary of the theorem that architectural beauty is achieved only when form simply follows function.

The sameness of modern apartment houses has stiffened the critical tendency to find deterioration in any case, and has made the critics exaggerate in retrospect the differences between houses that were built in our cities one hundred to fifty years ago. To be sure, there are some older sections of our cities in which buildings were erected one by one, on streets that were laid in the beds of the old settlers' paths. These in turn, may have followed Indian trails. As the cities grew from their earliest settlement, however, their unplanned street patterns were left behind. A growing population needed increased transportation to bring in food and raw materials. The grid street patterns of the newer sections of American cities provided a simple transportation scheme that cut the land into equal sections, each easily divided into building lots of equal size and readily marketable. The land platting made standardization of building design easy, and cut to a welcome minimum the cost of laying utilities in the bed of the street. In the same way, of course, the producers of clothes increasingly prepared them in advance to standardized sizes, instead of cutting them to order to suit the individual customer.

By the end of the nineteenth century, hardly any urban area in America was still being developed with custom-built homes. Any variety that can be found today in the row houses that went up in the 1880's or 1890's was produced, not by their original builders, but over the years by their individual occupant owners, who changed the roofs, or the stoops, or who added a room here or there. The repetition of forms in residential buildings is the most serious esthetic problem in the cities; but, contrary to the critics, it is not a new problem. It is not even a problem caused by, or related to high-rise apartment house construction; the repetitive dullness of one-family developments is identical except that it is horizontal instead of vertical. As long as sixty or seventy years ago, only the wealthy districts or the really undesirable districts, demonstrated natural variety of residential structures.

The survival of variety in the second kind of district—the

undesirable district—has been offered, notably by Mrs. Jane Jacobs, as a model for the solution of the esthetic problem of the urban residential building. To understand the relevance of this prescription we might examine the history of West Greenwich Village—Mrs. Jacobs' prototype.

West Greenwich Village is a section of the borough of Manhattan, between the Hudson River and Seventh Avenue. It was close to the West Side docks, and hence had attracted sufficient industry and heavy commerce so that by 1830 its land use patterns discouraged residential occupancy by the wealthy. By the same year, however, much of the industry that might have moved into the area found other sections of the city nearer to the busiest sections of the waterfront, and thus more desirable.

The presence of some industrial buildings discouraged expensive residences; the presence of residences discouraged industry. The area remained somewhat neglected, a number of small single-family residential buildings interspersed among industrial structures and warehouses. Few tenement houses of the type built in the late nineteenth century were ever built in the West Village. Along the Avenues, low, semicommercial buildings remained. Stores moved into the ground floors of what had once been wholly residential structures. The very mixture kept land values low, and rents down; an added attraction for artists, writers, and young professional people, a number of whom settled in the area.

In the years after World War II, under the stimulus of a nagging housing shortage, a number of families discovered the West Village area. They were able to buy small buildings which originally had been intended for single-family occupancy but had been converted into rooming houses or cut up into small apartments. The new owners purchased these buildings for their own use, and, sometimes, as an investment, they fixed up one or more of the floors for rental to others. The attractions of the older houses in the side streets, and the pride at having discovered a treasure in the unconventional setting were cementing forces among the neighbors. To this must be added the force of Mrs. Jacobs and her writing, which, like the descriptions of a good novelist, has led all who read about the West Village in her words to see it through her eyes. Having observed many other American cities struggling with the esthetic problem of residential repetition, Mrs. Jacobs was provoked to analyze and distinguish what had solved this problem in her own backyard.

Clearly what distinguished the West Village was the number of old houses which were restored. Clearly, also, one could not advise the cities of America, "Build more old buildings." Mrs. Jacobs looked about her to see what other characteristic distinguished the West Village from the less felicitous sections of her city, and others. Its dominant characteristic was the intermingling of industrial and residential buildings. Mrs. Jacobs coined a phrase to describe this phenomenon: mixed primary uses. Recognizing that these mixed uses were related to the present attractions of the West Village—and that all new developments lacked this mixture—Mrs. Jacobs generalized that the difference between a lively city and a dead one was the incidence of such a mixture. The connection, in fact, between the mixed uses and the charms of the West Village was, as we have seen, not that the intrusion of industry into a residence section was attractive; but rather that the mixed uses were literally repulsive. In other old but unmixed sections of the city, the market value of older buildings had long since soared; if the land itself had become very valuable, the old houses had long since given way to apartment house development. To confuse the characteristic that led to the survival of the buildings with the qualities that made them beautiful is to succumb to a curious kind of logical fallacy, much as though Mrs. Jacobs had visited Pompeii and concluded that nothing makes a city so beautiful as covering it with ashes.

Mrs. Jacobs' interest in mixed uses of land was valuable to her also, however, because it presented her with a thoroughly satisfying target of criticism: the city planner.

Although her attack on city planners included a number of other charges, none has so irritated them as her strictures against the separation of different types of land use. In the first place, her lay readers have almost unanimously misunderstood what she is saying. Mrs. Jacobs is not simply praising the great bazaar of city life, and urging people to live on or near colorful streets jammed with stores selling jewelry, hats, hams from distant smokehouses, books full of pictures, or miniature schnauzers. She is suggesting that a good city is a twenty-four-hour city, and that it becomes a twenty-four-hour city through encouraging the neighboring of wholesale warehouses (which work during the day) and residential buildings (which work during the evening and morning) and night clubs (which work during the night). Or truck terminals (which work during night and day) with office buildings (which work only during the day) and schools (which work during the day and sometimes at night) and residences and theaters (which work mostly at night though sometimes during the day) .

Probably very few of those who proclaim their adherence to Mrs. Jacobs' doctrine understand that this means that she favors the construction of a truck garage adjacent to residential buildings or schools. She justifies this not only on the grounds that the trucks will make the neighborhood livelier, but because the drivers will loiter around in the street, discouraging immoral persons from molesting the children of the people who live there. About the danger of traffic accidents, Mrs. Jacobs says nothing. Mrs. Jacobs' neighbors have come to understand, however, that she means what she is saying, and will support the construction of a theater on a block of small homes, no matter what the neighbors may think of the traffic it will attract and late evening noise that it will generate.

Mrs. Jacobs' writing on this subject is irritating not only because in these respects she is misunderstood by her readers, who,
if they bothered to understand her, would call her wrong. It is
far more irritating that, in some respects, she is right. The eye
does require diversity and refreshment; the mind does choke
on bland repetition; and Mrs. Jacobs tells us this with rare
poignancy. Yet, do her suggestions help? Even if we suppose it
true that mixing heavy industry and residential buildings is
desirable, how shall we get industries to locate near them? The
problem of the city today is to attract industry on any terms.

Many of the cities in the nation are offering all the inducements in their power, together with some charms that it has
been claimed are not properly in their power at all, to attract
industries to settle within their boundaries. One has only to
read the ads in the business magazines and the Sunday newspapers, to see what attractions local development bureaus
throughout the nation have found to be persuasive. Cheap and
stable labor, plenty of water, convenient access to railroads and
truck highways, room for expansion. The last two are surely not
to be found in residential districts. The fear of being trapped
by residential neighbors, with their fuss about noise and truck
traffic, is a compelling reason that drives industrial plants to
move in the first place. Shall the cities lure industries with tax
benefits and ample water, only to frighten them with baby carriages and anti-noise ordinances?

Even if the campaign to attract industry were successful,
moreover, the amount of land which industries might be persuaded to take in the central parts of the cities is so limited, in
comparison with the land taken by residential structures, that
they would not seriously provide variety to the residential
buildings. In New York, for example, more than four times as
much land is devoted to residential as to industrial use.

Similarly, the cities of America have encouraged the development of far more commercial property, usually in strips along

the avenues of residential sections, than is actually needed for stores. Vacant stores are commonplace. The balance is worsening, too, because the small retail store is, as everybody must know, being threatened and crowded out on the one hand by the large supermarket, and discount house, and on the other by the vending machine. Shopping centers, surrounded by parking lots, have become the most popular mode of retail distributing. The corner drugstore is going the way its lunch counter has already gone. Monster cut-rate establishments have opened in the downtown sections of the city, catering to the receptionist, who struggles happily home at night, pocketbook stuffed with the bottles of hair conditioners and eyelash curler bought with the money saved on Economy Size Aspirins.

All of this may be regrettable—the disappearance of the druggist who made up prescriptions, not merely counted pills; the fading of the measured counterpoint between housewife and butcher—all gone, to be replaced by the unanswerable monologue of advertising, calculated to prod an instant response to the brand labels glimpsed along the supermarket aisles. Still, the disappearance of small stores does not result from urban renewal's preparatory demolition; for the disappearance preceded urban renewal, and extends far beyond it. Nor can it be said that the supermarket is a plot, imposed on an unwilling citizenry by some monster Svengali, hypnotizing the people of the country (and now, behold, of Europe as well) to suffer against their better interests. Regrettable or not, in the supermarket and the singing commercial, a system of distribution has developed which establishes more demands than any other, and then proceeds to satisfy them, alas.

Unrelieved by industrial or commercial structures, the residence buildings must therefore provide their own esthetic interest. How? It is fashionable nowadays to say that the dreariness of the American city is caused by the construction of high-rise apartment houses; by which the critics generally mean buildings well in excess of six stories. Critics have told us that if the "inhuman scale" of high-rise builders were eliminated, beauty would be lured back to the city streets. This sounds both learned and easy to understand; it is neither. Nor is it true. *Inhuman scale* is a technical term imposed on the unwary reader. It calls attention to that eerie phenomenon in perception as a result of which the internal consistency of the sizes of objects at which we are looking, blinds us to a sense of their absolute size. An example is the astonishment we feel at the end of a marionette show, when we discover by the intrusion of a truly human form, that the dolls we have been so long assuming to be human, are actually only thirty inches tall. The criticism of the "inhuman scale" of high-rise buildings is intended to make the reader believe that he, like the marionettes, is overwhelmed by the size of these buildings, because they are simply too high for comfort in relationship to the size of his own body. While this impression may disturb an Australian aborigine, whisked blindfolded from the outback and unbandaged in the Chase Manhattan Plaza of New York City, I do not believe that, after even a few idle moments in the twentieth century, the spectator is overwhelmed by the high structures. The observer relates them to the size of his own body no more than he relates a hilltop or a tree to the size of his own body. A door which turns out to be three stories high, a door handle two feet long, a chair eight feet high, a footprint size 29—these are far more upsetting to the observer. These are inhumanly scaled; but the parts of the high structures—the windows, the doors—are of normal size.

Incidentally, the length of a building's facade is far more likely to overwhelm the observer than is its height. He measures the length by the fact of his own activity, walking. To be oppressed by the height—to become fully conscious of it—he would have to try to fly over it. The only serious pain that has ever been inflicted on me by the trick of scale in a building was inflicted in Washington by the Department of Justice building. This structure, only a few stories high, has literally been built on an inhuman scale. The windows, with their iron grills, are immense, but both windows and grills appear to be of normal size, because they bear precisely the same size relationship to the building's stones that normal windows bear to the stones or brick of a building of ordinary length. One walks along the Department of Justice building, measuring one's speed by normal standards, and finds oneself getting nowhere. Eventually, in pain, one can only assume that the building must be inhabited by a race of symmetrical giants.

One vertical feature of many modern buildings has been oppressive to the observer: the total lack of a *top*. The theory that beauty means the dismissal of the nonessential has been interpreted by architects (and their clients) as a permission to drop the useless cornice. Some buildings, having eliminated the cornice, replace it with nothing else, no parapet wall, no capstone, not even a television aerial. Gargoyles may be anachronistic but let us at least have something that tells the eye that the building has been stopped by deliberate intention, not by exhaustion of money or hope.

The attack on high-rise buildings, it should be noted as we talk of residential structures, is not leveled merely against their appearance. More significantly, I believe, it is leveled against their utility for low-rent housing. I have no objection at all to high-rise residential buildings for agglomerations of adults or teen-agers to live in; I can see positive advantages in the view, the noiselessness, the saving of ground space for light, air, and landscaping. Just so long as baby carriages can be crowded into the elevators, the high-risers present no insuperable difficulties to families with nurses and governesses who can escort the children downstairs, reminding the boys to take off their caps and keeping them from committing upper-class nuisances in the elevator.

In those low-income housing projects which are not specifically designed for occupancy by old people living apart from their children, the lack of nannies presents problems. Elizabeth Wood has pointed out that if we raise a mother eight or ten stories above the ground we deprive her of the power to inspire terror in her offspring; the shouts from the window do not chill her kids to instant attention in the playground. They sound rather like a vague and distant greeting.

No one can conscientiously lay down a fixed set of rules for achieving harmony and comfort, pride and ease, beauty, if you will, in the long stretches of residential buildings in our city. A natural fear of repetition has goaded most designers and developers (sixteen models to choose from—this is one of the persistent cries in the newspaper ads), as though, like women at a cocktail party, the controlling fear is that someone else may appear in precisely the same dress. I find that a development scheme which purports to provide variety through the alternative combination of identical forms, merely emphasizes the emptiness of its original conceptions: if the living room can really be placed on either side of the front door; if the roof over the dormer window can as easily be hipped as straight; if the window in the study can as easily be bowed as not; then the building is wholly unimportant in either case. It is presumptuous to intrude itself on the observer who may struggle to unravel the secret code used by the developer in designing his subdivisions—first house: two peaked dormers and a gray roof; second house: two hipped dormers and a red roof; third house: two peaked dormers and a red roof; fourth house: two hipped dormers and a gray roof. Walking down such a street is like taking the Army General Classification test: you are given the first few numbers in a series, followed by dots. Then they challenge you to fill in the next in the series.

The great esthetic advantage possessed by nature over civilization is its ability to produce random variations. The human mind cannot frame anything merely at random, without the help of an associative process. If, to satisfy certain forms of higher mathematics, you need random numbers, not selected in any order or sequence, you must buy a book of them, whose randomness is guaranteed.

If a single designer wishes to vary a common form, like the residential building, human limitations mean that he must do it with purpose. He must, for example, alternate high and low buildings because the two are needed for different kinds of occupants: the high building for the aged, the childless, or the wealthy; the low building for the modest families with children. Then the low buildings themselves must be varied with the naturally random, with trees.

The main esthetic argument in favor of low rather than high buildings, is not, it seems to me, the scale, but rather that the trees more nearly balance the size of the facade, unless the high building can be placed by itself in a mass of green; the tower in the park. Low buildings which stand close together on very wide streets, where no trees grow and where even the unity of the cornice lines is broken by gasoline stations and used car lots, advertisements and novelty siding—these comprise the ugliest urban vistas in the United States, a personal judgment which I shall not modify to please those who tell me these views are a kind of pop art.

The other argument for low buildings is that embellishment of the small facade is easier; here, and here alone, is there some relevance to the question of human scale. Surely the human figures loitering in marble or sandstone on the pediments or around the cornices of large buildings must be immense to be seen at all. If immense, they are simply not human. If the embellisher relies on mythical or legendary models, they look all too likely to catch their togas in the revolving doors. No one has developed a satisfactory style of ornamentation in and for the modern idiom. In the 30's, under the aegis of the WPA, a new architectural mythology, sometimes sculptured, sometimes painted in post office lobbies, emerged in which not Ceres, Vulcan, or Demeter, but Labor, Industry, and Agriculture honored the government by removing their clothes, at least above the waist. Their high purpose was manifest by this total lack of seductivity; they stood or strode as stolid and inhuman as the families of models who demonstrate union suits in the Sears Roebuck catalogue.

Impatience with Victorian floridity has made it undignified to treat the ornamentation of architecture, on the theory that the form of the building itself, hewing to the concept of its use, is an artifact so beautiful that any additional adornment would only mar it. And there are modern buildings so perfectly resolved (I keep coming back to the Seagram's building) that even a postage stamp on the exterior would be defacement. But in residential areas, which will continue to remain largely unbroken by stores and factories, we must deal not with an occasional and majestic structure, very different from its neighbors, but with endless thousands of buildings, large, small, and medium-sized—frequently, in response to land economics and zoning, lumped together by size. They all look alike. If the endless repetition of simple forms is the embodiment of ugliness, if this is what reduces urban man to a sense of individual meaninglessness, then the repetition of form, not "human scale" or the size of structure is the primary artistic problem with which we must deal in the city.

Yet some of the handsomest city blocks I have seen contain nothing but a row of identical or almost identical buildings. Some of the most exciting urban landscapes, the Piazza di San Marco at Venice, for example, consists largely of a continuous facade of identical columns; the Cathedral, the Campanile, and the Palace of the Doges are set in contrast to these other two sides of the square that stretch unchanging into the distance with a melancholy rhythm that has often suggested the passage of time. If all the buildings on the Square had been designed to flash their separateness, the Square would be chaos. But the harmony of repetition is achieved only when there is repetition of *accent* as well as size; simple, unaccented facades without emphases are not harmonious, only boring. I am convinced that the contemporary building, with bland window openings set into plain brick walls, no cornice lines, no vertical interest—the standard apartment house that is going up across the country—is objectionable not so much because it looks like every other apartment house ("*another* glass box") but because it is a dull building, and would be, were it erected all by itself in the middle of a desert. If we look at a block of identical fronts that conveys a sense of harmonious composition, we discover that the harmony is produced by an accentuation: of the roof line; of the window lines; a decorative stress at coherent intervals.

There have been a number of elegant apartment houses built in the United States since the war, on which the builder, either for his own satisfaction, or because he believed it important to his clientele, spent time and money to achieve a structure that one would take pleasure in observing: the designer found a way to accent the facade by a change in materials or texture, or by an assembly of elements related to and yet separable from the usefulness, or the structural dignity of the building. Most builders, however, have relied on the assumption that the modern idiom is uninteresting, and that like the office builder, he will attract more customers by labor-saving devices inside than by attention to the outside. Then, again, the economics of the construction industry have tended to make decoration, when it occurs, an adjunct, laid over the building rather than a pattern in the shell of the building itself. Since the skilled mechanic of the building trade is now a middle-class citizen—himself, indeed, a customer for the building he is erecting (a phenomenon, incidentally, which has probably never before occurred in human history, and whose social implications are not to be just waved aside with a demand for more beauty or less restrictive building codes) —nothing must interfere with the swing of the work. The setting of elaborate window frames and lintels, stone on brick; the shifting of courses and bonds of brick to provide accent; the external emphasis of vertical members in the facade— all of these interfere with the swing of work. They must be avoided.

As the extreme housing shortage that has pinched middle-class citizens since the war has eased, and competition has returned to the urban rental market, some builders, especially those who were not building on sites with prime attraction, have attempted to provoke interest by some external decoration, the internals—air conditioning, automatic dishwashers, walk-in closets—having been pretty well matched out. I recently noticed a new six-story apartment building, designed in a modern jargon, with no roof line at all, its windows pushed into the flat brick walls like square currants in an unbaked cake. After all the solid work had been accomplished, the decorators were called in, to hang on the building, without visible means of support, a monstrous, shiny, streamlined porte-cochere, big enough to shelter a fifty-foot Cadillac sedan with two Jaguars swinging beside it. Perhaps to protect the orange bricks of the facade from the spray cast up by cars big enough to use this entrance becomingly, the builder had inserted the inshore end of the stainless steel canopy into a pink and white splashboard, fanning out as high as the second-story windows, and ending in a series of jagged spikes, like a sunburst in a movie travelogue. It is easy to say that the same money spent on window details, vertical elements, and structural emphasis would have produced a better building. Probably, however, the porte-cochere cost less, and, in the builder's view, would create more interest. This dismal result is not going to be changed by the mere wringing of hands.

Such garish modernism has led people to believe that things

were generally better in an earlier day. It is important to distinguish the precise differences. The stone-faced row houses built on speculation in the 80's and 90's for families who could afford to pay well for them, but not well enough to afford custom buildings, provide us with some of our pleasanter blocks, despite the repetition of form. One must remember that the stone carvers, brick layers, and stone masons who erected these buildings were recent arrivals from Europe. They built 4,000 square feet of floor space for each middle-class family; they lived, themselves, in a tenth of that space in the tenement houses. As a result, the speculative builder could afford to pay for the elaborate window frames, carved cornices, stone stoops, and elaborate doorways that break what would otherwise be simply an endless brown facade into a series of meaningful spaces and intervals.

It is not the past itself that has produced fine cityscapes, but, rather, the customer could afford labor on the decorative elements of construction while the man who built it returned each night, as Thoreau said, to something "little better than a wigwam." Even the apartment houses of the 1920's were erected at a time when the difference between the workmen's pay and the earnings of the renters justified some spending on exterior emphasis. Lewis Mumford may despise Park Avenue as merely a high-priced slum, but another observer may disagree respectfully, pointing out that the wide street requires high buildings to frame it in satisfactory proportions. When the Park Avenue apartments were built, their designers insisted on breaking up their facades with emphases which were, indeed, extraneous and in many cases intrinsically absurd, but which, nonetheless, have maintained the eye's interest down its long vistas.

These, then, are the two great problems that face the architect of the modern city building: high cost of labor and the lack of any clear standard for decoration or emphasis of the facade. The problems are accentuated in the case of government buildings by the belief that government exists to serve the people, and that display and excessive cost are the sequels of corruption and autocracy. It should be no surprise, therefore, that the one kind of building which presents all of these problems in their greatest intensity, which goads and envenoms the critics more than any other is the public housing project. "The dreary deadlock of public housing" says the *Architectural Forum,* in captioning a discussion of what can be done to improve the design of the projects, and make them lift the hearts of their owners and tenants.

Despite all the criticism it has received (some justified, some not), public housing stands remarkably enough in the best position to stimulate significant attention to the esthetic problems of residential construction. This conclusion flies directly in the face of all the despondent words of the urban critics. Why do the urban critics so detest it?

They detest public housing because it appears institutional; having been produced by "cataclysmic money." No question about the fact that public housing projects resemble institutions more than do privately owned buildings; but the poignancy which accompanies this observation may merely mean that to the physical resemblance the observer attaches an unwarranted emotional significance. It may be that institutions are not shamefully but well designed. In any case we should explore the points of resemblance between public housing and institutions. There are perhaps three.

One point of resemblance is that public housing, like institutional buildings, neglects the regular street patterns of the city, and develops a plot plan in which the building is not oriented rectilinearly with reference to the street. In the case of the institutions, the orphan asylum, the hospital, even the prison (other than the ancient City Gaol which must be located near the courthouse and police headquarters) this new orientation reflects the fact that institutions were built generally on cheap land, which they could use extravagantly in order to provide the maximum light and air to the buildings and their inhabitants. The typical urban residential structure was required to use land economically; light and air were imposed on it only to the limited extent of the law. It is interesting that the anti-street location of the institution—first applied on a wide scale by public housing (admittedly the pioneering was done by private owners, including the big life insurance companies and a few nonprofit or limited-profit sponsors of cooperatives or planned communities) is now being copied by the developers of private luxury apartment houses, which are now frequently set back from the street pattern, and oriented to a private driveway instead of a rectilinear public street grid.

This same characteristic has also been under attack on the grounds that public housing is destroying the street, a form of human settlement whose disappearance—at least in its most familiar manifestation—must be regretted by every lover of cities. There is no escaping the truth that the street is disappearing. The urban street as community facility is primarily a commercial phenomenon in the United States—it is the great bazaar, a stretch of continuous shops which one visits in turn. Its point and method is individual specialization, and it was doomed not by large-scale residential developments, but by the growth of patent medicines which meant that the drugstore proprietor could turn from compounding prescriptions with mortar and pestle to sell perfumes and hairsets, beach balls and thermos flasks. The street is dying because butcher, baker, greengrocer, fish dealer, delicatessen store proprietor, and stationer have been amalgamated into the chain store and the supermarket and the discount house, whose store window is the television set or radio. The chain store and the discount house have neither mystery nor promises to offer the passing stroller. Everyone remarks that the great walking street in his city—the Champs Élysées, Fifth Avenue, Walnut Street—are not what they once were, but no one bothers to note that this decline is not peculiar to his own city. But even then, the downtown streets have by far the best of it, for the largest cities can still, though barely, support the independent specialized establishments that can make the outdoor corridor useful and busy. In the outer sections of the city the street is dying. The institutional look of public housing in this sense is only a manifestation of an attempt to find a new kind of street lined not with a solid front of buildings of identical height, but with buildings of varying height (in accordance with the varying needs), with walkways and open spaces. Public housing—because of the legislative unwillingness to mandate subsidies for commercial enterprises—has characteristically been unable to handle the stores that are needed as part of the residential structures, but this is now beginning to come.

A second characteristic resemblance between public housing and institutions is the solid, safe look of public housing, its appearance of a permanent stability at minimum maintenance costs. Given the choice between raising the spirits of the onlooker—or the tenant—and lowering the costs of maintenance by solid construction, the builders of public housing—that is to say the local municipal authorities and the federal government which guarantees the financing of this work—have generally chosen the latter course. They have designed for permanence rather than beauty, though not always.

Not that all public housing projects are the same. In Marin County, California, for example, a small public housing development was placed on a hillside. It consisted of a number of small buildings with pitched roofs, angled into the slope of the hill. The buildings harmonized with the fall of the land, provided an interesting design of small flat planes against the undulating background, and established a standard which private developers might well have emulated. The buildings won a prize from the Public Housing Administration, and were roundly criticized by the federal government's General Accounting Office because they were allegedly extravagant.

In Washington, D.C., the National Capital Housing Authority has refused to build any projects which do not resemble the best of private development; this means, in Washington, that the Authority has insisted on low buildings, with attractive roof treatment, the small buildings being distributed on semisuburban sites within the District of Columbia, wherever the Authority can find land cheap enough to justify the type of construction they believe in. The last project approved came within $50 of the limits which the federal agency that finances public low-rent housing has established as the maximum cost per unit. The housing is handsome; but the suitable sites are so few that as many families are waiting for apartments in public housing in the District of Columbia as are living in them now. And unless the Housing and Home Finance Agency is willing to change the dollar limit on the cost of construction, there will be no more public housing built in the District.

In New York City, the Housing Authority, working perforce with high land costs, has been able to come within the cost limitations of the federal government only by building very tall buildings, and spreading the cost of the elevator, the roof, the footings, over as many apartments as possible. Congress has placed a top limit of $4,250 as the cost of a single room in public housing; the Housing and Home Finance Agency has gone further and set a top limit of $20,000 per apartment. In New York City this hardly pays for the cost of rehabilitating older buildings—which the Authority has done with great thoroughness in some cases—to the standards that are imposed by the requirement that the buildings have a projected new life of 40 years. It has time and again required the redesign of proposed new developments which originally were planned with architectural innovations that proved too expensive when put out for bids. It has had the effect of increasing the stultifying conventionality of staff thinking, because the staff of the Housing Authority has too often found that any new way of designing results in higher costs which will not be approved by the federal government. Although the Authority has successfully experimented with good design—low buildings, for example, in the Pomonok housing development with a most attractive roof treatment that, in my mind, compare most favorably with the widely praised buildings of the nearby Fresh Meadows project of New York Life Insurance Company; sky terraces, on the Luna Park project; crisply designed single-building developments, such as 131 St. Nicholas Avenue in Harlem—it is now finding itself forced to go to thirty-five-story apartment houses which, whatever their architectural interest, seem hardly appropriate to the low-income families they will contain.

Of course, $4,250 per room sounds like a lot of money to the senators from Idaho and Nebraska. The $20,000 limit per apartment seems high enough in the Marlboro country, where land costs are low and the same figure would build a ranch house surrounded by a big spread of land. But substitute land at $10 a square foot (more, on occasion) for land at $200 an acre, labor at $5.50 an hour for labor at $2.50 an hour, and you find you can't build single-family homes in the city itself. You must build houses strong enough so that they can rest on top of one another; sufficiently firesafe to protect life; sufficiently permanent so that the government will not have to renew them in less than fifty years. This leaves precious little money for clarity of architecture, experimentation in ornament, generosity in construction, the human touches that would make the public projects an accomplishment of general pride.

Despite this record, the local authorities, if they can only get the support of their mayor for more generosity—or even more extravagant design—are somewhat freer in spending this money than they would be if it were the city's own. They are held back primarily by the third factor that makes public housing appear institutional. Like an institution, it obviously has been provided to serve, not customers exercising free choice in a market, but a specific income group that has little, if any, choice, in the free market. Public housing is a reminder that the realities of American life fall short of the American dream of independent yeomen walking erect in their own world. Public housing is a reminder that part of the dream remains to be realized—the narrowing of the vast difference in the scope which different families enjoy in pursuing their happiness. Public housing is a reminder that the dedication of public powers to completing this achievement may change not only the physical aspect of cities, but many of the forms of the society that fills them.

Because no private institution fills the same role—the provision of homes for low-income families—public housing offers a unique opportunity for high quality in design of all the forms of housing. It alone is free from the economic pressure that debases standards. It should set a high standard for all contemporary architecture, all modern structures to copy. Fear that public housing would compete economically with private enterprise set much of its present form. Yet precisely this competition should be welcomed by private enterprise. If government-owned housing, stimulated by incentive subsidies for new and striking architecture, develops new public awareness of the significance of architectural achievement, it would seem to follow that consumers will become more and more willing to pay premiums for living in better designed and more beautiful homes.

All of these energies are potentially available through a generous use of public housing, serving a vital social need through an institution that has actually—despite its unquestioned disappointments—worked well when it has been treated amply. It is altogether galling that the criticisms of public housing by the humanitarian critics are so loosely phrased that they are serving as the perfect excuse for keeping this institution from achieving its full promise.

Good architecture requires generosity of spirit, and it is lost in the city not by accident, but from conflict. The difficulty in providing adequate funds to make public housing beautiful is only a more dramatic rendering of the same difficulty that appears in the case of so many institutions. Shall taxes be spent on beauty, or on public health services; shall the building unionist be a middle-class citizen, so that his work must be used sparingly? Or shall he be reduced to a narrower share of the total wealth, so that architects and builders may be able to use his services with generosity, or even extravagance? If one really feels that the hourly earnings of building tradesmen should be reduced in the interest of beauty, how in the world shall such an edict be made effective?

The disappointment that is unquestionably felt by the observer of many if not most new buildings, results from no mindless destruction of the landscape—the favorite explanation of the editorialist. It results rather from the conflict between the people who work in the structure, and those who want to admire it. It results in the end from a tussle as to who shall control, or receive, the bounties of the American production system. It would be well to remember that this is no trivial conflict, to be decided in the cause of beauty by gentle persuasion or the wagging of outstretched fingers at tea parties at which the American landscape is decried, however accurately, as a mess. Invocations to beauty can only be effective when the partisan is willing to pay higher taxes to achieve it, and to defend the use of these additional revenues for the production of beauty, rather than, say, for more beds in the hospitals. The partisan of architectural beauty had better be ready to explain to the Metal Lathers Union why it should not insist on a six-hour day in constructing the Whitney Museum; and to defend the mayor who has been found guilty of extravagance by the newspaper editorial writer who has been told of artful but nonessential mosaics in the new Junior High School. Architecture is a mixed art in that it involves the work not only of the artist himself, but of many others; it demands space, not only on the wall of a room, but on the land of a city.

To recapture, in the midst of the twentieth century, the atmosphere of extravagance that characterized the age of Louis XIV is not simple. Nor could one, if one wanted to, return to the relationship between producer and beholder that characterized the American construction industry seventy-five years ago. To insist on beauty in American architecture means to cut deep into the economic fabric of American life and into the whole structure of political values as well; it suggests that except for rare buildings erected by private institutions for their own celebration, great architecture can be achieved only through political choices. These will be hard to achieve, for they will cut against the prevailing ethics; they will cut against the worker, trying to improve his economic lot, and seeking to turn each additional dollar intended for extra beauty into wages to be paid for the regular flow of work. Such decisions will cut against the pragmatic turn of mind characteristic of this nation's history, in that they will prefer money spent on intangibles to money spent for concrete benefits like school seats, subway cars, and hospital beds. Such decisions will cut against the notions of simplicity in government and public service without ostentation—the motive which dissuaded George Washington from becoming a king, and prevented L'Enfant's plan for the city of Washington from being carried out. These are the same sentiments that provoke ribald laughter whenever the mayor's Cadillac is mentioned in any city. Let all those who stand up for architectural beauty in the city recognize also that they are asking their officials to stand up for the silk hat against the snowball; for waste and, perhaps, graft, against simplicity and economy. The battle for beautiful architecture is not against the villains of popular conception—the greedy landlords, and the selfish politicians. It is, nonetheless, a battle which must be fought and won if people who combine taste and sensibility with the power of choice are to be kept in the city. Without them, the city's promises to its other residents become, as we shall see, impossible to keep.

IX. WHEELS WITHIN WHEELS

MANY components of a city are highly desirable, but only two are absolutely essential. One is people, and the other is transportation. Sometimes the critics need to be reminded that without transportation the people would be unable to build shelter, or feed themselves, or have water to drink, or power to light their homes. Without transportation, urban men would choke on some of their own waste products and find themselves buried in others. Transportation makes cities possible.

The assumption by critics that cities necessarily deteriorate has led them to write about technology, which grows constantly more vital to the cities, as though it were a distressing law that could be repealed, like Prohibition, or a state of affairs to be overcome with prayer and protest, like segregation in public accommodations. They refuse to understand that the problem is not how to ban technology and its products, such as the automobile, but how to use them to widen human chances in the city as a whole. Instead of determining the best use of each transportation method, the critics ask the officials to choose—People or Automobiles, People or Jobs, People or Public Utilities. They do not like to be told that automobiles move only with human guidance; that men must work if their lives are to be satisfactory; that public utilities must be supplying public needs, or they would long ago have come to a stop, like windmills or planked roads.

Believing that there is a right and wrong in technology, they believe that transportation has a virtuous side on which all angels belong. This belief becomes particularly confusing when it obscures the fact that transportation does not simply mean bringing people back and forth from the suburbs to the offices or the department stores. It means also the carrying of goods in and out of the city by rail or truck, and the influence of this pattern on employment. It means also the transportation of electric power and drinking water into the city, and the transportation of wastes out of it.

Most critics in good standing agree that automobiles are bad and should be replaced. Typical is a man I know who has written repeatedly about the incompatibility between the automobile and the central city. The central city, he tells his readers, is doomed unless cars are prevented from entering it. Of course he lives in the central city, and he keeps his car in a garage around the corner from his home. This doesn't count, he tells me, because he needs his car in his work. It has not occurred to him that anyone else might be in the same position.

The nonpracticing critics who decry the automobile have not noticed that earlier forms of transportation were also expected to kill the city. The Roman chariot, the mounted knight, the horse-drawn wagon, and the steam locomotive were each as menacing, in turn. A large part of every central city had to be dedicated to vehicular use when cities began to grow in the nineteenth century. Almost one-third of the total area of Manhattan, laid out in 1811, is given over to streets, including sidewalks. After the automobile was invented, even this generous provision was insufficient; special limited-access express systems had to be built to take advantage of the automobile's speed and flexibility. To minimize accidents and speed movement, the automobile express roads had to be placed either above or below other street patterns. In either case, some cleavage of the city resulted along the route and a large new increment of land was pre-empted. The percentage so pre-empted rises as one nears the center until, as in Los Angeles, if you have enough freeways converging, there is hardly any downtown at all. In New York City, the highways were placed where they would cause the least interference, along the waterfront. This has given rise to the theory, expressed with special venom by Peter Blake, that passenger-automobile expressways have cut off New York City from its waterfront. I can hardly think of a large city whose cargo-handling waterfront is laid out so that its pedestrians can visit it with impunity. If automobile highways do not cut them off, then railways do, carrying freight to and from the piers. If, unfortunately, there are no railways, heavy trucking performs the same office. New York, Chicago, Cleveland, New Orleans, Philadelphia, all working ports, have been built so as to cut off the citizens from the central section of the waterfront; nevertheless, it is the automobile specifically which gets blamed for this state of affairs.

In Western cities, like Denver, the Eastern eye is dazed by the absence of the walking street; downtown is chopped up by parking lots and broad highways with staggered lights. Hideous business signs have dictated the very shape of the buildings they are intended to promote: under the sign that resembles a hamburger a stand has been built in the shape of a roll.

The urban critic feels that the downtown city has been ruined for pedestrians by the automobile. The facts, however, are rather different: the Western cities were never built for pedestrian access because almost no one of consequence ever lived in the downtown city. For the rural families, horseback riding or carriage driving were the only ways into the city. The dirt roads that favored the horses' hoofs splattered the dresses of ladies, as they tripped from one store to the next on the duck-boards which were the late nineteenth century equivalents of sidewalks. Only feminists and whores were seen downtown on foot. Hitching posts in the streets established the pattern which parking meters continue. Those who lament that the automobile made the downtown of the Western city less com-fortable to the pedestrian have forgotten that the pedestrian could scarcely get to it before the automobile carried him in. Until that remarkable development, the peddler was needed to bring the city to the country.

Victor Gruen, another critic, has told us that automobiles should be excluded from the central city because they are not really desired by people generally, but merely inflicted on the feeble-minded public by a conspiracy of automobile and steel manufacturers, unions, rubber planters, and oil millionaires.

Surely no one argues that the building of highways does not involve the employment of the nation's labor force, or that the automobile industry has no connection with the prosperity of a number of other major industries from steel to rubber. Yet, the economic history of the nation reveals that other industries occupied positions that, in their own time, were equally sig-nificant. They vanished in the absence of public demand on a part of the consumer. The railroad industry, for example, was established with public subsidies that probably exceeded in relative size and scope those granted to the automobile in-dustry in the construction and policing of roads; they did not prevent the public from turning to automobile transportation when the advantages of this invention became real.

Much of the criticism of the automobile as a transport de-vice stems from the belief that federal and state funds lavished on automobile roads would have been better spent on mass transportation facilities in and near the major cities. No one remembers that the money spent on highways is collected from the buyers of gasoline and the licensees and registrants of vehicles. Mass transportation obviously demands less public space per individual body carried, and so it would seem to be far more economical in its use of urban land. A single automobile, with only one person in it, requires about 150 square feet of street. This is far more than the street space required per body by buses; while railroads, erected apart from the street, are even more economical.

These facts have been reported innumerable times by those who draw from them the conclusion that mass transit, being more economical, is morally preferable to the private automobile. Those who preach this have probably on no other subject relied on economy to carry their point. On other subjects, they demand that a solution be chosen for its quality, not its cost. The standard of comfort in the automobile, with its private space, freedom to smoke, a profusion of scenic variety, leg room, fresh air or air conditioning, and radio entertainment, is so seductive to the American citizen that one has about as much chance to lure him away from it into the bus or subway on the grounds of economy as one would have to lure guests from the Waldorf Astoria to the YMCA by telling them how much money they might save.

In addition to these merely physical qualities, automobile transportation affords psychological satisfactions not generally available on the subway or the bus, except perhaps to the few passengers who, in the subway, are able to crowd into the front car and peer ahead at the tracks as they come into view from the dark void ahead. The satisfaction is that each man at the wheel is master of his own destiny, captain of his own soul. On an objective scale it may be ridiculous that anyone should be reduced to inflating his *amour propre* by sitting at the wheel of an automobile wedged into a mass of other stalled machines. At the wheel of each sits another man feeling equally self-determined. But the absurdity makes the feeling no less real; on the contrary, the absurdity merely emphasizes how few are the occasions in modern life when one has the opportunity to exercise that individual control and individual choice which the philosophers of democracy and the sellers of soap agree are the most important attributes of free men. Besides, the traffic jams are almost never quite as bad as they appear, and there are delays on subways and buses also, delays that one must endure under far more unpleasant circumstances.

This last statement will depress those who believe it possible to design urban mass transit systems that will be more beautiful, more efficient, more convenient, and far more comfortable than any in common use. When this has been accomplished, the same philosophers believe that the systems will be so much more attractive to so many people that the added fares of the transit system will make it self-supporting or nearly so.

It is my thesis that this is nonsense. Transit systems can be made more beautiful, more efficient, and more comfortable, but this will also make them more expensive. The very qualities that are needed to increase their attractiveness to the off-hour user (certainly no one would attempt to crowd more people into rush hour rapid transit than now use it), are the qualities that, as we shall see, would increase its operating and capital losses. I don't believe in the nostrums that have been suggested to meet these losses. As the fares rise to meet the losses, the passengers drop off and the deficits rise further.

When people talk of increased comfort in the subway, they frequently refer to the Stockholm subway system, and suggest that much the same sort of system could be achieved in the United States. I have traveled by subway and bus in many of the world's capitals, and agree that Stockholm's subway approaches the ideal of comfort and silence. It's a new system which reflects the habits of an orderly, homogeneous people. Strategically, its major function is linking the extraurban developments with the central city; it serves, in effect, as a commuter railroad in a nation in which all railroads are state-owned. The willingness of the central government to provide financing for the Stockholm subway tells us something of the importance of this one city to the nation as a whole, an importance far greater than the relative importance of any single American city. Stockholm people, self-deprecatingly, tell us that their beautiful subway, built during World War II, represents also the wisdom of remaining neutral when the rest of the world is at war.

One cannot understand the design of the Stockholm subway without noticing that it is the result of the suburban arrangements of the city, and that these in turn reflect the significantly lower automobile ownership in Sweden than in the United States (20 percent of Swedish families own automobiles; over 50 percent of American families own them). Each of the Stockholm suburbs clusters around a pedestrian mall in which people do their shopping. This clustering is possible because of the extent to which high-rise apartment cooperatives are acceptable in lieu of the single-family homes of the typical American suburb. The assumption that what works in Sweden will work in the United States requires that one neglect the presumptions that underlie and explain the form of the social system of the nation. Surely in America the dream of owning one's own land has been a motivating force in the spread of population. Perhaps the dream may give way and with it the right of self-determination so zealously guarded by suburban villages; but neither has given way yet.

Given the American dedication to the single-family home, a dedication embedded deep in the American grain, the advantage of the private automobile for land development is far greater than one would believe reading the works of the critics who claim that the automobile superhighway has been imposed on a prostrate city by a vast outside conspiracy. Automobiles, not rapid transit systems, make possible a truly well-distributed development of the city's land space. The highway, fed by the regular street pattern, drains population from a widespread, low-density-developed area. In the semisuburbs of the great cities, each home has its own garage. Mr. Smith can as easily drive to his home ten blocks from the superhighway, as Mr. Brown can drive to his, five blocks away.

The case is very different with mass rail transit. To transport large numbers of people economically, the rail systems had to combine individually drawn train cars into trains. The great weight of these trains makes stopping them difficult. Safety demands a space of time between each train. This means, of course, that rapid transit lines consist of a number of large stations, with open track between. One can ride on the mass rail transit system to the station nearest one's home, and still have a very long trip to make after getting off at the nearest station. If a bus is added, because it can stop at every block, one may still be several lateral blocks away from one's home at the end of the ride.

The rapid transit lines fanning out from the city center have unquestionably helped the city to add new land space by minimizing the cost in time of putting it to use each morning; a close look at the pattern of development, however, reveals that the buildings and homes did not develop equally along the new mass transit lines. The development, rather, consisted of a series of rings, each centered around a single rapid transit station. The land lying further away from the stations, or between them, was not developed until later; its development could not be achieved until a local street pattern became real, and not merely a fiction on a map, and until that local street pattern was connected to the major attractions of the city by a respectable highway network.

The case is almost as striking when one deals with commuting distances to the remoter suburbs. Although the enemies of the automobile describe the difficulties and social costs of providing parking spaces in the city, they have forgotten that even the commuter who travels by train must, in most cases, use his automobile to get him to the station in the suburbs. The suburban American town has, on its own scale, a problem of great seriousness in providing adequate parking space near the station. Unlike the Swedish suburbanite the American commuter does not live in a high-rise cooperative within walking distance of the station. For him the question is not whether one should leave the car at home or take it with one and park it; the question is rather, *where* shall I park the car?

Thus, our attempts to design a more attractive transit system are self-defeating. If we want speed, we must limit the stops until they are put so far apart that automobiles are needed to get to them. If we want convenient stops, we get slow trains. No matter how attractive we want the train schedules to be, the pressure of American geography molds us into a system not too different from that which has already failed to attract. Of course, railroad cars can be clean, when they are new—but they do not remain new forever. To keep them clean requires high maintenance charges; to replace them regularly, high capital expenses. As a result, off-hour service is bound to be expensive to run, and relatively slow to ride on. It will operate at a loss. An excessive requirement of land means that parking cannot be provided at its intermediate stops. This almost unavoidably means that the off-hour visitor to the central city will prefer driving (especially so if he carries packages, or he expects to), and that automobile highways will be built to accommodate his travel and parking garages to accommodate his car.

The proposition—that parking garages in and near the downtown business section are desirable—elicits shocked outrage from most of the critics who claim, in addition to what we have already examined, that only an anti-urban heretic could possibly bring automobiles into the downtown sections of the city. These, we are told, belong to the pedestrian only.

And so they do, on Sundays, when, as Wordsworth put it, all that mighty heart is lying still. During the week, urbanity requires both pedestrians and vehicles to produce the contrast of tempo and color, of purpose and shape that is the very throb of city life. It is noteworthy that the same people who urge that the architectural city must be planned with the principle of random variety, seem not to recognize the importance of the same quality in the streets where it can be achieved under modern conditions much more easily than in the permanent structures beside them.

The heretical view that traffic is an essential element of the urban scene, and not just a noisy distraction, came over me while I was inspecting one of the pinnacles of the anti-automobilists' achievements, the Ljinnbann, a shopping mall in central Rotterdam. This is a section of the city that was rebuilt after its destruction by German bombs during World War II. The Ljinnbann consists of a long series of interior courtyards running down the center of several city blocks. On both sides of each courtyard, shops open into the courtyard—their backs are to the automobile streets; they face the pedestrian way inside. The Ljinnbann is attractive, colorful, cheerful; I had looked forward to shopping there, but discovered that for me, something was missing; after a while, I concluded that I missed the tempo of traffic, the variety of shapes and colors of automobiles, trucks, taxicabs, motorcycles; instead of relief at having escaped from them, I found myself thinking that I was not in a city, but at a summer resort, a place in which, for all its charms, I would not want to transact serious matters.

Of course there are those who believe that any problem involving physical arrangements can be solved with money. When asked where the money would be found to build and operate all-day-long express trains and provide new cars more frequently, they suggest tapping the authorities owning the highly profitable bridges and tunnels for automobile transportation. There is a real question as to how profitable the bridges and tunnels would be under the less favorable financing that might result from their being saddled with transit losses. Even if there were continuing profits from the automobile facilities, these would scarcely match the transit deficits, for the cost of an automobile facility is primarily and almost entirely the original cost of construction. The automobile user does his own driving, maintenance, fueling, and cleaning. The mass transit facility, today, represents not only a basic capital cost, but almost inevitably a continuing operating deficit, and a deficit so large that the highway tolls simply disappear into it. The basic reason for this is simple: instead of being operated and maintained by the riders, transit vehicles are operated and maintained by highly organized workers. Their productivity is hard to increase, because they are used at efficient levels only twice a day. Unless the cities achieve the unlikely courage to place a measure of control over these unions (even if such controls work), the future of mass transit is dubious for any purpose, and the prognosis for cities dependent on it is grave indeed. Incidentally, the uneven hourly demand for mass transit makes local bus transportation difficult to operate economically although the level of invested capital is much lower than the capital needs of rail systems.

Even cities where the transit system was installed years ago, and where the operating conditions would appear to be most favorable, operating costs are continually outstripping the fares collected. In New York City as recently as 1946, raising the five-cent fare was considered to be political suicide. The fare is now fifteen cents and going higher. But one must also understand that this fare covers only the bare cost of operating the trains. All capital charges, including not only interest on and the amortization of the basic debt for building the system, but all the costs of acquiring new equipment and modernizing the existing equipment, must be borne by the city. These costs are not covered in the operating budgets of the subway. In addition, the city quietly meets, out of its own general budget, the cost of a number of items which might very well be considered more rigorously to be a part of the true cost of operating a rapid transit system. The city, for example, pays for the cost of maintaining a large special force of transit policemen who are expected to keep order in the subways. San Franciscans boast that their new subway system will avoid these labor problems because it will be automated. But the automation would replace only the motormen on the trains, not the guards or the maintenance workers or the change makers or the car cleaners. The motormen of New York's subway system learned, in the course of a disastrous strike, that they are only a small and impotent minority among the workers in a subway system.

European subway systems are frequently cited as examples of the savings to cities that are implicit in mass transportation as opposed to automobile transportation. Of course, it is most helpful to the force with which this argument is put forward to have avoided visiting Europe in the past several years. Private automobile traffic is piling up in the streets of Paris; it has always piled up in London as anyone will know who is old enough to have seen Fred Astaire, in *Damsel in Distress,* dancing his way in and out of the taxicabs caught in the London traffic jams. In any case, European subway systems close down around midnight. It is difficult to imagine a passenger-carrying railroad operating under conditions less favorable to the passenger, and more favorable to the management, than the New York City Transit System. At rush hour on the Lexington Avenue line, going home in the evening, the fare entitles the rider to barely enough floor space for the placement of his two feet together. He has a clouded title to the air rights above his shoes. While he suffers, the motorman and the conductor operate a train which, at rush hours, may take in revenues of as much as $360 per hour. Their combined wages do not exceed $7 per hour. How can such crowding not be profitable?

The answer is that a city transit system, if it is to provide attractive service as an alternative to the private car, must run not only at rush hours, but throughout the day and night; it must spread its lines, not only through the densest sections of the city, but also, in many cases, through intervening miles of factory areas which produce almost no traffic except at shift-change times. Its tunnels, underground, require constant patrolling to patch leaks, maintain switches, change electric light bulbs, clean tracks. Those bulbs, incidentally, unlike street lights, burn twenty-four hours a day. Its stations require attendants, even at off hours. There must be guards or police to keep the passengers safe, and, perversely, the fewer the paying passengers, the greater the need for guards.

This is not all. The intense concentration of heavy loads on narrow steel tracks requires continuing attention to prevent their coming loose from ties. Compared with this, the maintenance of automobile roads, whose load is distributed more or less over their entire surface is much easier. Some snow plowing in the winter; a little landscaping around the edges, and the city is finished with it.

The effect of these facts is already clear. A number of commuter railroads serving New York City from the New Jersey side—the Erie-Lackawanna and the Lehigh Valley—are begging the ICC for permission to go out of the passenger business. The New Haven Railroad, which brings commuters into the city from the eastern edge of Westchester County and Fairfield County, Connecticut, is already in the hands of trustees. Although no payments are being made on its fixed indebtedness, the railroad claims to be running a cash deficit each month, and its continuation clearly depends on the willingness of the government through whose land it passes to support it with gifts. The judge who is supervising the operations of the trustees recently castigated the governors of both these states on the ground that they have hardly glimpsed the amount of money that would be needed to keep the railroad running. It can be predicted safely that by the time enough money has been provided to meet present expenses, wages and supply costs will have risen again.

Those who quail at the complexities of three-dimensional chess are unqualified to discuss railroad accountancy. In chess, at least, the moves of the pieces remain fixed. But the assumptions of railroad accountants vary to suit what they are trying to prove and to whom. The simpleminded may believe that a loss in running a railroad for one year may be measured by the drop in cash in the bank. Even correcting this naïveté for the obvious omissions like the difference in the inventory of supplies or the accounts receivable and payable, the whole question of depreciation has been left out. Depreciation is of crucial importance to a railroad because of the tremendous size of its capital investment in relation to the raw materials and direct labor it actually uses. If the rate of depreciation for the railroad *as a whole* is difficult to determine, the case is still worse when the accountants try to calculate the profitability of a specific train—does it pay to run it? Or a specific number of cars on that train—should it include six or eight? Or of a specific station—is it worthwhile to keep it open? How much more does a car deteriorate when it runs than when it merely stands empty in the yard? What rate of general and administrative overhead shall we apply to the direct costs of putting two extra cars on a train?

The mood of the accountant, or the nature of whatever he may be trying to prove, determines his answers to these questions. They remain complicated even when the capital charges are paid by someone other than the railroad's owner, by the city perhaps, as in the case of the New York subway.

Despite mechanical efficiency, I see no reason to believe that

newly constructed transit systems would operate more economically. They are bound to require labor forces, no matter how
highly automated the train operations may become. To the
extent that city life depends upon transportation, the transit
unions pose a sharp, unified threat to the life of the city, and
can resist with great effectiveness any effort to cut down the
manning tables. A transit strike paralyzes a city dependent on
public transportation, and it would seem that federal subsidies
would be an invitation to further intransigence by union leaders.

Many Sunday-supplement articles have extolled the glories
of a monorail system. There is dramatic appeal in the design of
transit cars balanced on a single row of wheels. This dramatic
appeal has probably led to the belief that trains hanging from
or resting on a single elevated track would be much cheaper
to build and operate than conventional trains. While the initial
cost of a monorail might be lower than that of a conventional
two-rail system, there is no reason to believe that an overhead
monorail system would be any less objectionable to people living or operating stores along its route than were the old
elevated railroads of Manhattan. These railroads played an
important part in the growth of New York City and it has been
said of the Sixth Avenue Elevated Railroad that the city's two
happiest days were the one on which they put it up, and the one
on which they took it down. In Seattle, for the 1962 World's
Fair, an overhead monorail system was built linking the downtown business section of the city with the Fair grounds. The
track was a heavy concrete beam. A two-car train traversed it
on rubber wheels that gripped it from the side, as well as from
the top. The ride was silent, swift, and delightful for the rider.
The storekeepers underneath it have been urging that it be
taken down; for them it is a blighting nuisance.

It has also been argued that a monorail system could
be placed on the right of way acquired by a city for a super-

highway automobile road. This is persuasive until one remembers that the automobile highway has been built, generally, away from the intraurban centers of population; it cuts through the parts of the city with the lowest values, and the lightest concentration of significant land use; no city tolerates the destruction of its most important factories and residential sections for superhighway use. Most automobile drivers must drive their cars a significant number of blocks to get from their homes or their places of work to the superhighways. If the new mass transit lines follow the superhighway lines, passengers on the monorails will be asked to walk difficult and inconvenient distances to reach new stations from their homes. No matter what they are told by the urban critics, they will take their cars and drive all the way instead.

We have not even touched the far more important user of the automobile—the industrial and commercial man. Most of the inveighers against highways talk about passenger automobiles, and pay no attention to trucking; or if they do talk about trucking, they lament its effect upon railroads. If trucking has helped to impair the moneymaking of the railroads, it has compensated for this handsomely by enabling small manufacturers who are not located on the railroad to stay in business competitively. The truck is a godsend to the economy of the city, in general; without it, the cost of distribution in the city would be astronomical. The older ports, without rail facilities adjacent to their piers, would be out of business altogether; the chains of related industries in a metropolitan area would be broken.

In fairness, however, one must recognize that it is the truck traffic that creates the greatest off-hour congestion. I am not primarily troubled about the time wasted by drivers and passengers in private automobiles during rush hours; the decision to use their cars at rush hours, rather than public transit, is their own. I think that a revision of toll systems during rush hours, to penalize cars with fewer than two people in them, might help. I am very much concerned, however, with provision for walking-distance parking near the city center and with off-street loading berths for trucks. It is being urged that tolls from bridges, tunnels, and superhighways, to the extent that they exceed the operating and financing costs of such facilities, should be used to subsidize mass transit. The deficits in mass transit, however, are so overwhelming that the toll surpluses would disappear. I think the surpluses on the bridge and tunnels should be used to construct parking garages near the midtown business district for short-term parkers, and to provide loan funds for off-street loading facilities for trucks.

The combination of highway and transit ownership in a single authority has been often suggested as the way to end competition between transit facilities. Those who propose this often do so in the belief that highway profits should finance subway deficits. But the authority owning both would soon find itself forced to push the construction of profitable facilities to keep pace with the losses on transit. The combination would not end the competition but stiffen it. Public authorities that must sell bonds in the marketplace are at least as sensitive to the nuances of economics as any other form of enterprise, including the state stores of Russia.

Perhaps this country will someday provide for nationwide subsidies for mass transit and suburban railroads on a truly effective scale. I doubt it, however. Every state has, and needs, automobile highways; the cities which require mass transit or commuter rail facilities are few in number. As long as the overwhelming majority of railways are able to operate profitably under private management, the industry will not be nationalized, and new rail subsidies for *all* railroads are not in prospect.

A partial rail subsidy, for commuter railroads only, is also unlikely. Since the suburban train user is, almost by definition, a man of wealth far above the national mean, voters or their elected representatives would question why they are being asked to subsidize the rail transport for those Americans who wish to live apart from their urban fellow citizens of lower social standing and smaller income. This means to me that we shall have to get along with the automobile; not a real hardship, I think, for it has made habitable large sections of our cities which otherwise never would have been used. The automobile provides the nation's only real hope of achieving a reduction of the crowdedness with which Americans live in cities to something affording a comfortable pattern of shared playspace and open space—perhaps the London limit of forty homes per acre. The automobile truck in the city is keeping alive a large number of urban commercial and industrial organizations which would otherwise move elsewhere. The automobile provides an urban atmosphere, a sense of pace and excitement in the city, and it satisfies what is simultaneously an economic necessity and a profound psychological need—an instrument, one of the few, which man controls himself, and in whose design he takes pride.

The urban officials must plan for the intelligent and ample use of the automobile and the truck in the city. They must develop this policy over the outcries of the voters most directly affected by new roads. The officials must measure realistically, and not by slogan, how much the new highway will cut down the significance of the downtown section, and how much it will save the salvageable part of that significance. Anyone who thinks that the American municipal official would prefer to decide against the voters who live in the way of the new highway, or municipal parking garage, in order to collect federal funds, is ascribing magical qualities to money, that it never quite achieved anywhere other than on the pages written by the urban critics. Finally, there is the possibility that new technologies will bring smaller vehicles, non-gas-producing power systems, perhaps even remote control powering or direction of individual cars. Perhaps we shall even have new collapsible parking systems made possible by remote control powering. Who knows?

We do know, of course, that the automobiles may ultimately kill us all, unless a way is found to control the poisonous gases that come from their exhaust pipes. In this contribution to the pollution of the urban air, automobiles are joined by the power companies. The airborne wastes launched by the latter pose another technological transportation problem with political overtones.

Consolidated Edison—the little old electric company in my home town—occupies a strangely ambiguous position in the minds of good citizens. On the one hand, they are made uneasy by it; it belches forth smoke, heats the river, threatens them with atomic energy, and runs its wires across the landscape. On the other hand, it is dedicated uniquely to the public service under stringent government control. When good people in my city want to suggest a policy that will eliminate bad landlords, improve decayed buildings, and guard against exploitation of tenants, the very same citizens who inveigh against Con Edison, suggest cheerfully that housing be made into a public utility. They have never explained what makes a public utility which does not exist better than the existing public utility of which they are always complaining. For years they complained that the public utility that they do know is forever raising its rates and polluting the air. Now they are outraged that it is threatening the countryside. In this last connection, a terrible confusion has arisen. Despite the happy notion of the community of interest among Americans of goodwill, a real conflict rages between saving the city and saving the country. It will not be settled by bland and soothing words, or moral imperatives.

The question of how to conserve a natural environment that will support human life, spiritually as well as physically, has fascinated Americans for the past fifty or sixty years. Since the frontiers to the West were closed, and it became clear that natural resources were limited, men have claimed, with vanity that was only slightly exaggerated, that they belonged to the only natural species which had the capacity to change the environment significantly. Although other animals like coral and beaver have shared this dangerous gift, the boast was sufficiently relevant to the rate at which the natural environment was being changed, and not for the better, to entrain vastly practical consequences. The conservationists have wrought miracles in the United States; and not only in the setting aside of important tracts of land to be preserved against damaging or destructive use. The conservationists also managed to inculcate conservationist practices in many of the users of the land—the lumber companies, some of the major farming interests, and the hunters and the fishermen. The conservationists have been most successful with private interests when the latter were susceptible to their own economic fears of depletion; they have been least successful when the exploiters were under relentless economic pressure to operate cheaply on the short term, to graze their herds in the national reserves, for example, or else succumb to international or other competition.

The achievements of the conservationists have been remarkable. Species of birds have been brought back from the edge of destruction, the bison and the antelope have been saved, ever-renewing forests have been replanted. The similar tasks remaining undone are so tremendous—saving the topsoil from wind and water erosion, cleaning the air from smoke and smog, freeing the waters from pollution, and disposing of solid wastes throughout the nation—that any unpleasant suggestion about conservationists or their programs has a definitely ungenerous flavor. But one must note that the history of the conservationist movement, the nature of the enemies of conservation, and, perhaps, the turn of mind that inclines people to this kind of work, however important it may be, have inclined them to make some rather characteristic overgeneralizations. These generalizations are most frequently about matters that affect cities.

It is shocking to find oneself writing that conservationists can be wrong. Yet they can, even though this lines up the writer with the bad cowmen, the billboard designers, and the peddlers of used cars along the highways. I think conservationists start with a basic distrust of human beings. They distrust those who are forced to earn a living by the exploitation—in the broadest and least pejorative sense of the word—of natural resources. I once heard an Audubon Society lecturer sigh, while demonstrating the sad effects of overgrazing on grass cover, and the consequent wind erosion of Western lands, "All this, just so some men could have jobs." How fortunate, thought I of the lecturer, that he was able to earn his living differently. His participation in the sins of the sheepherder was limited to wearing woolen clothes. With the development of orlon, he can even equate conscience with comfort. There is, on the part of many conservationists, an automatic readiness to find guilty any proponent of change in the natural order, without balancing the change fairly against human needs.

I am enough of a fisherman to share the conservationist's resentment of change. The river I fish in northeastern Quebec is entirely wild. Not a man lives on the Kaniapiskau from its rise near the Labrador border until it finally empties into Ungava Bay on the northern rim of the continent. A float plane takes one hour to fly to the nearest settlement; yet during a recent summer, Quebec Hydro, the electric power company, established a survey camp on one of the arms of the river. Its young men sported above us in a helicopter, thrashing the air about our heads; trees were cut to take sights; bench marks were established, and as one fished under that lonely sky he could sense that someday all this would be gone. A monstrous dam several hundred feet high would block off the river, impounding thousands of acre-feet of potential energy on the beds of lichen, the spruce-covered ridges and eskars, the white water rapids and falls, the rocky islands. The dam, someday to be built, would anonymize this land, burying its many destructive features under a vast abstract hydraulic head. We hear of fish ladders, but for the brook trout, ouananiche, lakers, and pike of this northern country, for the wolves, the bear, the mink and carabou, the dam would mean extinction.

I share the conservationist's bitter resentment against this total extermination of land that, for countless ages, has been disturbed only by the soft footfalls of a few Indian trappers, a land practically inconceivable in its vastness, a land of total human silence.

Yet this is only one side of the story. The power from this dam, generated quietly, and without smoke, will someday surge through heavy overhead lines 400 miles south to the St. Lawrence, and then south again to the cities of New England and New York. Millions of people live in those cities while daily the dust and sulphur fumes in their city air pushes inexorably up to the point of danger. No one has solved the problem of filtering the pollutants of coal or oil smoke from the fuel chamber exhausts of the power stations, especially when burning conditions change, due to a sudden change in power load when a dark cloud passes over the city or on an unexpectedly warm morning, when a million air-conditioning sets are turned on all at once. The smoke is sometimes heavy and black; sometimes it's washed out with a plume of steam. But the particles of fly ash blow across the city, sift through the edges of the window frames, settle on the roofs. They blacken the inside of the lungs, and one can as yet only guess at their long-range influence on the life cycle of the city man.

Much as I treasure my fishing trips, my fellowmen in the cities have their own claim on the wilderness. And as the pressure of increased population rises relentlessly, the issue before the city is no longer how to conserve the wilderness for those who can reach it, but how to conserve the human species altogether. It seems to me that in their resistance to hydro power, to high-tension overland electric power transmission, to the provision of greater access to undeveloped land for mass recreation, all of which mean compromising the pure wilderness, some of the conservationists are themselves opposing a fair try at the most serious of conservation problems. And how few of the urban critics, believing in the wonders of community of interest, have dared to stand up to them.

Two kinds of conservation are needed to keep alive urban man who is choking on his wastes. Both involve problems in the transportation of wastes out of the city; one deals with airborne wastes, the other, with waterborne wastes. To some extent the waste problem can be lightened by attention to transportation at the other end: to transporting into the city only those products so pure that the wastes can be eliminated altogether. It is regrettable, but true, that the transportation of wastes is so lacking in glamor that it has attracted far less attention, sympathy, and moral fervor, than the preservation of scenery and natural species. No one wants to say that there may well be a conflict between the preservation of scenery and species on the one hand, and clean water and pure air in the cities on the other. While the area of conflict may be narrowed by great wisdom and greater generosity, elements of conflict will remain. I find myself on the side of the cities.

The most pervasive airborne waste with which the cities must contend is the waste produced by electric generation. The degree of their dependence on electric power sometimes escapes the attention of city dwellers. It is on the other hand, perfectly evident to anyone who lives in a modern country house, where the water is pumped electrically from an artesian well: the heat depends on an electric motor to vaporize oil, and a spark gap to ignite it; and the refrigerator and stove are energized by a distant generator sending power over lines that are vulnerable to lightning. When the lights go out, so that the householder cannot read a book, his alternative diversions— the television set, the phonograph, the doorbell—fail him. After a break in the power line, one does not simply regress a few years and give up the deep freeze or the slide projector. The break drops one instantly into a remote historical period, in which water must be fetched by hand, sanitary plumbing disappears altogether, and food can be cooked only in the fireplace, by candlelight. Country dwellers have, of course, one advantage over their urban brethren: when the power fails, they can get into the automobile and drive to the city. When power failure hits the city, all internal transport stops; elevators are caught between floors, and the subway trains are stuck between stations.

Cities may get their electric power from several different sources; the one option they lack is cutting down their total power requirement or even stabilizing it at any given level. In engineering offices men spend their days thinking up new devices to increase the urban dependence on electricity. The art of brushing one's teeth by hand fast becomes as obsolete as scrimshaw work; the day is almost here when slicing a steak without an electric knife will be as quaint as a man's fly that fastens with buttons.

In most of the cities of North America, electricity is generated by the rotating power produced in high-pressure steam turbines, for which the steam is heated by burning pulverized coal, or oil, or natural gas. Atomic power aside, one would hardly design a power station today for one of the major cities unless it were capable of being energized by at least two of the fossil fuels. The wisdom of this flexibility became apparent during World War II, when the fuel administrator of the federal government advised the cities that he could not guarantee railroad cars of tanker capacity for future delivery of coal or oil. The cities, having power stations which could burn coal, were able to pile up tremendous reserves of it; the fuel flexibility kept them going through the war. Being able to switch back and forth between coal and oil subsequently has permitted the utilities to minimize their fuel costs. But both coal and oil contaminate the atmosphere, and there seems to be no sound reason for believing that air pollution from either will be completely eliminated technologically. If the cities are to control the menace of air poisoning (the word is used precisely, though the process may be a slow one) , the men in charge of generating electricity—or those in charge of controlling *them*—must find another source of power.

From time to time, the suggestion is made that natural gas can be used with great economy in a gas turbine, eliminating the whole steam-generating phase of the electricity-producing cycle. This would mean that no coal or oil would be used, and that air pollution could be stopped without, according to the engineers who have recommended it, raising the cost of power. Unfortunately, this suggestion would at best mean only that the obnoxious dust will be replaced by unbearable noise. No one who has stood near a turbo-jet airplane while it warmed up, could relish the prospect of living nearer a similar stationary noise maker one hundred times larger. Finally, the available natural gas is so much more readily suited for the consumer's kitchen that the Federal Power Commission is unlikely to permit its use on a giant scale, and permanently, for a purpose for which other fuels are equally suitable with greater flexibility.

A second alternative to coal and oil, and air pollution, is atomic energy. The suggestion that steam-generating stations powered by atomic fuels should be built within the city has generally been greeted with local cries of outrage and indignation. Unfortunately, atomic power—perhaps because of its military background—seems to the public far more dangerous to human life than a little dusty air. But if atomic energy is so dangerous to the public, the same public is already endangered by the atomic reactors that already exist in many American cities, buried in the physics laboratories of the great universities. The engineers, in designing an atomic power plant, pose themselves a rather stiff safety criterion: what would happen to an atomic energy plant if it were hit, dead on, by a jet airliner, flying at speeds in excess of the maximum flown today, and loaded several times beyond current load limits. The atomic plant is so designed that even such a disaster would not set off a chain reaction. But the public does not yet believe this, and, in fact, atomic energy is competitive economically only with the very largest conventionally fired steam stations. Incidentally, the failure to provide competitive power costs does not simply reflect on the profits of the utility company; it reflects also on the housing costs of the city, and the ability of its manufacturers and workmen to compete with those in other cities.

All of these pressures lead the urban utilities in the North inexorably to a single conclusion: to reduce air pollution significantly they must generate power outside the city, and transport it to the city as electricity. This means coal or oil plants near the coal fields or oil fields, or it means hydro power backed up to huge dams. And either one of these alternatives means high-tension lines cutting across the rural landscape. If the urban air is to be made harmless, the rural atmosphere will be threatened by power lines. Many conservationists apparently consider saving the rural atmosphere more important than cleaning the urban air. They are determined to resist power lines. This resistance is growing. The conservationists propose now to require the burying of extremely high-voltage transmission lines in rural areas, at such great expense that it would make the long-range generation of electric power uneconomical, or drain off federal subsidy funds that should be devoted to more serious conservation matters.

These members of the conservationist movement are moved by their memory of wilderness. They feel that the high-tension electric power lines that transport electric power from remote generating stations to the cities mar and disfigure the country-side. No one charges that the lines actively endanger anything. My own view is that the lines are simply a nuisance to people living near them. The alternating current which is inevitably used for long-distance transmission of power sets up interference in nearby radio and television sets, although this is reduced by the latest technology. As the transmission distance becomes greater, the voltages necessarily become higher, in order to minimize transmission losses. As the voltages rise, the towers must rise also, to support heavier copper cables at greater distances from the ground. The high towers dwarf ordinary buildings as they pass by.

This means that high-tension lines are preferably routed through wild country. Across wild country, the high-tension transmission lines seem to be much less noticeable than they are running across suburban landscapes. Those conservationists who view the primary objective of their movement as the preservation of wilderness mobilize in opposition. And here we have the conflict between rural and urban values. If the conservation of wilderness means keeping intact a place untouched by any reminders of man's effect on his physical environment, its pursuit in North America must be quixotic. Even in the remote fastness of northern Canada, far overhead the jet planes leave their vapor trails in the sky, reminding the solitary ground observer that he is but four hours from Orly. Man's satellites pass overhead in all parts of the globe, and the ether is filled with a constant chatter of voices and code. The untouched Garden of Eden is no longer with us, and the struggle to maintain it can be carried on only at the cost of the city man.

212 | Part II: Hard Choices

A more relevant activity is distinguishing between those elements which destroy the landscape needlessly, and those which hardly affect it. I should oppose the cutting of highways through national or state parks, unless to provide access to them; I should oppose billboards everywhere, cutting the motorist off from his vistas of the land; I should oppose sprawling developments and the use of highways as shopping streets, except in carefully planned circumstances. But the march of electric power lines across the landscape (they cannot be put underground except at formidable expense and, in the end, the burying scars the countryside with a track of denuded shrubbery and trees) must continue and spread, to save the lungs of the men in the cities. We cannot have both clean air within the city, and a countryside without electric power lines. The argument that rural virginity is more precious than are urban lungs is only beginning. But it will become one of the vital issues affecting the entire future of the cities.

If air pollution control demands, among other measures, the urban right to transport power across the country, water pollution control, fully as serious, requires a wholly new force in the government of this nation.

Air pollution, for the most part, affects the air breathed in by the voters of a specific local jurisdiction; one can assume that if some means is found ultimately of controlling the noxious fumes emitted by the internal combustion engine, the municipalities can, by their own efforts, control the nuisances that come out of their own chimneys.

The growing campaign against high-tension lines imperils the cities because the high-tension lines pass through land which is under the control of other jurisdictions. The Federal Power Commission now has the authority to require that the state and local governments give their permission for the erection of power lines. Already, however, suburban legislators would shift or abrogate this right, and pro-conservation newspapers, like the New York *Times,* apparently unmindful of the consequences, support them. If the rural constituency gained control over the erection of lines from which they do not benefit, the cities would be in an impossible position. If another commission of the federal government were given esthetic veto power over the rulings of the Federal Power Commission's power line approvals, we would have total confusion.

In the normal course of events, air pollution is a local problem (except, perhaps, for a federal requirement for automobile exhaust purifiers on automobiles shipped or driven across state lines). The air pollution produced within a single city is dissipated within a short time. It does not blow down, in high concentration, on the next city downwind. Furthermore, the gross quantities of material to be strained from the air are small. If their producers catch them, they can easily be disposed of. The disposal of the city's solid wastes—its garbage and trash—involves vast tonnages which have already overloaded the imaginations and the budgets of municipal officials. Wastelands and marshlands are disappearing beneath what is euphemistically called sanitary landfill. How to avert this destruction—and the air pollution resulting from incineration—should be the major long-range national goal of the conservationists. There is no answer in sight.

The immediate problem of waterborne waste—sewage—and water pollution is scientifically solvable. It is merely politically damned.

Unlike polluted air, dirty water is contained within the fixed banks of a river, or lake or bay. In the river, its flow is all in one direction; in the lake or bay, its spread is limited by the shape of the body of water. If the body of water is large, probably more than one independent city is using it for the same purpose. Since there is almost always another city upstream from any city you can think of, the taxpayers can always find a plausible reason for arguing that spending *their* money on sewage treatment will be futile. Sewage treatment of their own wastes won't even clean the river before their eyes: it was poisoned by their upstream neighbors. One cannot even praise sewage treatment as farsighted altruism. Unless all cities on a river invest in it, nothing is put right for anybody.

Without detailing a long and dreary treatise on sanitary engineering, let me only say that the waste disposal systems of most American cities combine storm and sanitary sewers, and that the whole complex of pipes and chambers is subject to storm flooding, which carries polluted water into the river, lake, or bay where the city stands. Unless the city is located on a small body of fixed water in which it will itself feel the results of its own, and only its own, lack of sanitation, the chances are that it will move only slowly to appropriate the money necessary to erect the treatment plants and catch basins necessary to clean up the effluent.

Nor is it likely, except under such circumstances, that any system of low-cost loans from the federal government, combined with well-meant threats, will succeed in moving cities to invest property, time, and tax revenues in the correction of water pollution. How is a city to be coerced to do something its taxpayers do not wish to do, unless a direct correlation can be shown between the health and happiness of the city and the expenditure of funds? Sometimes, it can be argued that the erection of a sewage treatment system will reclaim a filthy shoreline or waterfront for recreation. One would expect that the advocates of adequate recreational facilities would be able to rally political support for such an enterprise. But they don't. They do raise money, and support for buying a choice piece of land for a wholly new municipal golf course or park. I suppose one would like to see one's name over the gates of a new park—but who wants a sewage treatment named for him?

While there has been a great deal of writing about the use

of regional compacts between cities and counties, or even states, in the accomplishment of specific developments—harbor authorities, water development authorities—the sanitation compacts that have been entered into by states or counties have simply never worked. The Interstate Sanitation Commission, consisting of representatives of New Jersey, New York, and Connecticut, has been attempting to clear up water pollution problems in the New York Harbor–Long Island Sound complex for years. The Commission from time to time hands down orders to cities in the region, demanding that within a specific period of years each succeed in removing pollution from its sewer effluents. As monotonously and regularly as the Commission hands down its decrees, so monotonously do the towns, cities and counties refuse to pay attention to them. What is to be done with them? Where is the penitentiary to which we can commit New York City? Shall Camden send Philadelphia out of the room? Without any real self-interest in spending money on treatment plants, how are the local wills to be made to bend for the benefit of the remote general interest?

The federal government has also been easing the conscience of the Senate on water pollution matters by promising special help to those states, or parts of states, that join with other states, or parts of other states, in regional-planning bodies. This high-sounding pastime has never got very far, because of the vast confusion in the minds, even of experts with some experience, between planning and execution.

The federal government has attempted to pass legislation controlling industrial water pollution. It gets nowhere, or almost nowhere, because the industries claim, with perfect justice, that the cities and towns are worse offenders. If everything waits for the towns to control this pollution, we shall never make a start. For even if a planning agency gets the time to consider long-range matters, it has no direct way of positively commanding other agencies to carry out its plans. Specialists in the organization of city governments argue about the best way to overcome the difficulty: should the planning body be a branch of the executive government, subject directly to the mayor, so that the latter will be disposed to force the carrying out of its plans? This may be indeed a prudent hope. The plans, however, are hardly likely to be any better than the chief executive himself. Those who argue for the independence of planning for the total physical environment of the city, make the point that, even if the plans are not fully executed, over a long period of time they come to color the thinking and frame the perspectives of the several action agencies. Even if the plans never get adopted with the label and imprimatur of the planners, they, or part of them anyway, creep into the future, nameless but alive.

If these difficulties in bridging the gap between plan and action are to be found when we are dealing simply with the matters in a single city, how much worse to try to impose a plan of water depollution on several cities, even when these are found within a single state. Worse yet, when found in several states.

This suggests to me that water depollution can only be handled directly by the one governmental force able to execute a program in a number of different cities, spread over several states. The federal government must take on the responsibility of building and operating sewage treatment plants and depollution programs in the navigable waterways of the country. This would mean that the federal government would itself acquire the sites for the plants and operate them directly, in connection with the municipal sewerage and drainage systems. The federal government already has assumed responsibility for the construction of major dams for flood control conservation, power, navigational, and recreational purposes throughout the nation. Polluted water is, in many ways, as serious a deterrent to the fruitful use of the waterways of the nation as is the flooding which the Army tries to control with its dams and levees. It is as serious as the erosion of the headlands and valleys that the Bureau of Reclamation tries to remedy with its system of dams. Neither of these agencies turns over the ownership and operation of its systems of public works to local municipalities, states, or ententes between regions. Why should the ownership and control of the means for cleaning the polluted waste waters of the cities be treated differently? Nor is there anything significant to be said for local control of a sewage treatment plant; there is no real issue here that a federal bureaucracy is determined to run such establishments in a way which will ignore local sensibilities, traditions, and needs of self-government.

Other programs, such as low-rent housing or highway development, involve the federal government in providing funds and subsidies for state or city governments to use in developing facilities that meet federal standards or facilities that join together to compose a federal network. Direct federal ownership in these cases is impractical, not only because of local sensibilities, but also because local state courts may not uphold the federal government's right to acquire land by condemnation for purposes which are not specifically set forth in the constitution. But the danger posed to the national security by the millions of tons of human and industrial waste will not wait for the assuaging of local sensibilities. These have no proper place in any case in a program concerned almost wholly with technological problems. In the case of water treatment plants, however, there should be little trouble in using the powers of local government for site acquisition, provided only that an agency of the national government constructs and operates the plant. A national authority, or a regional authority established by the federal government, capable of issuing its own bonds would be practical. It might sell its own bonds to be liquidated by service charges to the cities. There would hardly be opposition to the construction of such plants—there is no opposition to them now, only to the spending of local money on them.

The conservation of human life and health in the cities—the very survival of urban man—depends in great measure on the prevention of air and water pollution. Clearing up urban air depends greatly, not only on what happens in the cities themselves, but upon the ability of the cities to bring in their electric power requirements by overhead transmission lines. Already the order of battle is in the process of formation: the conservationist and suburban interests will not readily assent to the construction of the lines that are needed by the cities.

Elimination of water pollution—with its vast promise of recreational facilities opened to new use for the whole nation—will require the federal government to take direct action in an area of government in which it has so far not dared to move directly. And the elected officials of the cities must be ready to permit the direct entry of the federal government into the cities with vast sums of money for water treatment.

Join regional compacts and clean up our waters, cry the conservationists—asking for something which the cities are clearly incapable of accomplishing. Even the conscientious reader of the urban critics has little notion of what really must be done so that he can breathe clean air, and swim in the bay, river, or lake that's only a short drive from his urban home. No single excoriation of industrial pollution, no snide remarks about the power lobby, will begin to clear the air or cleanse the water.

Reclaiming polluted waters on the appropriate scale is an enterprise involving perhaps half a trillion dollars, and putting millions of men to work. It will remake the American map. Without reconstituting the wilderness of the past, it will nevertheless make possible a handsome, dignified, common future. But it will require local elected officials to assent to federal measures they have never easily assented to; and to oppose those who, in the name of beauty, would permit urban man to choke.

X. | THE INCOME GAP

THE Lower East Side of Manhattan, in this respect no different from at least one venerable section in every other large city, is the territory of the immigrant poor. Once the stage for the Americanization of the Germans, the Irish, the Jews, and the Italians, it is now a Puerto Rican and Negro neighborhood. A few old Jewish traces survive amid *bodegas* and *carnicerías:* on Second Street, a faded synagogue hides behind dusty, boarded-up windows, identifiable only by a small sign hanging from its locked and rusty gates; on Ridge Street, in a three-story building that seems abandoned, bearded butchers pack the city's most fragrant salami; on Attorney Street, a winery in the cellar of a tenement house specializes in the bottling of sacramental vintages; the sweet smell of fermented grapes drifts down the street, past the corner bar where an orange poster in the window proclaims Cerveza Rheingold. The smell of wine in the street may remind the visitor of the opening of *A Tale of Two Cities*: the wine cask broken in the Paris street, and the desperate citizens on hands and knees to lap up the precious liquid.

The resemblance between prerevolutionary Paris and mid-century New York stops at the smell and the poverty. No one here is prepared to storm the Bastille; no one is quite sure what New York's Bastille is, nor even whether one still exists. A few Jewish families—the very old and the seriously disabled—linger in the neighborhood, perhaps one to each tenement house, a single Greenberg alphabetically separating Gonzalez from Guitterez, but the rest are gone, except for those who return each day to work here. Ten blocks away, many families who may once long ago, it seems, have lived in these very buildings, now own terraced apartments in a large cooperative sponsored by the garment trades unions.

The significance of the change in the identity of the poor is not simply a linguistic matter. The neighborhood has not merely substituted Spanish for Yiddish; a Puerto Rican community (whatever that may be) for a Jewish community (whatever that may have been) ; or a Negro community (ditto) for an Italian one. The people who deserted this neighborhood, and left poverty behind them, now think very differently about it, and the quality of their thinking in large part defines the city's current ability to deal with poverty, its most persistent and nagging social problem.

Thirty years ago, when the poor spoke with a different accent, the American economy was faltering so badly that people of unquestioned talent and adaptability were looking for work, any work at all, let alone the work for which they had been educated. No one in this neighborhood, except in moments of extreme personal frustration, construed his inability to find work as a purely personal failure; no one railed against unemployment primarily on the grounds that it stigmatized him. He wanted money first; status, perhaps later. How to improve the economy was a far more natural question than how to improve oneself in order to extract more money from it.

Even on the city scale, and everyone in those years knew that economic problems could not be solved on the city scale, the major criterion for deciding to build a proposed bridge, tunnel, airport, or housing project was simple: would it put people to work? No one suggested that a place of employment, a factory, should be smashed to make way for a home. One-third of the people in the nation were ill-housed, but it was understood that theirs was part of a general economic problem. There were practically as many people living in the Eastern cities in the 30's as live there today. Though there were no more homes, many of them were vacant: lack of money forced families to live doubled up, or tripled up. This did not stigmatize them, because the difficulty was general; but the generality made it no less uncomfortable.

Thirty years ago, on the Lower East Side, and in a dozen sections like it in other cities, a thousand articulated theories accounted for the state of the world. Over a glass of tea, or on the benches of Seward Park (across the street from the present 20-story, middle-income cooperative), men explained to each other how the conditions in which they found themselves were linked with the condition of the entire world as it approached cataclysmic war. Poverty was the result, certainly, of capitalistic exploitation, and would be ended only with the end of the capitalistic system. . . .

Or it resulted from the control of large sections of the American economy by corporations which prevented an equitable distribution of goods, in order that their own profits would be greater. . . .

Or poverty resulted from the absence of, and could only be eliminated by an increase in, labor solidarity, or cooperative organization, or Zionist self-determination, or collective security with the Soviet Union, or Social Democracy.

Then, curiously, the cataclysmic war produced neither disaster nor chaos. People were not reduced to wearing animal skins while living furtively in ruins, as predicted by H. G. Wells. On the contrary, the war, as if by accident, produced unparalleled prosperity; physical abundance arrived for almost all the

East Siders, without in any way confirming the theories they had developed to explain its absence. The pre-occupation that thirty years ago seemed to be most serious and universal—the study of world economics (or almost any other universal theory) to explain the human condition—turned out to have been only a youthful indiscretion.

Within a few years after the war, as the prosperity began to look reliable, the people of the Lower East Side had crept out into the sun, and found that it was good. They moved from the old tenement houses to Queens, from Queens to Long Island, perhaps, and learned that there was far more room for them in the system than they had thought. Psychology became much more interesting than economics. They concluded from their own experience (which often involved hiring people as well as working for them) that anyone who had not managed comfortably in the postwar years could scarcely plead that it was someone else's fault.

In the past few years the members of this new middle class have been reminded that some people are still living in squalor, once again in the very sections of the city they had themselves abandoned. It has been an unpleasant surprise for them to discover that poverty did not end with their own personal good fortune. The rise of poverty as a political issue has called to their attention that people are still living in the dark and dingy buildings they once inhabited; buildings that were old and decrepit when they themselves lived in them thirty years ago. Once again the former poor are being asked to take up the question put away years ago without ever having been quite answered: why is there poverty in the midst of plenty? It would be astonishing if the first impulse were other than irritation, as though someone had revived the recollection of a disgraced ancestor, or a slightly shameful episode from one's youth.

As the persistence of poverty poses heavy economic burdens for the city as a whole and for its middle class—not to mention the human and moral overtones—the attitudes of the new middle class toward the present poor become increasingly important in the development of programs for dealing with them. Urban political programs involving housing, employment, and education, and a strange amorphous activity called the Anti-Poverty Program, depend in large measure on the ideas which middle-class citizens currently hold of the people who earn too little money in the city to live, not luxuriously, not even generously, but merely on an acceptably human scale.

Perhaps the most important current middle-class idea about the cause of poverty is the absence of any idea at all. Their own experience of prosperity prevents the newly expanded middle class from believing any longer that systematic exploitation is the cause of poverty. If poverty cannot be blamed on a system, then the poor must somehow themselves be responsible. Recognizing from their own experience that failure to have achieved prosperity in the postwar world would be the result of personal failing, the members of the new middle class understand that their primary reaction to being poor today would be a sense of shame. They assume that the current poor feel the same way, and many of the most civic-minded middle-class citizens propose to attack the problem of poverty primarily by removing the imagined stigma from being poor. In this way, for example, so runs the implied theory, no one will know that they are poor, and it won't hurt so much. This theory springs more from the recent experiences of the new middle class than it does from their recollection of how it felt to be poor when they were poor. An empty pocket is no less painful because the man beside you thinks it full; in fact, the sense of its emptiness may be all the greater by contrast.

A second consequence of the absence of a general ideology to explain poverty is that one understands that the resentments of the poor will be less generalized, and more personal. One expects greater bitterness, together with the inability to organize the bitterness into effective action. Perhaps the intense fear of crime in the cities today springs not only from the statistics, which on close inspection hardly confirm this to be a period of lawlessness as extreme as even that of fifty or one hundred years ago, but from the awareness that individual or petty gang crime is a reasonable response—perhaps the only reasonable response —to poverty in the midst of abundance, when there is no theory to account for its persistency and no promise of its end.

Finally the lack of ideology to explain poverty leaves the Anti-Poverty Program without the benefit of a central strategy.

Certainly no one can devise a specific solution to the poverty problem unless he has a clear idea of what he is demanding. The very vagueness of the demands of those interested professionally in ending poverty indicates that those who make them have no clear idea of why some people are poor today. "We want human renewal instead of urban renewal," says Father Henry Browne, a Roman Catholic priest on New York City's West Side. What is human renewal? Father Browne suggests that it means finding people decent homes to live in, at rents they can afford to pay, and providing them with something else, on an emotional level, that will make them feel a part of the mainstream of life. But what will, in fact, make them feel a part of the mainstream? No one tells us. The Philadelphia Housing Association, discussing the housing problems of the poor, tells us that the "causes of poverty are complex: racial discrimination, unemployment, lack of education, social maladjustment, all these play roles of varying importance." Not a word about economics as a whole.

Yet economics must be the primary cause of poverty. The continued existence of a Lower East Side—Puerto Rican if no longer Jewish—where people cannot afford toilets or bathtubs must be the result of economic shortcomings. Not enough wealth is being produced, or it is somehow improperly distributed, if poverty continues to exist. People affected by economic poverty may be affected also by other personal problems. But *all* poor people are suffering from the shortcomings of the production and distribution system. There are such shortcomings and they deserve attention first. The American economy, miraculous though its achievements have been, is imperfect. It depends, as we have seen, on the wastage of irreplaceable assets. Its heated activity depends on military expenditures, that will not be easily replaced if for some reason (like peace) they should be curtailed. The economy is also falling short because its full productive capacity is not being used while there are still unfilled desires for goods and services which cannot be translated into economic demand.

Urban critics concerned primarily with the problems of the poor have recently been talking enthusiastically about ending poverty by simply handing out cash money to the families who need it, usually describing this process by a circumlocution, such as "family allowance" or "negative income tax." For special unemployable groups, such as the aged, the young, and the disabled, and the mothers of dependent children these cash payments are essential. The notion that salary supplements for the employed should be paid to those whose earning falls below a stipulated figure has the virtue of simplicity, in every sense. *Cash* income is not real income. The guarantee of a stipulated annual wage for those only partially employed, or employed in industries that lack enforceable claims against the national product as a whole, merely stimulates the better situated workers to demand higher wages, carrying with them the price level of the whole economy. This is especially true in the cities, where some unions, like the Transport Workers Union, have almost unlimited strategic powers. Expecting cash distributions to the poor to make up their deficiency in real income would make sense as economics only if the rest of the economy were subject to wage and price stabilization.

It is important to understand what translates desire into economic demand, or what blocks the translation. Without a sense of the central importance of economics to poverty, cities not only may fail to adopt programs to mitigate poverty. With the blessing of the critics, the cities may even positively encourage poverty with the noblest of motives.

If personal problems, or cultural deficiencies like illiteracy, fully explained the existence of poverty, the inability of stable families, headed by reasonably stable working individuals, to earn a decent standard of living would be an enigma. Yet there are millions of these in the cities. Their problem is that the corners of the economy in which they work simply do not provide the necessary income.

It would be easy to present a number of reasons why the unions have found these industries difficult to organize. The difficulties of uncertain occupation, small shops with a high organizational overhead, and the possibility of corrupting the officials of the unions are a few of the reasons. There is also a more important reason, the general lack of invested capital, the purely local character, and the low cash flow of the industries themselves. Those who work under these hardships are the hardest workers to unionize; their work history is relatively unstable, they personally have all too often felt the antagonism, on racial and personal grounds, of the members of other unions, and hence they have less confidence than the workers in other earlier organized industries that unions are in fact a potentially constructive force on their own behalf. Their income runs so close to the bare minimum wage that they cannot set aside the funds to pay union dues and other union expenses. They lack historical background that might make them feel conscious of being part of the labor movement. But the big unions will ultimately get around to the unskilled corners of the economy. They have nowhere else to expand.

Attempts to increase the economic power of the workers in these industries by raising their uncertain wages as a matter of local law, have been successful in principle, but at high cost to the individual worker. The mobile industries move elsewhere. Among the underpaid, underpaying urban employers, only the more efficient enterprises will survive higher minimum wages. Probably, their efficiency will be the result of their ability to replace labor with machinery; and the increased power that they will derive from the death of their weaker competitors will only strengthen their ability to effect further labor savings through automation. If the minimum wage is raised by local or state action, the consequences may include the movement of the industry, or parts of it, outside the jurisdiction of the law. This may give a measure of personal satisfaction to the sponsors of such legislation. They can boast that their city or state will not harbor substandard industries. But only rarely does anyone manage to consult the people who lose their jobs as a result of this exercise in civic pride.

If minimum wage legislation only speeds up mechanization and economic concentration, increasing short-term unemployment, what will help these marginal enterprises and their employees? Primarily, these enterprises are affected by the general level of economic activity in the city. If employment generally is high, the service industries are busy. People have money to spend on maintaining their clothes and on eating in restaurants —both activities employ marginal workers. With similar economic results, people with money order their food delivered to their homes, employing marginal workers in doing so, and, similarly, complete odd jobs around the house. The high level of original purchases means a high level of scrapping; the waste industries flourish. To maintain a high level of employment in the marginal industries, and to provide higher wages in them, whether by union or legislative activity, a high general economic level in the city must be maintained. Building construction, which involves a high percentage of local labor to total value produced, has been stimulating a high level of economic activity in the cities of America since World War II. It is no service to the underpaid workers in the marginal industries to urge cessation of construction of housing, schools, roads, on the grounds that these destroy the homes of the poor, or interfere with their neighborhoods. This does not mean that any specific project must be supported as originally proposed. But in reacting to proposals for reconstructing the city, one cannot forget their economic implications even for workers only indirectly affected.

Yet it can be shown that the construction programs now under way fall far short of stimulating a high enough level of economic activity even to maintain the marginal work force at present levels. New programs of tremendous scope will be required. These might include programs to conserve the natural assets of the nation, including federal construction of nationwide anti-water pollution, anti-sewage control works. A program of tremendous size, promising years of expanding employment opportunities in construction might open the doors of the construction trades unions to new members drawn from the marginal industries. Some such expansion of economic opportunity is essential for men who are not now earning living wages. In the absence of such an expansion, all the talk about training and education as a cure for underemployment will merely determine which members of the total work force are to be the ones left out in the cold. A Negro revolution intended to increase job opportunities for Negroes must create job opportunities in general. Lacking this, the Negro Revolution will be followed, or accompanied, by a White Revolution (the so-called white backlash) of those who feel themselves about to be displaced economically to make room for Negroes, however just their claims, and however long delayed this attention to the redress of ancient wrongs. It is remarkable that such a manifestation has not yet shown itself overtly in the Northern cities. Perhaps it will not be altogether averted by a vast program of nationally financed construction, but such a program will be an important element in averting it.

If mechanization continues to grow on the farm, people will continue to flock to the city. In contemplation of this continuing population increase, the most strenuous attempts to enlarge economic opportunities will never keep up with the swelling human tide. And no matter how hopeful one may be about the future American urban economy, many stable people employed full-time will still be unable to pay for what they need to live. The cities, with the federal government's help, are filling this income gap by providing services. These include hospital and health services, day care for the children, so that both parents can work, subsidized housing, perhaps even more direct support, such as supplementary welfare payments, and transportation in the city provided at less than cost.

Most, if not all of these services, are provided by teachers, social workers, and housing managers who are paid better than the people they help. The helpers are better organized. The city's own employees have become a group as powerful as the construction unions. The essential municipal financial problem is how to provide the funds to pay organized workers serving clients who are unorganized and underpaid. Most of the taxes that the municipalities can levy on the activities within their borders—real estate taxes, for example, sales taxes, permits, and license fees—fall as heavily on the poor as on the rich, which is another way of saying that they fall more heavily on the poor. Because they are not graduated in line with income, the taxes affect the business establishments which are likely to employ the underorganized worker, and limit his ability to demand better pay. Each municipality, at all costs, must avoid placing high taxes on the wealthier industries which, by definition, have a choice of location, and might either leave the city, or refuse to come to it if it were trying to attract them. Real estate taxes, of course, appear to be levied against property and wealth; in fact, they are, after a time, passed on to tenants; the lag, representing extra costs to landlords, only stiffens their reluctance to pay janitors and other service employees who, in the low-income residential sections of the city, are very likely not organized.

Despite all these discouragements, the federal government has been assisting municipal programs supporting the standard of living of the underpaid; these programs do succeed in raising their self-esteem provided only that the families are reasonably stable. Families of this general category, in spite of monstrous discouragements, do well in public housing, for example, and their children—whether they are Puerto Rican, Negro, or other —are making the same progress toward middle-class standards that has characterized former minority groups for whom American society opened up. If the cities are able to find the federal funds with which to provide more effective services for those who use them, the families they help will organize themselves, perhaps with outside help, to fortify their position in American life.

One can be hopeful about the prospects for the stable family. But behind the underpaid stable families—where problems can be met by increased earnings and services—lurks a group for whom no real help is in sight, and whose very existence is as mysterious as their numbers. These are the families or part-families so disorganized that they cannot work; these are families so disturbed that their members cannot keep up the pattern of regular family life. These are the families whose existence can be found in the reports of continuing criminal recidivism; in the annals of the welfare department; in the chronicles of truancy and juvenile delinquency; in the lists of evictions from public housing projects (or, if they have not been evicted, in public housing projects that have become notorious for shabby physical conditions and tenant destructiveness) .

It is easy, at a comfortable and safe distance, to describe these families in abstract terms that place the blame for their condition on government, or the indifference of their wealthier fellow-citizens. It is easy to develop any number of simple prescriptions for dealing with their problems, prescriptions whose simplicity is in direct proportion to the distance of the theorizer from the people he is theorizing about. But when he is confronted with them in the flesh, even the most fervent moralizer is likely to find that his theories are more moral than practical. The difficulties presented by these broken households can be inspected from a number of different aspects: as work problems, in which case one confronts not only a lack of training, but a lack of motivation to undertake training. A job-training counselor for Mobilization for Youth, an organization concerned with the plight of youth on Manhattan's Lower East Side, especially school dropouts, in New York City, said to me, "It isn't just that my kids don't know how to do the job, but that they've never lived in a home in which anyone ever worked. They see no reason why anyone should work; they never had an opportunity to watch a man in the house get up and go off to work. For them, the whole cultural tradition of the working-man in the western world isn't there, and we have to try to start over and build it in a few months."

Those children of the disorganized households who support themselves by theft and robbery choose crime as a way of life because its loose working hours and sporadic concentration are within their emotional capacity. No other work is. Delinquency, especially theft, has been presented as an economic loss to the community. The FBI and other agencies, private and public, interested in the problems of crime, have made enough calculations to add up the so-called social cost of crime. If crime were all cost to everyone involved, it could not continue. Forgotten in the calculations is the apparent fact that articles stolen must be sold, if the theft is to have significance. If a customer wants to buy them, he must have some use for them. Sit on the grand jury in a large city, and you will hear endless accounts of stolen television sets, typewriters, articles of clothing, even furniture. The thefts are evidence that a market exists somewhere for these objects, provided that they can be sold cheaply enough. Even if the seller procured these articles without paying for them, he can sell them cheaply only provided that another condition is met: the labor which transports the articles from the point of theft to the point of sale must itself be for sale very cheaply. This cheap transport labor is provided by the clumsy thieves who spring from the disorganized households. They are the only members of our society so lacking in ability to organize their time and their efforts that they are willing to embark on the trivial thefts and occasional muggings that feed the second-hand market. To the extent that the property they take is covered by insurance, the world has even socialized the cost of the distribution system that provides objects for sale to those who, presumably, cannot afford to buy new television sets, typewriters, and even jewelry and furs. In most cases, the missing items are replaced by their original owners—with a consequent stimulation of the economic system.

It is commonly thought that narcotics addiction is responsible for this kind of petty crime, on the theory that the perpetrators need the money to support an expensive habit. As a matter of fact, the correlation between narcotics addiction and crime is so high in the major cities of this country that the narcotics explanation of criminal etiology is self-defeating. If 80 percent of the thieves in New York are narcotics addicts, the notion that the addiction causes the theft is the equivalent of saying that if there were no narcotics there would be no theft at all, or almost none. This is palpably false. It seems much more logical to believe that the delinquency engages a personality unable to function regularly in a money world; while the narcotics help to make tolerable the resulting physical and moral blows. It is interesting that Synanon, one of the few schemes which has demonstrated any real success in treating narcotics addicts— even then in only a highly selected sample of those addicts —begins by making the addicts members of a rigorously ordered household in which they are expected to perform very specific household tasks in a meticulous way in order to gain respect and love. The artificial household created by Synanon is more real in its impact than the actual households which we read about in the cases presented by social workers. The household commonly described in accounts of multiproblem families has one standard attribute: no one is ever expected to do anything; no one has the responsibility of preparing meals, washing dishes, appearing at any particular time to eat, or go to bed, or purchase or clean anything. And if there are no duties, there are no rewards.

From the point of view of public health, these disorganized families present, in the cities of the United States, a disease as real as the pandemic infectious diseases that have, in such great measure, been eliminated. In New York City, in 1964, there were some 200,000 households supported in whole or part by public assistance. It has been estimated that approximately one-half of these were troubled, multiproblem families who would, under the most favorable economic circumstances, have been unable to earn their keep, for reasons having nothing to do with physical disabilities. Those 100,000 households represent some 250,000 people, 4 percent of the population.

Most people who are interested in these depressing statistics view them with equanimity, or even pride. After all, they tell themselves, these families were always with us. The only difference is that now we are taking care of them with welfare allotments.

I think this bland assumption is open to challenge. I suggest that the multiproblem, disorganized families present the modern city with a wholly new social problem, hardly glimpsed, let alone analyzed. Of course, there have always been disorganized, multiproblem families in the cities. The crucial difference is that as recently as 1900 they were a self-limiting problem. They were killed off by the communicable diseases that accompanied poverty, filth, and degradation. As recently as 1900, four of every ten deaths in the United States was caused by diseases like tuberculosis, diphtheria, yellow fever, cholera, and scarlet fever; in 1953, only one death in every thirteen was caused by the same diseases. The death rate from tuberculosis alone was reduced by 95 percent in the fifty years from 1900 to 1950. It seems quite reasonable to believe that these diseases were communicated in the crowded, airless conditions under which the urban poor lived. And it seems equally reasonable to believe that those most likely to contract, and then succumb to, the communicable diseases were the poor whose homes were the most disorganized, whose children were the worst fed, whose standard of cleanliness and order was the lowest. Medical triumphs of the last one hundred years have solved their problems of physical infection. They have simultaneously created a tremendous problem of social maladjustment. The medical men struggled for centuries with the problems of physical disease, but no one has been willing to believe that the problems of family disorganization are as deep, as complicated, and will take as great an investment of time and money to cure.

Admittedly, the coincidence between the falling curve of death by communicable disease since 1900, and the rising curve of the multiproblem family as supported by public assistance does not prove that there is a causal connection between the two. I am willing to assume, however, that the high death rates from infectious diseases, violence, and accidents in the cities up to and including the nineteenth century, limited the number of multiproblem families. One has only to read the accounts of New York slums in the mid-nineteenth century, to find the inevitable Mrs. X living in the cellar with two other broken families, while animal bones were boiled in the corner to make soup, and sewage gathered on the floor. Mrs. X, our guide tells us, has had twelve children, two living. Today's Mrs. X's may have fewer than twelve children, but the majority of them survive, and have children of their own. One need not believe in a genetic theory of inherited inferiority to accept the fact that the children of a broken home will tend in their own lives to repeat the only family pattern with which they are familiar. I have no hard and fast information on the rate of second- and third-generation illegitimacy in welfare-supported families, but those who have written informally on the subject—such as Julius Horwitz in *The Inhabitants*—suggest that this is a familiar pattern.

If family disorganization is a social disease which was once limited by the action of other diseases either caused, like rickets, by the very conditions under which the disorganized family lived, or, like tuberculosis, which flourished under these conditions, the disappearance of the limits presents modern urban society with a medico-legal problem of awesome dimensions. But while society was waving flags and playing bands to encourage the medical profession to attack the infectious diseases, no one has bothered to look at the disorganized families long enough to see that they constitute an unsolved health problem, requiring theoretical analysis and experimentation and not just good nursing.

I suspect that there is another reason that accounts for the slowness in subjecting the disorganized family's problems to serious scrutiny. That arises from a confusion between the intellectualized perception of modern man's alienation from his environment, and the disorganized family's alienation from conventional life around it. Alienation has become an intellectually stylish way to describe the futility of purely individual existence in a world in which satisfying work has been divided into fragments separated from man's natural state. But, I would guess that the multiproblem family would be equally troubled in any human situation, and equally alienated from any set of cultural values. This distinction is not always clear to the young intellectual.

He imagines that the inability of the disorganized family's members to keep a job is the product of a passivity or conscious rejection of the demands of society, a rejection to which he himself is sympathetic. The young woman puzzled by the contradictions and the uncertainties of present sexual mores, believes that the illegitimacies of the disorganized family, which she has heard of but never seen, are the free expression of a conscious rejection of mere conventionality, a rejection which on her own part is never quite as easy as promised. But this is a mythical view of the disorganized family. Nothing done by families in this state of disorganization is done from choice; one has the feeling, talking to them, that the fact of choice itself is beyond them.

From the point of view of housing, the disorganized families make a vivid impact on what happens in the city. One cannot clear slums without moving these households. We are told that we cannot fairly move them unless we can lighten their problems. Since we cannot cure their problems any more than Galen could cure diabetes, we would be unable to rehouse even those families who can be helped, if we took these strictures seriously. By inserting these strictures, urban critics like Herbert Gans confuse the clear fact that most of these families live in bad housing, with the notion that their problem is a housing problem, or that it can be solved by any procedures with which modern medicine or social work is familiar.

The New York *Times* not long ago published an article describing the home from which had come a nine-year-old boy whose battered body had been discovered in New Jersey, and, after a six-day interval, identified by his mother.

"Mrs. I." the *Times* reporter wrote, "said her husband was

in jail for larceny and narcotics addiction. Since he has gone, she said, she had lived with four other men, by whom she has had children. One of the men became 'very jealous' of a successor, she said, and stabbed her twice, and his successor six times. He is now in jail, she said.

"Mrs. I. now lives with the man who was stabbed, J. M., in a sparsely furnished five-room apartment that rents for $72.30 a month. Three of her eight other children live with friends or relatives, while the remaining five live with her and Mr. M. . . ."

No one can dispute the existence of their housing problem; it seems equally obvious that finding them a new apartment with enough rooms for eight children will not mean that this household will be then able to organize itself for a life in which the children will ultimately be able to support themselves, even if one assumes a world free of racial and national discrimination, and brimming with economic opportunity for all. I believe that in their numbers, Mrs. I. and her children present the American city with a problem it has never faced before: a hundred years ago, when Mrs. I.'s home lacked plumbing, when the cause of tuberculosis was unknown, when the government provided no food for the indigent, and private charity barely touched the fringes of the "respectable" poor, Mrs. I.'s children could hardly be expected to survive infancy. Those who did survive would not only be likely to have developed the greatest natural immunity against infectious disease, but also would have developed some kind of talent for survival. In my opinion, no city can survive in which Mrs. I. is saddled with the burden of raising children in the midst of her own disorder. I make this categorical statement in full recognition of how difficult it is on occasion to distinguish Mrs. I. from another, similar mother who, despite similar economic problems, manages to maintain a decent, loving home. While the distinction may not always be easy, it can be made within a range of error that should be acceptable, by psychometric tests that are already available. I suggest that the American city will ultimately be forced to deal with Mrs. I., providing an artificial home environment in which her children can be raised away from her. I suggest that in many cases she will welcome this as help, even if in some, a court order to protect their safety may be necessary.

Such an act requires no new legal groundbreaking. There are ample statutory provisions for depriving natural parents of their children for neglect; endangering the life of a child is even grounds for criminal charges against the parent. The selection of a proper home for children by the state is a commonplace in divorce actions, in which the judge must sometimes determine which parent the child shall live with, or, in some cases, may even decree that the child be raised by some relative other than either of the natural parents. I have heard bitter disapproval of actions taken by specific judges in making these decisions, but I never heard anyone say that the judge had no right to make it. If the state has a legitimate interest in selecting between parents, I think it has an even greater interest in removing children from a household so disorganized that its products are natural subjects for the most serious personality disorders.

Probably, the main reason for the reluctance of the state to remove a child from his mother's physical custody is the total lack of any public institution that offers a better prognosis. It is inexcusable that American cities, with federal subsidy, have not sought to develop institutions where children can be brought up in a surrogate family that will provide more guidance and affection than their real family. Private agencies, with sketchy resources have managed to accomplish this: the Wiltwyck School —a small boarding school for disturbed children from neglectful homes, on the outskirts of New York City—is a good example. So is Synanon to which I referred earlier. We can also point to the success of group analysis, in which a small number of people with complementary psychological disturbances, form fleet-

In general, Housing Authorities, using public money to provide decent homes for people of low income, have a choice of roles. Either they can try to provide decent housing for the stable impoverished family; or, alternatively, they can regard themselves as simply operating a public facility, like a park, to which anyone must be admitted until he commits a misdemeanor. The second alternative sounds democratic; but in fact, the analogy to the park is wholly false. If someone commits a nuisance in a park, it is a simple matter to call the police, and have him removed. But once a tenant has been admitted to a public housing project, no matter how big a nuisance he becomes, getting rid of him is a long and difficult job. In the meantime, he does incalculable damage, not merely to the physical property, but to the tone of life of the project and to the other tenants. However generous the design of the projects, and however humane their management, the disorganized family does not respond to these influences. This may seem a harsh judgment, but the available data seem to support it as this excerpt from a report by a local public housing project manager to the New York City Housing Authority indicates.

"I visited with the Housing Assistant at 11 A.M. Charles (age 18) was in bed. Vincent (age 16) was sweeping the floors. The three young children were all at home. The place was very dirty; the kitchen floor did not look as if it had been mopped in months; the windows were filthy; and in spite of Vincent's efforts, the place looked very bad. Mrs. M. (mother) expects confinement next month. . . .

"[Six months later] Kitchen disordered and dirty, insufficient food for family. Window broken and not reported. Two children home from school because they have no clothing. Bed linen dirty and bedroom smelly. . . .

"[Two months later] Tenant of apartment below complained of water coming down in his apartment. Investigation showed Mrs. M. had a toilet stoppage since morning which she had failed to report . . . and she had permitted the children to use the toilet all day."

It is probably the fear of having neighbors like this which discourages stable low-income families from living in public housing. Keeping these families out of public housing, however, does nothing to improve their behavior pattern in the private housing in which they happen to be living; it is simply the fact that in small, bedraggled buildings, their disorder is not so apparent; and when their landlords are the private operators of slum buildings, well-meaning citizens tend to set a very low value on their criticisms of their tenants. Probably this attitude is unfair.

Meanwhile, any housing authority that tries to keep such troublesome families out, lacks a magic formula for discovering them in advance. The New York City Housing Authority, after extensive consultation with private agencies in the social work field, drew up its formal admission standards. The standards are embodied in two lists of undesirable characteristics, or personal history events. The first list is of "Clear and Present Dangers" that the Authority considers grounds for automatic rejection from consideration as a tenant. The clear and present dangers include drug addiction, sexual deviation, illegal activities "within the last five years," a history of disturbing neighbors and destroying property, and "behavior which endangers life, safety, or morals."

The Authority's second list includes what it describes as "potential" problem traits. Applicants evidencing one or more of these cannot be admitted without favorable findings in a more complete evaluation by the Authority's Social Service Division. On this list is found out-of-wedlock children, alcoholism, a common-law relationship when there is no bar to marriage. Only the most casual private landlord, the one least interested in the condition of his premises, fails to make a somewhat similar investigation of his tenants. But even these investigations are far less than completely accurate; some families are excluded who might well be good tenants; some are admitted who turn out to be problems to their neighbors and the Authority. There seems to be a correlation between the architectural attractiveness of the buildings erected by a public housing authority, or a specially favorable location, and the quality of their maintenance and the high interest and morale of their tenancy. This should not be taken to mean that the buildings themselves are therapeutic; it merely means that it is easier to fill desirable buildings with desirable tenants.

All of this has great significance for city planning and city housing program policy decisions. The significance is that housing cannot be expected to solve the problems of the multiproblem family, the family whom the Authority considers ineligible for its projects. The family that is so disorganized that it cannot live with neighbors is, in most cases, a family in which children do not belong. To suggest that decent housing not be built for low-income families who cannot afford private homes because one is unwilling to undertake the surgery required by the disorganized families is to postpone the solution of problems which can be solved.

If guaranteed annual incomes and the negative income tax sound humane, the notion that the poor must be allowed to work out their own destiny sounds democratic. But despite the protestations of those who utter these words, in essence they come back to the hypothesis of the new middle class that was once poor: that the cause of poverty is within the control of those afflicted by it, and that the economy as a whole is so successful that no one can claim that his failure to participate in its fruits is not his own fault. Organizing the poor to assert demands outside of the economic mainstream of urban life is, generally, to face them in entirely the wrong direction. They are told to demand better homes from landlords who have no funds with which to accomplish this. They are encouraged to participate in city planning, though their very poverty disables them from renting the apartments or buying the houses they might desire, while the fact of their poverty does not in any way change the federal or state laws that generally define the level of subsidies that can be provided. They are taught to demand greater services from the city administration, although this simple demand does not provide the new funds with which it can be met, while the demand itself, if successful, would result in the imposition of new taxes which, in the end, hurt the marginal industries and their workers more severely than anyone else. In short, if the poor are to participate fruitfully in the process of reducing their problems, this must mean primarily that they must participate in the general economic progress needed to narrow the income gap between them and the rest of the population. Obviously, this is not in their power alone.

To narrow the income gap between the poor and the middle class, the cities must provide vastly increased economic opportunities; for example, the construction of a total national waste treatment program which would, under direct federal auspices, provide wholly new waste collection and disposal systems. Construction of such a system would not only represent an inescapable investment in the future health of the nation, but might, if developed with statesmanship, open direct employment opportunities in the construction fields for many young adults now only on the edges of the job market. In any case, the flood of federal money into the cities, in the course of accomplishment of such a program, would raise demand for the services of marginal industries in which many of the poor are employed. Unionization of these workers must be encouraged, and, in connection with this, federal minimum wage legislation can be helpful if its short-range difficulties are overcome by a high level of employment generally.

The cities nevertheless must supplement these direct economic measures with services provided by the federal government, including new low-rent housing for those who can use it cooperatively. Health, educational, welfare, and transportation services must also be provided to narrow the income gap; it seems likely that new labor legislation must be enacted if the powerful unions of municipal employees, providing these services for those who cannot afford them, are to be kept from exploiting the strategic monopoly situation in which their leaders find themselves.

Finally, the cities must dare to attempt something entirely new to break the chain of disorganization and discouragement that links the disordered household to delinquent children, and delinquent children to a disordered household in the subsequent generation. At the least, this will require inspired development of a new kind of boarding institution, intimate and humane, in which the children of these households can be raised, physically apart from their own inadequate homes. Perhaps, in the final analysis, this first step which will help to clarify the difference between the disorganized poor and the economically poor, is the most important strategically, as well as the most difficult politically.

XI. | THE INADVERTENT SYSTEM

THE new awareness of the continuing poverty in the cities has changed American urban politics. The poor themselves demand greater attention to their problems and a novel share of the welfare services of the city—in a word, more sanitation, educational, and park services, per capita, in their section of the city, in addition to the hospital, mental health, and fire services with which the poor have for a number of years been more expensively served per capita than have their wealthier fellow citizens.

The poverty planners and administrators in Washington are demanding that the poor themselves direct the operation of programs intended to relieve poverty in the cities. Whatever the intended significance of the federal instructions on participation by the poor, the effect has been to impress city officials with the importance of according the highest priority to municipal programs dealing with the immediate comforts of the poor.

Finally, the spokesmen of the poor within the cities demand that decisions on city policy and city planning be judged solely by whether each one specifically hurts or helps the poor people most immediately affected. No matter what its intended long-range effects, if a proposal will force relocation of the poor—

favor over their continued presence the expansion of universities or hospitals, or provide where they once lived new sites for homes for people of greater income—it will be opposed, vigorously, clamorously, and on moral grounds. The outcry of the spokesmen will stir the consciences of the most civic-minded, politically oriented, and articulate citizens. The troubled conscience will find expression in newspaper editorials, protests, and, ultimately, postponement or cancellation of the proposal.

The poor must be served first, because their need is the greatest. This is the simple slogan of the spokesmen of poverty, and it almost perfectly expresses an ancient and honorable American principle—that the government's aid should be given only to those whose very welfare depends on receiving it. Surely this guides the cities to a more generous attitude to those who are fatally handicapped by age or illness. But if this tenet is applied in this simple form to the general problems of the city, then there is no moral alternative to Herbert Gans' dictum: middle-class citizens need not be encouraged to stay in the city, so that a uniformly impoverished constituency will demand services which its own elected officials will be minded to confer. To evaluate Gans' suggestion one cannot avoid asking whether the interests of the urban poor in general (not merely the handicapped poor) are served by according the achievement of their present comfort an absolute primacy over any other determinant of municipal policy. This intensely practical question cannot be answered without a look at its implications. Assuming that the problems of the poor have first claim on the services of government in the cities, what can the cities do for the poor other than to raise their present comfort? Have the cities served the poor in any other way? If so, in what other way?

To examine the method and end of the city in dealing with the poor, we should call on a systems engineer who would look at the human urban collectivity coldly, as though it were simply an assembly of processing systems. What, asks the system engineer, is the purpose of a system? What are its inputs? What are its outputs? How does it work? How can its efficiency be increased? Looking at the human system of the urban city, a systems engineer might well conclude that its essential purpose is to transform the rural man into an urbanized man. Its human purpose, in a word, is educational. Its inputs include, on the one hand, the floods of impoverished people who have been leaving the farms since the close of the Dark Ages, and, on the other hand, the various institutions and activities that are necessary to their education. The output is an urbanized work force, capable of contributing to, and demanding a fair share of, the city's products and services (those the city buys as well as those it produces). Looked at from this point of view the present comfort of the poor is not the sole criterion by which the value of an immediate political decision can be measured. We may find that comfort may be one requirement of a successful educational process, but it is by no means the whole of the process. The criteria by which any immediate proposal can be judged depend on an understanding of the educational process.

That the educational effectiveness of the city came about inadvertently—that no one planned it—may give rise to the impression that the city is inevitably educational. But it is not. Imperial Rome, the city whose decadence has so exasperated Lewis Mumford, was a city which no longer fulfilled an educational function. Perhaps because of its disorderly growth, the city failed in its later days to provide for the systematic urbanization of the new arrivals. Instead of being led to become a participant in the effective processes of the city, the new arrival remained unabsorbed, untaught. And so did his children. Instead of education, the city provided entertainment; instead of dignity, delectation. And creating pleasure for the mob became a determining factor of political life for the declining empire. Behind the disquieting race riots in Northern cities of the past several summers, behind the statistics concerning inadequate family organization and inadequate training, lies the possibility that the American city may, similarly, have exhausted its educational potential, with the same dreadful consequences for the future. Applying oneself to the analysis of the human system in the city—which is to say the city's functioning as an educational institution should then become an urgent matter for the urban systems engineer.

If the engineer were summoned to the aid of the city, he would, after unfurling the slide rule from his breast pocket, categorize and describe the elements common to all successful educational systems. From this list it may be possible to derive some ideas about the city of value not only to the urban critics, but to the city officials and those who elect them.

One element in a successful educational system of any kind is the *model*. The model is a human figure so respected by the person to be educated that to emulate him he will submit to the boring rigors of education. Without effective models, only the exceptional student will submit.

The model may in some cases, be fictional or historical—never seen at all, but only read about. In the present American city, secularized and anti-royalist, in which an article of common faith recites the unique importance of the individual man, the effective model is usually a living person with whom the person to be educated can readily identify.

Nathan Glazer and Daniel Moynihan discussed models in some detail in *Beyond the Melting Pot*. They pointed out that new arrivals took as their models those members of their own groups who attained economic success or public prestige in the city. No mighty struggle with psychology or social dynamics is needed to show that the bars of race and color are preventing the emergence of effective models for many current arrivals in the city from the country. Those rural Negroes so fortunate as to have a stable family origin may use their own parents for preliminary models. But for that large number of new city dwellers who lack family stability, the blocking of the emerging of effective models—the crimping of the Negro middle class, confining it to an inferior section of American life—is an interference with the essential educational system of the city. Not only has the Negro middle class been denied access to the inner social recesses of American society, the country club and the Elks; the Negro middle-class citizen has also been denied the American right to spend his money freely, even until recently, to occupy an overnight room in a downtown hotel. Separate medical societies, separate bar associations, even a separate Contract Bridge League and Tennis Association, are evidences of the extent to which the successful Negro is prevented from becoming an effective model for those new arrivals who might be expected to identify only with him. The ability of the city to educate the current newcomer is thus blighted at the outset. No appeals for orderliness, no breast-beating by nonNegroes over the broken Negro homes and the heritage of slavery, no "reverse discrimination" to pay reparation for a century of indignities, can compensate for this crushing of the emergent models.

Successful education depends also in part on an atmosphere that emphasizes—or accepts—the student's own worth. A vindictive teacher, bullying and berating his pupils, seldom extracts their best work. Yet self-esteem cannot be established by the cruder flatteries; the student soon senses when the teacher talks to his own nondescript generalization of the class before him rather than to the unique quality of each student. Frank criticism of a student's failure to reach his full potential, when accurate, is far more constructive to his self-esteem than superfluous flattery.

For many of the current arrivals in the American city, its complex educational system must begin to operate on a state of mind already crushed with a sense of inadequacy, and unsupported by their own sense of the worthiness of their group. The slum conditions under which they find themselves—far worse than the general standard—embitters the sense of unworthiness and imperils the effectiveness of the modern city as an educational system.

This statement does not imply that previous arrivals lived better. Older immigrants lived as badly, or perhaps worse. But their sense of their true worth, based on a supporting cultural tradition, stimulated many to escape from the dirt and squalor around them. The new arrivals merely find their own evaluation of their unworthiness confirmed by the dirt, overcrowding, and decay.

Agreeable physical surroundings, sound homes, an opportunity for wholesome recreation, are important aids to the development of self-esteem by the new arrivals in the city. People who expected that better physical surroundings alone would complete the educational process, should have known better. It is as much as to hope that a handsome school building, without a faculty, curriculum, parental supervision, or a program for self-government, would alone educate illiterates for college entrance. But deciding that these other elements of education are needed does not make the building itself unnecessary.

A third element in any educational system is described in that itchy word *discipline*, which merely means that the learner must have the attitude of a learner. Over many long and tedious years, discipline was construed to mean that the pupil must always bow to the views of his master. It is hardly surprising that the divine right of teachers survived little longer than that of kings.

Despite the argument between the proponents of strong discipline in education, currently described as belief in a structured school environment, and those who believe in a nonstructured school environment, there is basic agreement that the student must be in a frame of mind in which he is prepared to accept education.

The city relies on some ancient prods to nurse the disciplinary attitude. In general, though not perfectly, it pays higher incomes to those willing to learn more. It promises public prestige to the talented or the educated. Lately, the city has organized special services—youth programs, extra-school preparation, family counseling—to deal with the laggards. But there are respondents who remain untouched by these methods, and for them the city reserves its own right to apply the disciplinary rules. Some may be applied by the withholding of benefits otherwise due—as in the case of the Housing Authority which will not rent to troublesome families. Other rules will be applied by force, which brings us to the educational value of the police department.

Because the city is as hard as rock, the process of urban education is a difficult one for the pupil, and there are failures. The police have always had to deal with some of them. Their method of dealing with the failures has a marked effect on the education of the other members of the same group. If they are too stern, their crudity may delay or wholly upset the process of urbanization. If they are too mild, on the other hand, they may permit a misleading impression to be formed about the ease of urbanization, or undermine the models in the view of those who might be emulating them.

Even the most bitterly bigoted Southern policeman shows a cheerful tolerance of the Negro who commits offenses against other Negroes. He reflects not human charity, but the kind of patronizing tolerance appropriate to dumb animals. His mildness is part of the process of perpetuating inferiority. Although the public outcry raised by Negro and civil rights organizations in the United States is concentrated against alleged police brutality (I say alleged because I have no way of knowing its extent), I find when I speak about urban problems to Northern middle-class Negro audiences that the police problem which really concerns them is the tolerant nonenforcement of laws in the Negro districts.

The police scarcely think of themselves as educators, and are ill-equipped by training or personality to examine the motives and consequences of the way in which they discharge their official duties. This tension has always been true of the relationship between the contemporary city police and all newly arrived groups. The problem is accentuated today for the Northern cities because the arrivals bring with them the recollection that the police were used in the South as part of the repressive power that kept the Negro in what was called his place. Even the middle-class Negro who is vitally interested in the arresting of crimes committed by other Negroes, has reason to wonder whether alleged offenders have been apprehended because they committed the offense, or because their skins were black. And he probably has had one or two experiences himself that lead him to the belief that the latter is more likely. With his self-esteem squashed by American prejudices, or just beginning uncertainly to sprout, it is hard for him to view these incidents philosophically, as part of the price of civilization.

What in the world prepares the city policeman to deal with these subtleties? He is not one of the eminent beneficiaries of urban civilization, but a semimilitarized man in a civilian world, not very well paid in comparison with many who ask favors from him, and not concerned with educating the uninitiated in the values of the order he is paid to protect. His life is very different from that of the civilians around him, which intensifies his clannish self-protection. Many of the people he must apprehend are armed. When he hears that groups of citizens are suggesting that, without personal experience in dealing with stopping armed suspects, they should review acts that he might commit at moments of intense peril, he feels all the more embittered. It does not seem practical to replace present-day

policemen with new civil servants differently trained and motivated. If one could replace them, presumably at higher salaries,
there is no guarantee that the new lot would stop the commission of crime more effectively.

Urban educational discipline is menaced by the crisis over
the police. The tragedy is that both groups—those who demand
the Civilian Police Review Board, and the police who fight it—
have much in common. This common area can be defined if we
recall that the police are a part of the total urban educational
system. The police need a civic organization like the PTA, not
to investigate major crimes (that, after all, is the nature of a
charge of police brutality—that a policeman has committed a
crime) , but rather, on the invitation of the local precinct com-
mander, to meet regularly for the exploration of mutual problems including racial feelings on both sides. Both sides can join
in the demand for changes that will make the police task less
lonely, the law enforcement pattern more nearly uniform. Although many teachers probably resisted them when they were
first suggested, the PTAs have not undermined the authority of
local faculties or their administrations. They have helped the
principals and the teachers to get proper attention from the
boards of education; both parents and teachers have come to
understand better each other's problems. In the process, the
education of the students has improved.

A fourth characteristic of an effective educational system is its
recognition of the fact already noted, that there are failures.
The educational system must be prepared to deal especially
with them. It is in this area, as we noted in discussing poverty
and public housing, narcotics and the broken family, that the
present American city has not risen to a pressing new challenge.
But the cities have been slow to realize it, and the urban critics
equally slow to understand its significance. The physical survival of the broken family—thanks to the physician and the epi-
demiologist and its own fertility, and thanks also to the assump-

tion of public responsibility to maintain, if not to cure, it—
obstructs the functioning of the city as an educational system.
Familial institutions for the children of the disorganized homes,
special housing developments for those households which cannot neighbor, and, perhaps as important as either of these, a
clear and consistent public definition of the difference between
the democratic and the merely disorderly, are needed to keep
the educational system working.

Finally, no educational system can operate successfully unless
its matriculates feel that their efforts are worthwhile. There
must be reward for successful accomplishment, not merely full
citizenship, but economic opportunity. The new arrival must
be prepared for fruitful work, not merely through the development of his urban traits and specific skills, but through the preparation of a healthy and bustling economy that must be waiting
for him. This has not yet been achieved. Its achievement appears to depend on programs of federal involvement in the city,
primarily in the field of conservation of water against pollution,
where the federal government can act itself. The support of
massive federal intervention in this area—and others like it,
perhaps coupled with a gentlemen's agreement for the opening
of the construction trades unions to large-scale apprenticeship
—is as important to the cause of effective urbanization as is universal suffrage or the abolition of racial bias in housing and
home ownership.

The city is an effective educational system only when at least
five conditions are met.

There must be models for the new arrivals; and the models
will not be in the city unless *their* models—the longer-estab-
lished middle- and upper-class white families—are there also.
They will not be, unless the city provides also for what they con-
ceive of as their own needs. This may very well require the
postponing or cancellation of some proposals for directly increasing the present comfort of the poor. Surely it means that the

city's institutions that provide the values cherished by the models—the universities, the theaters, the museums—must be encouraged to flourish.

The self-assurance of the new arrivals must be enhanced, with sensitivity to their wishes, but without permitting those wishes to destroy the complex whole. The disciplinary forces of the city must be brought into partnership with the best of civic life so that they will strengthen, not undermine the city's educational function. New, daring, and perhaps dangerous, because untried, ways must be found to deal with the human failures of the city's educational system. Finally, great economic activity must be generated, if the effort of education is to seem worthwhile to those who must undergo it.

The task of the elected official is to manage not one or another of these, but all of them at once. He must maintain them all in some kind of balance with the power at his disposal. He must maintain that balance even against the cries of each part of the population demanding that its own values are at all times paramount, and to be achieved first, last, and at all times. The official may perhaps develop his own understanding of the relationship by remembering the need to maintain the educational value of the city's human system. But where will he get the strength to keep the balance real?

XII. AUTOMATING THE POLITICAL MACHINE

IF you overemphasize the community of American city dwellers, feeling as most urban critics seem to, that all good city resi
dents share the same tastes and the same devotion to virtue, yo
fall into a fallacy about urban politics. You begin to assume th
what is good for the city is necessarily popular; or, contrariwi
that what is popular is necessarily good. This fallacy comes
full flower in the belief that the people—a description far m
ambiguous than it appears—possess some fine and fundame
wisdom that enables them, in the last analysis, if not earlie
decide what specific municipal decisions are good for t
however painful they may look.

If you believe that the people have this power, you car
believe that city politics can be used to help solve the pr(
of the city. Men can run for office successfully by putting
the people the real and painful choices which must actu
made. Or, turning the conclusion around the other w
must be ready to judge the merit of prescriptions for th
least in part by calculating their popularity. Accept th
a serious test, and we must face the melancholy fact
prescriptions so far presented in this volume must
For they could scarcely be less popular.

We have advocated the continuation of urban renewal, in the course of which we may displace poor people to make room for middle-class people; and all in the hope of producing racially integrated models. We have recommended an increase in public housing on which we propose to spend far more money than ever before, urging extravagance as the way to provide more interesting design. We have urged dangerous flexibility in the civil service system to provide stimulants for improved architectural design. We have urged taking an indeterminate number of children away from the homes of their natural parents or parent, to raise them in new, small, pioneering institutions. We have conceded that some human city problems cannot be solved at all with knowledge now in hand. We have urged the expenditure of tremendous sums of federal money on sewerage systems and treatment plants. We have condoned the construction of new automobile highways that will destroy people's homes in the course of construction, and have scoffed at the possibilities of a greatly improved rapid transit system.

If one conceives of city politics as the method by which the people choose their salvation by forcing officials to pledge themselves to execute proper policies, one must believe against all experience that a program made up of these elements can be made enticing to the voters. If one cannot swallow this chestnut whole, one must, in the alternative, believe that these suggestions are all wrong, a possibility which I refuse to contemplate. Or as the final choice, one must gradually come to the conclusion that humane city politics must depend on something other than the extent to which officials elected to office do what the people say they want.

A brief review of American city politics may lead to the conclusion that this last is the more precise view. If it is true that popular demand is not a guarantee of the value of suggestions made for the improvement of our cities, it then becomes neces-

sary to take a new look at how American city governments come into office. To what extent can they be freed of the exigencies of popular demand? A quick glance in this direction is not reassuring. The old political machines have rusted away. With them has disappeared the system through which the political leaders were able to win a moment's freedom from the demands of their constituents by buying them off with personal favors that were generally irrelevant to the formulation of policies. The politicians have few personal favors left in their power to bestow. As a result, a political campaign in the city is conducted very much like a political campaign for the Presidency or for Congress, through promises by the candidate that he will do what he understands the people want. But the people in a city are various, as we have seen. The power and scope of city government are so limited in comparison with those of the national government—its responsibilities being largely executive, rather than legislative, and so confined geographically that compromise and balance are impossible—that promises made by the candidates in a municipal election are even less significant than those made on the national scale. Thus, a governmental system of values that is entirely appropriate nationally may be extremely disappointing in the cities.

Enough of a record has now been made so that one can compare the achievements of the new no-boss governments with those of the old political machines. A fair look at the evidence suggests that the obsolescent political machines were capable of achievements in the cities to which the new, more responsive governments have not yet attained. This conclusion probably dismays any believer in good government who remembers how the old political machines once appeared to him. Only a few years ago all righteous citizens understood that their municipal officials were stout gentlemen with spotted vests, whose only civic concern was their own dignity. The immediacy of the targets of the politician—his unwillingness to become involved with the future—was the major complaint leveled against him by the municipal reformer.

In the Lincoln Steffens tradition, good citizens assumed that the municipal politician had no interest in the future beyond the next election. The good citizen, on the other hand, measured virtue in statesmen by the extent to which they accepted the future as an arena for action. The challenge faced by good citizens was to impose their view of the importance of the future on those who were running municipal governments. They solved it by pressing for the establishment of professional planning as a branch of local government. The reformers conceived of professional planning as a serene discipline, wholly outside the arena of political battle; and they assumed that the beneficent influence of professional planning would radiate through the city, leading politicians in strait paths for their names' sakes.

Thanks to these views, state legislatures throughout the nation, in the 30's and 40's, began to authorize or require each city to establish a department or board of commissioners whose function would be professional planning. In some cases these boards were empowered to review and reject specified kinds of proposals for physical changes to be made by city departments or by private interests when these required the exercise of public powers. Stimulated by the demand for trained planners, many American universities established schools or departments of city planning. Their graduates have, for a number of years, been working in the city, county, state, and federal governments. The several schools that train city planners place their emphasis on varying elements of the complicated physical, economic, structural, and demographic data of the city. Some planners regard themselves as a subspecies of architects. Some are specialists in regional economic analysis. Others are transportation experts. A growing number of planners are interested primarily in social problems. One result of this variety is that the planners often cannot agree on a definition of their work that is comprehensible to the lay listeners. No matter. Planning is simply a systematic concern with the future. Looking more carefully at the activities of city governments, even in their most venal post-Civil War period, we may be astonished to see that the politicians were, in fact, deeply concerned with planning. On reflection, this is perhaps not so surprising. The machine politicians had a good thing in their city, and were interested in keeping it going. Somehow the quality of this interest has never registered with the reformers; perhaps it was not couched in the right words, a circumstance which continues to cause misunderstanding between planners and politicians. No one seems to remember that the municipal politicians of the last century planned the water supply systems that have served American cities on the whole remarkably well; they established parks in built-up areas even without benefit of the royal patents and grants that made park provision considerably simpler in the London region. In the first half of the twentieth century, the municipal politicians of America planned and built highways, roads, and tunnels within the fiscal limits set by their own municipal treasuries; they even showed a remarkable willingness to put some of their own land and their own problems into the hands of interstate bodies or port authorities over which they had little or no control.

Many of these planned changes could be accomplished only by demolishing large numbers of houses, disrupting the lives of their occupants. In the case of tenants, no compensation was paid. Individual plants were uprooted; important private interests, such as ferries, were forced out of business by public competition. All of these acts involved a sacrifice of living citizens to future needs, but the municipal political machines never got credit from either the planners or the reformers for what they had done.

Of course the reformers may, in their hearts, have suspected that the politicians embarked on these planned changes because they expected to profit privately from the contract letting. Their suspicion of the public works achievements of the politicians was heightened by the failure of the politicians to understand the planners' language. Even when they adopted the planners' suggestions, the politicians did not claim that their hearts beat in time to the music of planning. The phrase *Master Plan,* which planners for many years uttered only as though they were hearing somewhere in the background a fanfare of trombones, made no impression on politicians whatsoever; and the feeling of the planners that their master plan would be largely a political embarrassment has caused most planning agencies to avoid preparing one although legally they are usually charged with the responsibility of preparing one.

Frequently, planners found that for mysterious and disquieting reasons the politicians turned down their proposals. Sometimes it appeared the politicians had not understood them; sometimes they said that their election captains did not like them; sometimes they turned them down as part of an elaborate political bargain involving several departments of the city government. Sometimes, finally, they turned down the proposals simply because some mysterious "boss" had passed the word. Despite this lack of power, the planners were also made uncomfortable by being charged with responsibility by the critics and even by the public for matters over which they had no control.

In the 1950's, politics in the larger American cities had begun to change drastically. The old machines had, as we have seen, lost their ability to refuel. New, younger people were coming to the fore, many of whom had gone to the same universities as the planners, although they had studied law or business administration, instead of architecture. These younger men and women vibrated to precisely the same ideas—they usually referred to them as concepts—as did the professional planners. They seemed to the planners to be willing to support their ideas, not because they were convenient, as on occasion the older politicians had supported them, but because they were right. The development of the new class of political reformers gave the planners hope that their recommendations would be followed as a part of the political process.

The type of young reformer who emerged in American cities in the 50's and early 60's has been well described by Banfield and Wilson in their bright book, *City Politics*. The writers discussed the reformers when the latter were on their way into power; their rise has been so rapid, however, that almost no one has had time to look at their accomplishments since they began to win elections to the city councils, or to play important roles in electing the mayors. Nor has anyone examined the implications of their accomplishments, or the lack of them.

The reformers won while announcing that they were free of commitments, and would refuse to contaminate themselves with patronage. They were free, in a unique sense, to attend to the desires of the voters who gave them their victory. The first point that should have been noted about the victory of the reformers was that it was too easily won. Someone should have been more suspicious, perhaps the reform leaders themselves.

Like the rulers of the emerging African states, they might have suspected that if their predecessors could so easily be dislodged, the ivory and gold about which they had so long heard would probably turn out to be less real than the problems. When the reform leaders throughout the cities began to win elections, they discovered that there was less to reform than they had believed before taking office: indeed, that is why they were able to win. Earlier reformers had long since cut down the spoils systems, and many of the moral gains that the new lot thought they were battling to achieve had long since been adopted. Public letting, rather than dubious inside dealing, was already the rule in public contracts. And if there was bribery in the course of the execution of contracts—sometimes because the specifications written by professional civil servants were impractically rigorous—the corruption was so far down the chain of command that the reformers were no better able than their predecessors to root it out.

The preexistent honesty meant not only that there were disappointingly few corrupt offers to turn down; there really wasn't enough work to be done in the way of simple housecleaning. Besides, many of the administrators in municipal government were civil service employees. When it came to making appointments the reformers found themselves very little different from their predecessors. They preferred appointees whom they already knew, even if this smacked somewhat of the old patronage system. Once taking office, also, the reformers discovered that they were now professionals, their business was now government, and they had to make a living at it, unless reform were to depend entirely on the privately well-off, which in itself sounded somewhat undemocratic.

For all of these reasons, the reformers, once in power, discovered that their only truly unambiguous battle lay behind them: the battle to take over the party machinery and get themselves elected. Most of the fervor and excitement of the reform movement in municipal government since the 1950's has been generated by intraparty questions. Many reformers were stimulated to enter politics in the first instance by the cold treatment they had received when they volunteered their services to their local Democratic Club in the course of the first Stevenson campaign. It was commonplace, in those days, for a new arrival in a local Democratic Club to overhear two old-timers discussing him in this cryptic sentence: "Is he a Democrat, or is he one of them volunteers for Stevenson?" Smarting from these snubs, the reformers took power in the party by concentrating, perforce, on the party's methods of choosing its leaders; their slogans really amounted to making the Democratic party safe for democracy. Since there is no list of program objectives in municipal government itself upon which reformers agree—except for the general objective that their programs are to be aimed at and with "people," a principle which is something less than precise when one attempts to apply it to the problems actually faced by municipal administrators—debates in reform clubs tend to concentrate on questions which might be described as theological. The club's membership will, for example, be urged to support one or another of two candidates for a party nomination on the ground of which of them is the more truly a reformer. The question has little or nothing to do with the attitude of each candidate toward current problems, but concerns rather the effective date on which he first demanded the direct election of district leaders, a vital first step in party democracy.

The earnestness with which the competing claims of the rival candidates are debated reflects another consequence of the lack of a program for municipal government itself. It follows from the lack of a program that anyone in political life, or even in political office, can become a reformer instantly merely by announcing that he now supports intraparty democracy. In no discernible way must his conduct in public office be altered because, as though in proof of the democracy of the reform movement, there is no set of ideas by which he can be tested for orthodoxy.

Naturally, the reformers adhere to the program of nationally supported changes in American life which have tended to raise the income and living standard of citizens through government intercession in the economic process. Thus, they have advocated the expansion of the social security system, widened welfare benefits, Medicare, better schools and more of them, a vast highway program, civil rights legislation. But these very programs were supported as well by their predecessors, the old municipal politicians, who adhered to them not necessarily on the basis of a theory of social justice, but because they made the job of running the city easier. Why, after all, should anyone whose business is government object to its enlargement? It is probably somewhat of a mistake, as well, to think that the pre-1955 political leader in the cities was totally unconcerned with social justice. He too was jealous of his place in the municipal history book, although he did not allow his kind of vanity to derail those who had contributed most heartily to his election campaigns. The pragmatic quality of the older politician's life, however, made it very difficult for him to fool himself continuously. As a rule, he knew when he was being venal, or, as he may have described it to himself, when he was forced by circumstance to follow a course other than that which his conscience might have dictated. The better machine politician, therefore, had kept his heavenly accounts in good order by performing perhaps one good or courageous act in compensation for five or ten of which he was not quite proud. This may seem a low average, but at least it is better than the case of those officials who believe that in always supporting popular causes they are being more democratic, and hence more praiseworthy, than they would be in defying what their constituents want, when they believe them wrong.

Some of the pioneering *municipal* social legislation, particularly in areas which do not involve the spending of funds, were put through by the so-called machine politicians, although the reformers are unthinkingly given the credit. New York City's Sharkey-Brown-Isaacs Bill, which forbade racial discrimination in privately owned housing, passed the City Council before any reformers had been elected to it; Mr. Sharkey, whose name is on the bill, was one of the old-time regulars of the Democratic organization in Brooklyn. It has been rumored that he was told to vote for the bill by the late Ed Flynn, Democratic boss of Bronx County, who telephoned Mr. Sharkey and encouraged him to support the bill on the grounds that "it's the right thing to do."

The point is not that the organization politicians were saints, but rather that the practical differences between the municipal programs they executed and those supported by the reformers were by no means so great as the reformers had expected before taking office. After only a short period of responsibility, the reformers discovered that a vast difference exists between the passage of national legislation of progressive tendencies, and the execution of that legislation on the local scene. Taking low-rent housing programs as an example, most progressively minded people may as a general proposition support government aid to create it. Their reaction may be very different when they discover that public housing means that the building they are living in will be demolished, or that the field in which their children have been playing kick-the-can will become the site of a housing project. It also turns out that the men, women, and children living in public housing have not always dropped their sometimes irritating evidences of humanity as a happy result of moving into fireproof premises: some of those who drank, continue to drink; the wenchers continue to wench; and those who threw paper (or worse) on the street and grounds may for some time continue this habit as well. Even if 90 percent of the tenantry is neat, orderly, and sober, they, by definition, leave no trace; the unsubsidized neighbors, of course, notice the other 10 percent entirely too much and assume they are noticing the entire tenantry. All the people who will be inconvenienced, disturbed, or displaced by the prospective construction of a public housing project know what will happen to them. They make their presence felt early and continuously; those who are benefited by moving in when the project is completed may choose, at some later time, to express their gratitude, but the official responsible for their condition is rarely around to hear about it.

This is the case not merely with public housing, but with practically every other progressive program for dealing with human dissatisfaction in the city by making physical changes in its fabric. The reformer soon enough learned, after succeeding to office, that he was elected not because he supported enthusiastically the general propositions that everyone else supported, but because he had criticized the incumbents who were administering those programs. No one had listened to, or would have understood, his *reasons* for criticizing them. The fact of criticism was itself enough. Once in office, however, the reformer was caught between his sense of the importance of the general propositions, and his pressing awareness that in practice these propositions were both imperfect and unpopular with the people affected, especially when they happened to be in his district. The planners, whose programs these were likely to be, expected from the reformer that solid ideological support they had not found in the old-line politician. They got from the reformer instead a ringing speech in favor of slum clearance, and an equally clear statement of why it was unsuited to his own constituency, unless certain conditions were met. The conditions were impossible under applicable laws, and largely impractical for other reasons.

Finally, the history of this contemporary reform movement has greatly affected the formulation of its policies. It did not start in response to a desire to make changes in the policies of municipal government, but rather in response to a desire to make changes in the internal organization of the party. The case made by the reformers against their predecessors in the political clubs was partly an implicit accusation that the old-timers were corrupt and dishonest. More explicit was the charge that they were undemocratic. The old clubs did not provide an opportunity for the membership as a whole to participate in the formulation of party policy (whatever that may be) or the selection of candidates for office. The reformers came to power in the old clubs by enlarging their membership and pledging themselves to give the new members what they wanted in the way of basic doctrine.

This sounds extremely forward-looking, almost the epitome of a progressive and humanistic attitude toward the relationship between the individual man and the state. It works reasonably well in the case of a party dealing with national affairs, and concerned with so many matters that the membership is able, generally, to work out a pattern of compromise on which no one must lose on every single issue. In municipal government, where there are few decisions to make, and where some of the decisions affect individual people with great force, compromises are much more difficult to effect. If you lose your decision, and your home goes down to make way for a new highway, no other victories will quite make up for the loss. The concrete nature of acts performed by local government makes it as painful to lose a decision because you are outvoted by your fellow-members, as to lose it because the leader of the club has turned you down cold. The fact that you lose democratically fails to soften the blow. The result is a certain instability of membership in the reform clubs—even greater, perhaps, than that in political parties, in general. The elected leaders of the reform clubs are quite conscious of their need to keep the disappointed in the club. This habit follows them into public office, where its major consequence is to inhibit action on tender matters affecting one's constituency, and to view the resulting hesitancy not as cowardice, but rather as a high-principled devotion to democratic methods.

One cannot test the value of a local government simply by measuring the extent of its use of democratic methods in reaching decisions. A democratic government is tested, rather, by the election which takes place after it has had an opportunity to put its own program into effect. Courage in local government consists of defying the opinion of those most intimately affected by a proposed change, when that change is necessary in order to carry out a crucial point in one's program. The reformers in office have rarely found this kind of courage—the courage to inconvenience a considerable number of their own constituents and supporters in order to achieve an essential part of their program. They have used uncompromising defiance only on issues like civil rights on which all their constituents are probably unanimous, and in which, incidentally, some measure of compromise and adjustment is probably necessary in order to make practical advances after the passage of high-principled laws.

Several years ago, a group of prominent New Yorkers, some of whom were identified with Reform Democratic politics, urged their fellow citizens to support a campaign for the acquisition and dedication of a public swimming beach on the ocean. This, they claimed, was "the Central Park decision" of our time. They were referring, of course, to the municipal action in the mid-nineteenth century by which the then city government of New York acquired the site for Central Park, and conserved it for park use. The park consists of almost 1,000 acres of what would otherwise be prime real estate in what is now the center of the city; beyond question its use for a park instead was one of the critical decisions in New York's history. Without Central Park, Manhattan would be hard to imagine today, and even harder to live in. I happen not to agree that the proposal to construct a public park on the Atlantic Ocean in Rockaway is a suitable analogue to the proposal to build Central Park. A more interesting question is whether the reform politicians who generally supported the citizens who favored the ocean beach would have been able to build Central Park if they had been in office in the middle of the nineteenth century.

At that time, several thousand families were living as squatters on the park site. We may assume that they were poor families, and that since they did not have title to the land they were living on, that they could not be compensated under law for the hardship of having to move. We may assume that the Central Park squatters were least able, among New Yorkers, to take care of themselves, and most in need of public assistance. On the other hand, let us look at who was to use Central Park.

When it was proposed to make the land into the Park, the center of New York City's population lay some five miles south of the land's southernmost boundary. There were no trains or rapid transit conveyances to bring people to the Park. Horses and carriages were essential to enjoy a facility which (one can almost hear it being said) would be built with money that belonged to *all* the people. Even those of us with the slightest memory for Currier & Ives will recollect the lithograph of skating and carriages in the Park, and recognize that this was designed for use by the wealthy people of its time. To push poor people from their miserable hovels in order to make way for the games of the rich—this might well be a description of the Central Park decision uttered by a hypothetical Reform Democrat of the mid-nineteenth century.

I am not suggesting that concern for the people affected by an improvement is misplaced; on the contrary, I suggest that their needs must be given important attention. I do, however, deeply object to the theory that the views of those most immediately affected by a public proposal are somehow entitled to special consideration. The intricate balance between public interest and private good is not that simple. In the long view of municipal history, and over the long life of any improvement, the number of people who will benefit from it cannot easily be calculated; their interest, however, should be paramount, and it is the weakness of the political leader who feels he must have public assent to what he proposes that he cannot solicit the assent of persons not yet born.

Beginning with Plato, there has been no shortage of students of government who proclaim that the weakness of democratic government is its inability to handle difficult choices, because the people personally affected adversely by certain choices will be unable to balance their hurt against the public good. People are swayed, so the anti-democrats have said, by their personal fortunes. It has been the theory of democracy that the special interests balance each other out, allowing for a bargaining process as a result of which some schemes enjoying general approbation will move forward. The democratic theory has never before been put to the test in American cities, men having for so long traded off their votes for favors. Certainly the theory will not work if each municipal official feels that the vetos raised by his own constituents are of primary importance; and if all the municipal officials hold each others' hands on the theory that no measure that displeases anyone's constituents can be considered humane or democratic. This, at least so far, has been the position of the reformers in New York City, who have either opposed outright, or attached impossible conditions to their approval of, the demarcation of sites for urban renewal, the construction of highways, or the approval of low- or middle-income housing developments. Not having majority control of the City Council, or of the Board of Estimate, the reformers were unable to block action on the matters they opposed. If they did attain such a majority, however, one wonders if any of these actions would have been taken. Had the reformers opposed the principles on which the actions were based—low-rent housing, urban renewal, industrial development with its need for effective transportation—their opposition to the specific proposals would at least be consistent with their general purposes. But they opposed these actions because they did not have the complete approval of the people involved. Their curious view of democracy apparently is founded on the belief that the consent of the governed must be practically unanimous, and must be sought, not in general and at election times, but in the case of every issue affecting the lives of the citizens significantly.

The old-time politician started with a different premise. Right or wrong, he believed he was uniquely well qualified to run his city because he understood its needs and the conflicting desires of its inhabitants. He dealt with the conflicts when he had to, by offsetting against each other the different goals of the several contending groups, and by relying on the importance of symbols of unity. He shamelessly used such banal abstractions as civic pride and boosterism to win assent to what some people feared, and sweetened the slogans when appropriate with Thanksgiving baskets and poll-watching jobs. He also recognized and was willing and able, in the past, to assume an additional responsibility with regard to his constituents. He felt he had some sort of charge to *change* them; he was aware that this was one of the roles of a leader, and while he was certainly not willing to go as far in changing the minds of his supporters as the planners, with their special interest in the future, would have liked him to go, he did not believe that whatever the voters said was necessarily right. He certainly never thought their wishes were binding on him. The result of these attitudes was sometimes surprising, even if the planners did not always notice it.

Only a few years ago I appeared at New York's City Hall to speak in favor of the proposal to construct on vacant land in the East Bronx three low-rent public housing developments. The income of the people who would live in these developments was not significantly different from that of the majority of the older families who owned small one-family homes in the neighborhood, homes that many of them had bought years ago and clung to through the long, hard years of the Depression. Nevertheless, the opposition to the new public housing on the part of the home owners was unanimous and virulent. What should the city do? Certainly it is hopeless to try to provide better housing in the central city, and to thin out the teeming slums of Harlem and Bedford-Stuyvesant unless new public housing can be built on vacant land.

I was interested to watch the borough president of the Bronx whose constituents were the home owners. As usual no one except a few pallid representatives of public interest groups from Manhattan supported the housing. The borough president, however, knew that the city administration felt that the construction of the housing was vitally important to city policy. I watched him squirming as his constituents followed each other to the microphone, cajoling, appealing, threatening him with reprisals at the polls if he permitted the city to go ahead with its low-rent housing. The borough president was not noted for his sagacity or his great courage, but he knew he could be reelected by a powerful machine, and he knew that if he wanted important favors from the city administration, he had to support the city in his turn. Ultimately, right out in front of his constituents, he voted in favor of the largest of the three projects, and against the other two.

When he cast his vote in favor of the project, his constituents rose to boo and hiss him in the hearing room. His face turned beet red, but I can remember him reaching for his own microphone, and saying to them, "I'm convinced that all you people really mean is that we shouldn't build any public housing at all, and I can tell you we're going to keep right on building it, because the city needs it."

It wasn't much of a speech, but it did have a certain educational value, and it did assert that there are things more important than giving way to the expressed wishes of the people most immediately affected. When my progressive friends celebrate the disappearance of the political machines and the bosses, I find myself wondering how we will get hard decisions made without them.

The basis of their power is gone, however, and it is not clear how long we shall have to wait until new officials, inheriting some of their willingness to assume responsibility without, perhaps, all of their vanity, come forward. I suggest that this new breed will not come forward until the reformers, and their constituents, discover that action which is taken imperfectly, against the expressed wishes of a large part of the people, is ultimately more popular than no action at all.

XIII. | THE LIVING END

BY eight, or ten, or eleven o'clock in the evening the last speaker says he is certain that having heard what the people want, the elected officials will (or will not) proceed along the lines they previously indicated in the decision, memorandum of understanding, opinion of the corporation counsel, Board of Aldermen, State Board of Review. Two groups slowly rise to their feet and with a last cajoling, threatening, fearful, unhappy glance at the officials, wander out of the hearing room, sticking their arms into the sleeves of raincoats that had shriveled during the long day, creased like press releases that people had crumpled beneath their feet, and dry like words used so often that all meaning has been pressed from them.

The cleaning women, janitors, custodians, policemen, watchmen, wiping, sweeping, yawning surreptitiously, take the center of the stage. Lights go out. The officials, ignoring the half-empty cardboard coffee containers, waxed paper with pickles, and cellophane envelopes of mustard left on their desks from the supper brought in from the one drugstore or all-night coffee shop in the neighborhood, pack their papers into attaché cases, and, mumbling goodnight to each other with a weariness that indicates their total surfeit with the sound of the human voice, a sound no more bearable than an air raid siren, leave through their own door.

At that hour of night no one official with the power to decide, can once again review the arguments and counterarguments, and musts and do nots, in which he has been left to soak. The burden is in the case he is carrying, crammed with the responsibility for making a decision which may be right, may be wrong, may be neither or both, that will offend, please, anger, placate, irritate. Newspaper editorials, telephone calls, casual words from old friends over a highball, a bland assumption on the part of someone who gave $4,000 to the last campaign, an emotional plea from an old woman he didn't know—all weigh on him, all make him hate to face the need to make a decision, even to lift and open the case holding his burden.

Yet sometime the decision will be made. Perhaps he will decide in favor (against) because more people supported the proposal than opposed it (or vice versa).

Perhaps he will decide in favor (against: pick one) because of a promise made during the last, very difficult election campaign.

Perhaps he will make his decision so as to win support in a future campaign, or in return for support that otherwise could no longer be depended on.

Perhaps he will decide on the basis of the urgent recommendation of the planning commission that has studied the matter and believes it knows what's best, even if it doesn't dare to complete and release the total plan of which it is a part, fearful that this will stir up a new big controversy in addition to all the small ones.

Perhaps he will decide because he knows the decision must be made, despite its unpopularity. Perhaps he knows that in the end, the popular will is only his will as he tries to determine what is best. Perhaps this decision is a commitment needed to ensure the city's future, even if, in this case, it prefers one group to another, and may even imperil his own position in the next election.

Walking down the steps to the car, the thought does not please him. He hates fights; he hates being unpopular; he hates the interior squirming, the sense of guilt, that corrodes him when he speaks to reassure the old woman that what she fears will never be done, knowing that he may very well be forced to order it. Of course he can hope that one group will settle for gaining at one gulp a little less than it has said it requires, and, perhaps more likely, that another group, already blessed, may give a little more than it wishes in order to maintain peace, to keep the city going. That, as he disappears into the car, dropping the briefcase on the seat beside him, almost showing strain not to look at it, is finally what he has on his side. The city hall, with its clock and empty flagpole, looms above him, lit by reflected light on the darkened city. The city exists, its institutions are alive. Perhaps they give to its people a sense of distinction, a knowledge of their own collectivity. Perhaps these qualities stiffen the people's insistence on their own survival and soften, just a bit, their unwillingness to compromise to ensure it. This thought gives him a measure of peace. With luck, like a man carrying water in a teaspoon, he might be able to keep it intact in his mind all the way home.

INDEX